A VOYAGE TOWARDS THE SOUTH POLE 1822-24

A VOYAGE TOWARDS THE SOUTH POLE

Performed in the Years 1822-24
CONTAINING AN EXAMINATION OF THE ANTARCTIC SEA
(1827)

by

JAMES WEDDELL

A Reprint with a new Introduction by
Sir Vivian Fuchs
Director of the British Antarctic Survey

UNITED STATES NAVAL INSTITUTE

ISBN 0 87021 889 1

This work was first published in 1825
by Longman, Rees, Orme, Brown & Green, London
This reprint is of the second edition
published in 1827

Reprint published 1970

Printed in Great Britain by
Latimer Trend & Company Limited Whitstable
for David & Charles (Publishers) Limited
South Devon House Newton Abbot
Devon

INTRODUCTION TO THE 1970 EDITION

James Weddell was the son of a Lanarkshire upholsterer living in London. At an early age he became an apprentice in a coastal vessel, and in 1808 he sailed in a merchant ship to the West Indies, where in the course of some contretemps with his Captain he knocked him down. Weddell was promptly handed over to a man-of-war to be disciplined.

This was the beginning of eight years' service in the Navy, where he made a sufficient mark to be promoted Midshipman and later Master. He left the service in 1816. Three years after this he was appointed to command the brig *Jane* (160 tons), in which he sailed south to hunt for seals in the South Sandwich Islands. From 1819 to 1821 he was engaged in exploring and surveying the islands.

This volume, however, is concerned with a second venture, on which he set out from England in September 1822. Still Master of the *Jane*, on this voyage he was accompanied by the cutter *Beaufoy* (65 tons) commanded by Matthew Brisbane. Apart from a few isolated occasions, the two vessels successfully sailed in company throughout a hazardous two-year voyage.

Today when we use powerfully engined ships with specially built hulls of immense strength, we look back with amazement and admiration at the fortitude, daring and skill shown by the early pioneers. Not for them the precision of satellite photographs which today reveal to us the ice and weather conditions, no radio or radar to show up icebergs shrouded in mist or darkness. In their frail little ships, with only the wind to drive them, men like Weddell ventured into unknown, icy waters, seeking knowledge as much as the profits from sealing.

Weddell himself was scientifically minded, but all he had for his measurements were his nautical instruments. Of these he made good use, charting many coasts and anchorages. His wider interests are shown by carefully kept records of the ice situation and constant references to the fauna observed. In particular, he brought back the complete skin of a seal which he erroneously called a sea leopard. This he presented to the Edinburgh Museum, where it was scientifically described and all that was observed. In this he was outstandingly different from most of the sealing skippers of his time, who were not only secretive about their activities to discourage competition from rivals, but were only interested in the profits which their cargoes would bring them.

In this volume the merit of the man and his scientific inclinations are displayed. In addition to the narrative and the accompanying charts showing his tracks and the coasts surveyed, we find appended sections which include 'Observations on the Navigation round Cape Horn', comments on the use of chronometers, a list of positions for places visited, and in particular a reasoned dissertation on the state of the Poles in the light of the knowledge then available. Finally in this second edition, Weddell includes an account entitled *Second Voyage*. This briefly relates the experiences of Mr Brisbane, who sailed in command of the *Beaufoy* in August 1824. On Weddell's instructions he revisited the 'Fuegians' and there is some account of the behaviour of these people at this time of their early contact with Europeans.

It is not known what happened to James Weddell after his return from the voyage here described, but it seems that he made other voyages in search of seals. He was not in

England between 1831 and 1833, but in 1831 Captain John Biscoe reported that a Captain Weddell was in Hobart in command of the cutter *Eliza*. On 9 October 1834 he died in London at the age of forty-seven.

VIVIAN FUCHS

Drawn from nature by I. Weddell. I, Clark sculpt.

Man and Woman of Terra del Fuego.

Pubd. by Longman, Hurst, Rees, Orme, Brown, & Green, 1825.

A VOYAGE TOWARDS THE SOUTH POLE,

PERFORMED IN THE YEARS 1822–24.

CONTAINING

AN EXAMINATION OF THE ANTARCTIC SEA,

TO THE SEVENTY-FOURTH DEGREE OF LATITUDE:

AND

A VISIT TO TIERRA DEL FUEGO,

WITH A PARTICULAR ACCOUNT OF THE INHABITANTS.

TO WHICH IS ADDED,

MUCH USEFUL INFORMATION ON THE COASTING NAVIGATION OF

CAPE HORN, AND THE ADJACENT LANDS.

WITH CHARTS OF HARBOURS, &c.

By JAMES WEDDELL, F.R.S.E.

SECOND EDITION,

WITH OBSERVATIONS ON

THE PROBABILITY OF REACHING THE SOUTH POLE,

AND AN ACCOUNT OF

A SECOND VOYAGE PERFORMED BY THE BEAUFOY, CAPTAIN BRISBANE, TO THE SAME SEAS.

LONDON:

PRINTED FOR

LONGMAN, REES, ORME, BROWN, AND GREEN,

PATERNOSTER-ROW.

1827.

TO

THE RIGHT HONOURABLE

LORD VISCOUNT MELVILLE, K.T.

FIRST LORD OF THE ADMIRALTY.

&c. &c. &c.

THIS volume, containing the Journal of a Voyage in the Southern Hemisphere, and which reached a higher latitude in that quarter than was ever before accomplished, is (with His Lordship's fostering permission) respectfully dedicated.

When the writer, a Seaman, views the noble exertions made under His Lordship's administration to ascertain the Geography of the Northern Polar Circle, he must deem it at once a debt of gratitude and a tribute of respect, humbly to offer him the account of researches pursued at the other extremity of the Globe.

J. WEDDELL.

A

VOYAGE

TOWARDS

THE SOUTH POLE.

CHAPTER I.

INTRODUCTION.

HAVING performed a voyage of investigation to a higher southern latitude than has hitherto been attained, I have thought that it might be expedient, more especially for the benefit of hydrography, to make public the principal occurrences of that voyage.

Our adventure was for procuring Fur-seal skins, and our vessels were the brig Jane, of Leith, of 160 tons, and the cutter Beaufoy, of London, of 65 tons, both fitted out in the ordinary way, and provisioned for two years. The former, with a crew of twenty-two officers and men, was under my own command; the latter, with a crew of thirteen, was commanded by Mr. Matthew Brisbane.

The recent discovery of New South Shetland

had led to a conjecture that Sandwich Land was a projecting point of a southern continent, or range of land lying east and west behind the islands of South Shetland: but this idea I found to be entirely erroneous; — as I sailed between these lands to the latitude of 74° 15′ south, and there left a clear and navigable sea.

It may not be improper to preface these pages with an outline of the investigations which have been made to the south of Cape Horn, and within the Antarctic Circle, prior to my setting out on this voyage.

Many navigators, in their passage round Cape Horn, had reached the 62nd degree of south latitude, but always too far to the westward for falling in with the range of South Shetland, till in the year 1818, Mr. William Smith, of Blyth, in his passage from Monte Video to Valparaiso, made, apparently by accident, a discovery of the islands which have been thus named. In an after voyage he had the boldness to approach closely, and ascertained this mass to be land; which discovery, he, with the honest feeling of an Englishman, reported to Captain Sheriff, the representative of his king at Valparaiso.

The only navigators who have, to our knowledge, explored the sea within the Antartic Circle, are Captains Cook and Furneaux, in their second voyage, which was towards the South Pole, in the years 1773, and 1774.

On the 17th of *January* 1773, Captain Cook arrived in the latitude of 67° 15′, in the longitude of 39° east. Here he found the ice in field, firm, and continuing as far as the eye could reach from the mast-head.

"We did not think it prudent," says he (vide Cook's Voyages), "to persevere in a southern "direction, as that kind of summer which this "part of the world affords was now half spent, "and it would have taken much time to have gone "round the ice, supposing it to be practicable."

On the 2d of *January* 1774, Captain Cook again arrived within the Antartic Sea, and having been beset with ice islands and loose ice, in the latitude of 68° and longitude 138° west, he bore up north-west, and re-crossed the Antartic Circle, steering various courses to the north and east, and then to the south. On the 25th of *January* he arrived for the third time within the Frozen Zone; and on the 30th of *January* had reached the latitude of 71° 10′ S. He again says, "As we could not go any farther to the "south, we thought it advisable to tack, and "stand back to the north, being at this time in "latitude 71° 10′ and longitude 106° 54′ west; "happily for us we had tacked in good time, "for we had no sooner done it than a thick fog "came on, which would have been highly dan-"gerous when we fell in with the ice."

Two Russian frigates, employed on a voyage of discovery in the year 1821, penetrated, as it is stated, to the 69th degree of south latitude, but were unable to proceed farther. The particulars of their voyage have not yet been made public in England.

Not expecting, at my sailing from London, to arrive at so high a southern latitude, I had not supplied myself with instruments which would have enabled me to extend my observations; but I was provided with all those in common use of the best construction. Of chronometers, I had one of eight days (No. 820.), made by James Murray; of which I shall speak in another place. One of two days by Murray and Strachan, (No. 403.) One of 24 hours also made by Murry, and they all performed sufficiently well to recommend the makers for their very improved mechanism in this useful art. My azimuth compass was patent, and, as well as the rest of my compasses, made by Mr. Alexander of Leith.

The great difference found in the variation of the needle within a short distance, about the latitude of 70°, may be worthy of remark, and will be mentioned in the journal as the observations were made.

Notwithstanding the inducement to which I have referred at the beginning of this introduction, of my being in a manner bound for the sake of the science of hydrography, to record the performance of this unprecedented voyage; I should, nevertheless, have done it only by means of an official letter to the Honorable Commissioners of His Majesty's Navy, had not the notices of foreign and unknown matters contained in my notes, appeared so interesting that the solicitations of my friends, (more particularly of my co-owners in the vessels and voyage, John Strachan, Esq. of Edinburgh, and James Mitchel, Esq. of London,) prevailed with me to carry my information to the press. I am further persuaded of the propriety of so doing, from my having had nearly two months' experience of the navigation in the immediate neighbourhood of Cape Horn, which is yet but little known: for although the cape has been rounded times almost innumerable, yet this has always been done at so great a distance from the land, that no accurate accounts of its coasts and harbours could be obtained.

A familiar knowledge of these shores must evidently tend to lessen the timidity which seizes the minds of some commanders in passing this cape; and an acquaintance with the anchorages, which are safe, must render the practice of relinquishing the passage, by bearing up along the east coast of Patagonia, during adverse gales, altogether unnecessary.

From my having been engaged five years, in navigating these seas, and having performed a passage of 26 degrees of longitude direct to the westward about the parallel of Cape Horn during the stormy month of *April*, I am fully acquainted with the perils and the conveniences of this navigation, and can offer my experience with the confident expectation of its being found useful.

The old and contradictory accounts which have been given us concerning the people found about the straits of Magellan, and the coast of Patagonia, may be wondered at; though the descriptions by Commodore Byron of the enormous size of these people, seemed to confirm all preceding statements.

There is little doubt that tall and stout men were seen on the coast of Patagonia by the voyagers; but it is more than probable that those with whom they communicated were chiefs, who were, perhaps, selected on account of their stature: for on no part of the coast have my officers, who have seen many of the Patagonians, found people generally, nor indeed any men at all, of the extraordinary appearance mentioned by preceding travellers.

The inhabitants of Tierre del Fuego have also been spoken of as if they were beings possessed of little more than animal instinct, and incapable of being instructed. This may, perhaps, be the case;—arising, however, out of the peculiar situation in which they are placed. Give them intercourse with foreigners, and they will improve in understanding; for I have found them to be not only tractable and inoffensive, but also, in many of their employments, active and ingenious.

The civil day being more intelligible to general readers than that called the sea day, I shall use the former in the following journal. The principal incidents related may be found to correspond with the ship's log-book, to the truth of which the chief officer of the Jane and two seamen have made oath before the commissioners of his Majesty's customs.

As I shall have frequent occasion in the course of the work to mention facts and circumstances which took place during my former movements in these latitudes, it may be necessary to state here that the two voyages to which I refer, were performed by me in the years 1819, 1820, and 1821, and extended to various parts in the southern seas.

It may be farther necessary to premise, that if in some of the following sheets I throw out an observation or reflection on the subject of the voyage, not perhaps strictly philosophical or scientific, I do so in the hope that it may yet be of a nature to challenge examination, and lead to more just conclusions in abler hands.

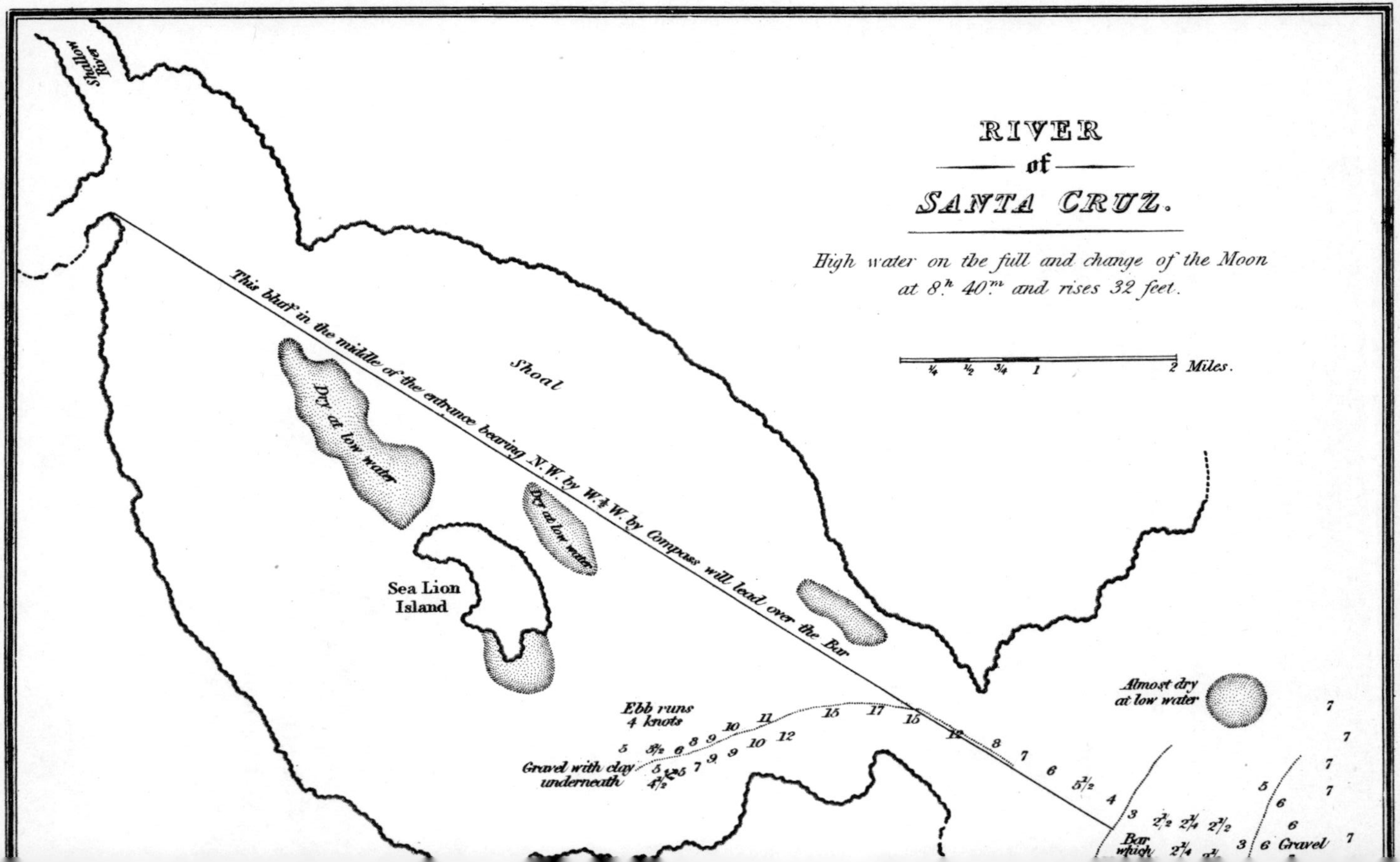
RIVER
of
SANTA CRUZ.
High water on the full and change of the Moon at 8.h 40.m and rises 32 feet.
¼ ½ ¾ 1 2 Miles.
Shallow River
This bluff in the middle of the entrance bearing N.W. by W.¼ W. by Compass will lead over the Bar
Shoal
Dry at low water
Dry at low water
Sea Lion Island
Ebb runs 4 knots
Gravel with clay underneath
Almost dry at low water
Bar which
Gravel

Land of Tierra del Fuego in Straits Le Maire.

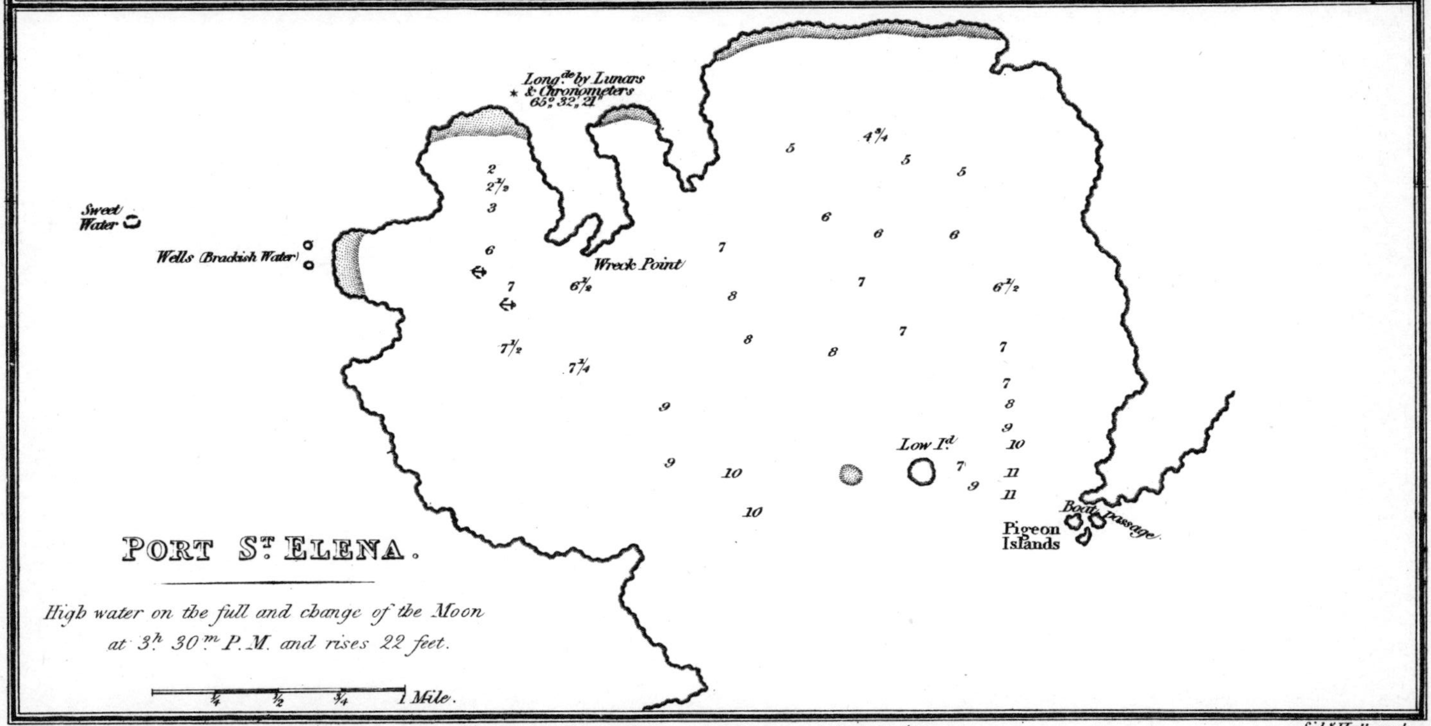

PORT St. ELENA.

London: Published by Longman, & Co. Paternoster Row, Augt. 1825.

Sidy. Hall sculp.

CHAP. II.

DEPARTURE OF THE JANE AND BEAUFOY FROM THE DOWNS. — ARRIVAL OF THE JANE AT MADEIRA. — PASSAGE TO BONAVISTA. — TRANSACTIONS THERE. — REMARKS ON THE ISLAND AND THE INHABITANTS. — DEPARTURE AND PASSAGE TO PORT ST. ELENA. — PROCEEDINGS THERE, AND DESCRIPTION OF THE HARBOUR.

ON the 17th of *September* 1822, I gave Mr. Matthew Brisbane his instructions, and at five o'clock in the afternoon both vessels weighed, and made sail out of the Downs.

We had the wind blowing fresh from the E.N.E. which by the 18th, in the afternoon, brought us off Portland. At 4^h P.M. with a Bill N. ¼ E. by compass distant fourteen miles, I took sights of the sun for chronometers, and departure for dead reckoning. The breeze continued to blow from the eastward, and steering a channel course, darkness soon closed from our contemplations the view of our beloved country.

As I had directed Mr. Brisbane to separate, when below the Bill of Portland, and to proceed direct to the Island of Bonavista, while I was to touch at Madeira, by the way, we allowed the Beaufoy to pass out of sight about midnight.

Nothing worthy of remark occurred during our passage to Madeira, except that in making

Porto Santo, I found that we had experienced an easterly current of 85 miles in ten days.

It was Friday the 4th of *October* before we arrived in Funchal Roads, and at half after seven in the morning I took sights for chronometers. The longitude deduced, placed Funchal centre in 16° 52′ 28″.

By the 5th in the evening, having (by the kind assistance of John Blandy, Esq. to whom I had letters of introduction), completed my business on shore, I returned on board, and at nine o'clock made all sail for the island of Bonavista, one of the Cape de Verdes. We took the trade wind at N. E. after clearing Funchal Bay, and carried it, blowing steadily, to Bonavista, where we arrived on Monday the 14th, and found the Beaufoy, with several small American and Portuguese vessels, at anchor.

Having to take in a quantity of salt, it was immediately set about, and by the 19th having received 36 tons, divided into the two vessels, and being in all other respects supplied and ready for sea, on the evening of the 20th both vessels weighed, and made sail to the southward.

While at Bonavista, I dined several times in company with the Bishop of the Cape de Verdes, who usually resides at St. Iago. He was at this period making his triennial visit, and with his retinue of priests, lived at the house of Senhor

Manoel Martins, who was absent on a mission to the Cortes, as representative of the Cape de Verdes. I found the Bishop a man of agreeable address, and by his winning manner calculated to make proselytes; indeed he attempted the conversion of an inmate of the house, an American lady, whose child he had baptized. She, however, with the common attachment that people have towards the faith in which they have been bred, repulsed all his endeavours.

The greatest respect was paid to this holy person by the principal inhabitants of the island; and great deference by the commonalty. Forbearance, suavity of manners, and rigid clerical discipline, appeared conspicuously in his character. When he rose from table he immediately withdrew to his room to study, and was seldom seen, except at table or taking a short evening walk, during which he was usually accompanied by a few of the chief people of the Island. Some of his priestly retinue were not quite so precise; for I could discover that when from under the eye of the Bishop, they were, like the laity, fond of the society of ladies, and open to their attractions.

The common people of these islands are, for the most part, intolerably indolent, and hence proceeds their miserable way of living. Their slaves, of whom they have many, are made to work hard, under the fear of the whip; for although, amongst all other nations, the Africans now enjoy a share of freedom, here no such blessing is afforded them.

Their principal occupation is making salt, and carrying on a small trade with the neighbouring islands, and with the ships that call here. The town of English Roads, which is generally called Bonavista, contains from forty to fifty houses; which, excepting about half a dozen, are rudely constructed of wood and clay, and mostly of negro-architecture. The colour of the inhabitants is from white to negro jet, comprehending all the intermediate shades; and they are so intermarried, slaves excepted, that they may be said to be but one family.

About three miles east of Bonavista, lies a town, called Nova Cidade, or New City, where the governor used to reside. It contains a neat church, and about 100 buildings, the most of which are huts. The Governor, whom I found here on a former voyage, spoke good English, and was extremely polite and communicative. He was an European, and a colonel in the Portuguese regular army; his age might be about 65, and he had been 42 years governor of Bonavista.

He informed me that the population of the island was about 3000, and that nearly 300 of these were regular troops. The soil, he said, was very prolific, when the rains fell at the usual seasons and were copious; but that they frequently suffered much from want of rain, and indeed sometimes of good drinking water: hence no vessel touching here can expect to procure that invaluable article. The mean of chronometers gave 22° 59′ 0″ for the longitude of the anchorage.

Sea stock of pigs, goats, sheep, and poultry may be had here, but all are lean and of an inferior breed: perhaps the best place for stock is St. Iago, where it is better fed, although somewhat dearer. I called at the latter on my last voyage, and waited on the Governor, who was on board a schooner of war, at anchor in the Bay. He was dressed in a general's uniform, and rather a good looking man. On my telling him that my object was to procure a supply of stock, and that the vessels should not anchor, he immediately granted permission to land, at the same time, recommending to my consideration the poultry yard of his lady, who, he assured me, would furnish me very reasonably. I was a good deal surprised to hear that a governor's lady should condescend to such a traffic, but immediately went on shore and proceeded to the palace. The door was guarded by a soldier, who refused me admittance; but on my business being announced, I was allowed to pass by this sentinel and two others, and at length arrived in the presence of the lady. I found her employed in getting out the stock, consisting of pigs, turkeys, and fowls, into the middle of the yard for inspection. According to the usual practice, she represented them as being fat and cheap, and I chose a number of turkies, &c. which were sent down to the boat. Our bargain was concluded in the house, over a glass of wine, and she politely desired her son, a youth of about fourteen, to play me a tune on the guitar, which he did with peculiar sweetness; after he had finished I settled for my purchase, and bade her ladyship good day.

Having mentioned this circumstance as exhibiting a singular union of rank and occupation, if not of pomp and avarice, I now return to my narrative by observing, that having weighed anchor at Bonavista, we carried all possible sail to the southward.

We had nothing remarkable until the 21st of October, when being in latitude north 14 degrees, we were not a little surprised to find the water up to the cabin deck; the cause was soon discovered to be a leak somewhere in the counter; and in consequence of coals being stowed in the after-hold, the water could not find its way forward. We immediately hove the ship to, brought her by the head, and finding the leak in the counter ends, succeeded in stopping it in a temporary manner.

An account of common occurrences on board a merchant vessel, and the ship's place in latitude or longitude over so obvious a track, can convey no useful or interesting information. I shall therefore hurry on to regions less frequented.

On the 23d of *October*, in the latitude of eight degrees north, the wind became light and variable, and continued so till we reached the latitude of five degrees north, when we took the S.E. trade wind. On the 7th *November* in the longitude of 30° we crossed the equator. The trade wind being far southerly we passed Cape St. Augustine, on the coast of Brazil, within 100 miles.

On the 14th, in latitude 14° S., we closed with a Portuguese schooner, having a cargo of slaves, bound to Bahia, and I boarded her. My officers were seriously impressed with the idea of making her a prize; but I was aware that we could not legally do so. This inability I much regretted, as we were of sufficient force to have relieved 250 fellow creatures from a cruel bondage. The men slaves were stowed in the hold, and almost suffocated by the smallness of the place; the women and children were seated on the lee-side of the deck, many of them shackled by the feet. As it was out of my power to render them any assistance, much as I deplored their miserable situation, I returned on board and the vessels separated.

This nefarious traffic is still carried on by the Portuguese, to a considerable extent to the southward of the Equator, in spite of all the humane efforts of Great Britain to put an end to it.

As far as the latitude of 24 degrees south, we had the wind frequently from N.W. to N.N.E. blowing in heavy squalls, with thunder and heavy rain.

At this season the route we took may be recommended for a quick passage, but, for the health of a crew entering upon a long voyage, the coasting passage is highly injurious. I had one man at the point of death by an attack of *tetanus*, brought on by his exposure to heavy rains.

We continued standing to the southward with the Beaufoy in company, till we reached the latitude of 40°; we then steered to the westward to make the land of Patagonia.

On the 10th of *December* we arrived off Port Valdees lying in latitude 42° 32″. I sent the chief mate to sound the passage into the harbour; but finding by his report, that there was only two and a half fathoms at low water in mid-channel, and that the tide ran rapidly across the entrance, I did not attempt going in with the vessels.

On the 11th in the morning, we made sail along the coast to the southward, touching at several places for furs.

On the 19th, we put into Port St. Elena. Our principal business here was to stop the leak in the brig's counter; in doing which, in order to secure the counter ends, we were obliged to unship the rudder and bring the vessel two feet down by the head.

The following day I sent Mr. Brisbane with the Beaufoy to examine St. George's Bay; and to meet me on the 28th, off Penguin Island. On the 26th, our business being completed, about noon we put to sea.

Port St. Elena lies in latitude 44° 34′ 16″ and longitude, (by mean of chronometers, compared with four sets of lunar observations taken eight days previous, 65° 32′ 28″.

The bay affords good shelter from S. by E. via west, to E. by S.; and, as the heavy and prevailing winds are between these points, this place may well be recommended to stop at for a few days. The winds are seldom from South East and generally light; and, the tide running strong across the entrance of the bay, the sea, during strong S.E. winds, is a good deal cut off.

As this anchorage is the most easy of access

of any on the coast, I shall annex a plan of it; for which I ran a base line of 400 fathoms, and took angles. In the valley marked A, I observed two holes which had been dug for obtaining fresh water, but what they now contained was quite brackish; farther up this valley, about half a mile, I found very sweet water, but not in quantity sufficient to supply a vessel without a considerable expense of time and labour.

Guanacoes are here very numerous, but not easily approached: they much resemble deer; their flesh is well tasted, and they are large enough to make them an object of consideration to ships touching on this coast in want of refreshments. We caught one which when cleaned weighed 120lb. and was, to my taste, very like well fed mutton. The difficulty of procuring these animals from their fleetness and watchfulness is such, however, that they cannot be taken hastily; but must be entrapped by lurking behind bushes about their watering places at the dawn of the morning. Hares, which are also numerous here, are much larger than in other countries. The tide flows at the full and change at 3° 30′, and rises about 22 feet.

On the 30th of *December*, in latitude 47° 54′ and off Penguin Island, in the afternoon, amidst several water-spouts, which are so dreaded by many, we rejoined the Beaufoy, and made sail to the southward.

We had now decidedly taken our departure for a voyage of investigation to the southward, and though we were a month later than I had intended, I was happy that we had made the brig comparatively effective; and was determined, should I not be successful at the South Orkneys, to prosecute a search beyond the tracks of former navigators.

I had given Mr. Brisbane my instructions how to act in the event of separation, and we now proceeded to the southward in company.

At noon of the 2d of *January* 1823, we were in the latitude of 51° 55′, and longitude 65° 7′ 15″, and this being the latitude assigned to the L'aigle shoal, discovered in 1817 by a Captain Bristow, I hauled up N.E. by E. ½ E. in order to obtain a sight of it; but with a run of 14 miles, and a view of 10 from the mast head, I saw nothing. Had it been accurately laid down I ought to have found it. This shoal must be very dangerous, as it lies in midchannel between the Falkland Islands and the coast of Patagonia; but as I have never seen it I cannot describe it. It is reported to be a patch of breakers about 300 yards in extent. Mr. Poole places it in latitude 51° 51′, and longitude 64° 50′, which, in my opinion, is not to be depended on; and therefore ships must be much delayed here in waiting, with a fair wind, for daylight.

At 8 o'clock in the morning of the 3d, the wind shifted suddenly from W.N.W. to south, and in less than half an hour we were brought to under a close-reefed main-topsail. The gale continued with great violence, and with a most irregular sea till the evening of the 4th, when it moderated, and we made more sail. The temperature of the elements during the gale was of air 39° 30′, and that of water 49° 30′. This was surprisingly low for midsummer, and the latitude of 53 degrees; but when we consider that a south wind blows over the frozen land of Shetland, the temperature of the air must of consequence be much reduced in the neighbourhood of Cape Horn.

On the 6th in the morning the wind again freshened at S. by E. to a gale, with a high and irregular sea, which, in the afternoon, stove two boats, washed away part of the bulwarks, and carried several things off the deck. This distressing sea was no doubt produced by a tide or current, as we were not more than 100 miles S.E. of the Falkland Islands. At midnight the weather moderated suddenly, and left us scarce wind sufficient to keep the ship steady.

The 7th being fine I communicated with the Beaufoy, and was happy to hear they were all well, and had met with no accident.

The wind continued blowing moderately from S. by E. to S.S.W. with passing snow squalls; and on the 10th, in latitude 58°, we saw five ice islands and an appearance of land in the N.E.; but as I had cruised over that spot on a former voyage I gave it no credit.

On the 11th at noon our latitude by observation was 59° 37′, and longitude by chronometers 46° 1′. The temperature of the air was 38°, and that of water 33°. Many ice islands were in sight which accounted for the temperature of the water being reduced.

At daylight in the morning of the 12th we saw some pigeons, and at 6 o'clock perceived the east end of the islands of South Orkneys *, bearing W. by S., distant about 11 leagues. We carried all possible sail to get under the land, but the wind soon became light and left us almost at the mercy of a heavy swell, in the midst of ice islands, which made our navigation truly hazardous. At 8 o'clock one of the eastern islands, which from its figure we named Saddle Island, bore S. 10 W., distant about 11 leagues.

During the 13th, the wind was light, and from the N.N.W., which in this region generally brings fog, and now obliged us to keep an offing. At 10 o'clock the wind shifted to S.E.

* Reported by me to the Commissioners of His Majesty's Navy, on my arrival in England, in 1822.

with clear weather. The temperature of air was 34°, that of water 33°. At daylight of the 14th we saw the land in the S.W., distant about 10 leagues; and by 7 o'clock we were within one mile of the shore.

I had landed on these islands the year before; but having a loaded ship, and no second vessel, I was obliged to relinquish a deliberate examination of their shores for that season.

Being now close under the land, I sent a boat from each vessel to explore them. We continued to tack the vessels about in a bay, which, from Saddle Island forming part of it, we called Saddle Island Bay. The ice bergs, which form in the bays in winter, and break away in the summer, now produced so much drift ice, that we had frequently to work ship to avoid striking it. This coast is, if possible, more terrific in appearance than South Shetland. The tops of the islands, for the most part, terminate in craggy towering peaks, and look not unlike the mountain tops of a sunken land. The loftiest of these summits, towering up to a point, I denominated Noble's Peak, in honour of an esteemed friend, Mr. James Noble, orientalist, Edinburgh. This Peak, in a clear day, may be seen at the distance of fifteen leagues.

On the 14th I made observations for settling the latitude and longitude of Saddle Island.

The latitude of its centre was found to be 60° 37′ 50″, and longitude by means of three chronometers 44° 52′ 45″ west of Greenwich. Two of these chronometers on the 12th agreed to the same second, and the third differed but 12″; hence it may be presumed that the situation of the island is correctly determined.

On the 15th in the afternoon, the vessel being close in shore and the weather settled, I landed on the south side of the Bay, and having climbed a mountain, was employed in taking a bird's-eye view of the country, when a dense fog set in, which in a few minutes shut the vessels from observation. I hurried down to the boat, and put off, hoping to get sight of the vessels before losing the land; but I was mistaken, for we soon lost the one without obtaining the other. My anxiety for the safety of the vessel lying among islands, in a thick fog, was great; but I was fortunately soon relieved by its clearing up, and allowing me to get on board.

Having seen some sea-leopards on shore, I sent the second mate to take them, who soon returned with six which he had captured.

This creature resembles the quadruped of the same name in being spotted. The drawing of one deposited in the Edinburgh Museum is annexed; and Professor Jamieson has kindly communicated to me a description of the animal. He considers

Drawn from nature by I, Weddell. I, Clark sculp^{t}

Sea Leopard of South Orkney's.

Pub^{d} by Longman, Hurst, Rees, Orme, Brown & Green, 1825.

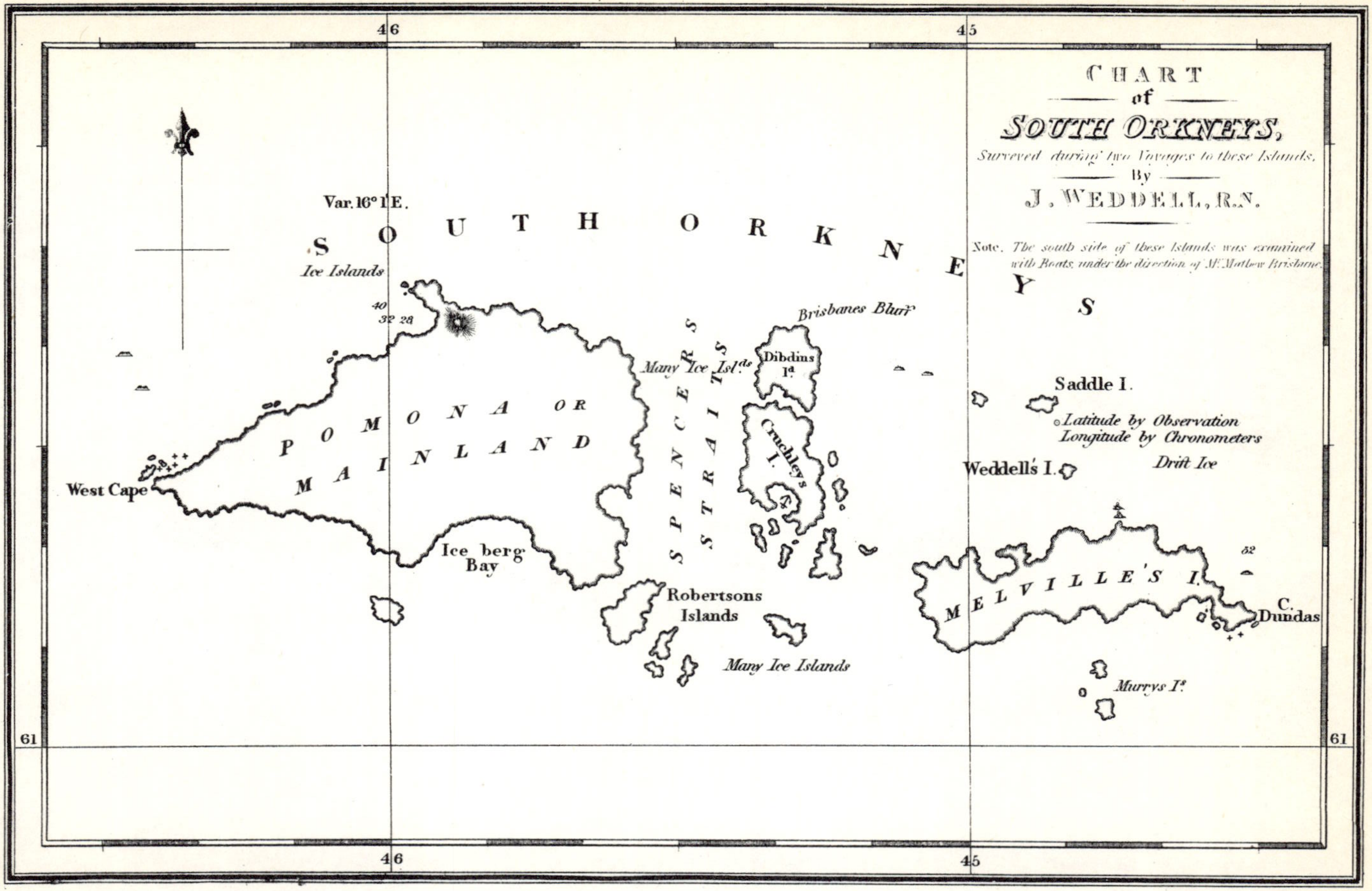
CHART
of
SOUTH ORKNEYS,
Surveyed during two Voyages to these Islands,
By
J. WEDDELL, R.N.
Note. The south side of these Islands was examined with Boats, under the direction of Mr. Mathew Brisbane.
SOUTH ORKNEYS
Var. 16° 1' E.
Ice Islands
POMONA OR MAINLAND
West Cape
Ice berg Bay
SPENCERS STRAITS
Many Ice Isl.ds
Dibdins Id.
Cruchleys I.
Brisbanes Bluff
Robertsons Islands
Many Ice Islands
Saddle I.
Latitude by Observation
Longitude by Chronometers
Weddell's I.
Drift Ice
MELVILLE'S I.
C. Dundas
Murrys Is.
46
45
61

it to be a new species of phoca, and gives it the following distinguishing characters :—Leopardine seal, the neck long and tapering; the head small; the body pale-greyish above, yellowish below, and back spotted with pale white. This species to be referred to the division Stenorhinque, of F. Cuvier; the teeth, however, do not quite agree with those of his Phoque Septonyx, nor with those of Sir E. Home, figured in Pl. xxix. of the Philosophical Transactions for 1822.

In the evening the boats returned, having coasted these islands for fifty miles. They had found but one fur-seal, and some sea-leopards, the skins of which they brought on board. This examination, though unsuccessful, afforded some hope, as the seal was an earnest of our falling in with more: I therefore hauled off the shore, to go round the west end of the islands for a further search.

On the 17th the wind freshened to a gale from the N.N.E., and at 4 o'clock in the afternoon we saw the land under our lee, distant but about five miles. I made the signal of our situation to the Beaufoy, and carried an oppressive quantity of sail to keep off the land: about midnight, however, it fortunately moderated, and the wind shifted to the S.S.W. We continued plying to the westward, examining the shores as we passed; and at 9 in the morning of the 19th we saw the west end, bearing S.W. ½ W., and straits running to the southward, which I called Spencer Straits, in honour of the Right Honourable R. C. Spencer; at the same time bore S.E. by S. ½ S.

The weather being frequently foggy and the winds light, we did not get off the western point till noon of the 20th, and at 3 o'clock I settled the latitude of this Cape to be 60° 42′ S., and longitude 46° 23′ 52″ W.

Not finding any animals in this quarter, I bore up to the east, to examine the other parts of the islands. On the 22d in the morning we were within six miles off the east point, which I called Cape Dundas, in honour of the illustrious family of that name. I presently despatched two boats to explore the shores, and in the meantime made observations for determining the position of this end of the Archipelago.

By a good meridian altitude I found Cape Dundas to lie in latitude 60° 46′ 30″, and, by chronometers, in longitude 44° 35′ 45″ west of Greenwich. Two miles from the shore, we sounded on a bottom of dark-coloured sand, with 58 fathoms water. About the Cape, where a little soil remained, there was a patch of short grass, and many birds assembled round it.

In the evening the boats returned with two seals and ten leopards' skins. They had investigated this eastern island thoroughly, and as we had now explored the whole of the group without attaining our object, I concluded that the seals we had found had migrated from some land, probably not very distant. My officers had besides ascended a hill, from which they said they had seen a range of land lying in the S.E. As I thought it probable it might be so, we stood in that direction, but on the 23d, in the morning, we were undeceived, for the supposed land was discovered to be a chain of immense ice islands, lying E.N.E. and W.S.W. We made various courses to the southward, and presently arrived at comparatively clear water. At noon our latitude by account was 61° 50′, and longitude 43°. The wind had shifted into the N.W. with a thick fog, on which we hauled to the wind to the N.E. under easy sail. In the afternoon the wind shifted to the W.S.W. and blew a gale, with strong snow squalls. We stood to the southward with little sail, and about midnight passed through a cluster of ice islands. In the morning of the 24th the wind moderated, and it became foggy, and we hove to. In order to avoid separation, the two vessels of necessity sailed very closely, our consort keeping constantly on our weather quarter. Our latitude at noon, by account, was 62° 35′: the weather continued foggy, with short intervals of comparatively clear weather, during which we always bore up to the southward. This very slow manner of sailing was teasing and unprofitable, but in these fogs it was risk enough to drift to the southward, lying to. In the evening, indeed, whilst enveloped in fog, the second mate called to me in the cabin, that breakers were close under our lee. I immediately prepared ship to ply to windward, but not seeing the broken water again, I concluded that what the officer saw was the breathing of whales; which must, indeed, have been the case, as when the fog cleared away nothing like breakers was visible.

On 27th at noon we had reached the latitude of 64° 58′, our longitude by mean of chronometers was 39° 40′ 30″. The variation of the compass at 10 o'clock in the forenoon, by azimuth, was 10° 37′ east. The temperature of air in the shade was 37°, that of water 34°; but in the rays of the sun, when clouded, the thermometer rose to 48 degrees. The weather being here so much more settled than in the lower latitudes of 60 and 61 degrees, could we but find land with produce, I had little doubt, but that in three or four weeks both vessels might have had their cargoes on board. As, however, we were to the southward of South Shetland, I stood back to the northward, considering it probable that land might he found between the South Orkneys and Sandwich Land; and as the summer season was now far advanced, it was advisable to examine those lower latitudes while the nights were yet but short, — since darkness added to fog makes navigation in an icy sea still more dangerous.

We stood to the northward with the wind between S.E. and S.W., and on the 29th at noon our latitude at observation was 61° 18′, and longitude by chronometers 40° 32′ 15″. The temperature of air was 34°, that of water 34°. Ice islands were our constant companions, and indeed they had become so familiar that they were little dreaded.

At 11 o'clock at night we passed within two ships' length of an object, which had the appearance of a rock. The lead was immediately thrown out, but finding no bottom, we continued lying to, till the chief mate ascertained it to be a dead whale very much swollen: such objects, seen imperfectly in the night, are often alarming.

We carried easy sail to the northward with the wind westerly, much fog and falls of snow. On the 1st of *February*, at noon, our latitude was 58° 50′, longitude 38° 51′. As there was no sign of land in this situation, we stood to the south-east, making an angle with our course, coming northward, which would enable us to see land midway.

I had offered a gratuity of 10*l.* to the man who should first discover land. This proved the cause of many a sore disappointment; for many of the seamen, of lively and sanguine imaginations, were never at a loss for an island. In short, fog banks out of number were reported for land; and many, in fact, had so much that appearance, that nothing short of standing towards them till they vanished could satisfy us as to their real nature.

In the morning of the 2d the wind freshened W.S.W. to a gale, which obliged us to lie to; snow squalls were frequent, and having many ice-islands to pass, we had to make various courses, and changes in the quantity of sail on the vessels. I carefully avoided the tracks of Captains Cook and Furneaux: and I may here remark how narrowly Captain Furneaux in the Adventure, in December 1773 and January 1774, escaped seeing South Shetland and the South Orkneys. He passed within 45 miles of the east end of Shetland and 75 miles of the South Orkneys: hence 20 miles, we may presume, of a more southerly course, would have given us a knowledge of South Shetland 50 years ago.

Running east in this latitude of from 60° to 61° we were constantly accompanied by all the birds common in these latitudes. Great numbers of finned and hump-backed whales were also seen; and penguins in large shoals, having for their resting-place some ice island.

Being determined to examine these latitudes thoroughly, we constantly hauled to the wind under close-reefed topsails during fogs and the darkest part of the night, bearing up to the eastward when daylight appeared. On the 4th in the morning land was believed to be seen in the N. E., resembling an island. The signal to that effect was made to our consort, and we carried all sail to ascertain the fact; but our pleasing hopes were again speedily dispelled by our illusive island sinking below the horizon. We returned to our former easterly course, and passed several ice islands, lying east and west. In fact, we found all the clusters to lie in that direction, which is caused, no doubt, by the prevalent westerly winds carrying them along to the eastward, and spreading them in proportion to their hold of the water and the surface they present above.

By the evening of the 4th we were within 100 miles of Sandwich Land, and within such a distance of the track of Captain Cook, as convinced me that no land lay between.

Our pursuit of land here, therefore, was now at an end, but I conceived it probable that a large tract might be found a little farther south than we had yet been. I accordingly informed Mr. Brisbane of my intention of standing to the southward, and he, with a boldness which greatly enhanced the respect I bore him, expressed his willingness to push our research in that direction, though we had been hitherto so unsuccessful.

The weather being dark and foggy we stood to the southward under close-reefed topsails only. At 10 o'clock the following morning the temperature of air was 37, that of water 36 degrees; our latitude at noon, by observation, was 61° 44′, and longitude, by chronometers, 31° 13′ 15″.

From having had a long course of dense fogs and fresh gales, the decks of our vessels were constantly wet, which produced amongst our seamen colds, agues, and rheumatisms. To remedy this in some measure, I had the ship's cooking stove moved below for their comfort, and good fires kept for drying their clothes; and by attending to these matters, and administering a little medicine, their complaints were soon removed.

I had allowed them three wine-glasses of rum a day per man, since we were in these seas; and their allowance of beef and pork was one pound and a quarter a man per day; five pounds of bread, two pints of flour, three of peas, and two of barley, a man per week. These allowances in a cold climate were rather scanty, but the uncertainty of the length of our voyage required the strictest economy.

During the 6th and 7th we passed many ice islands, one of which I estimated to be two miles in length, and 250 feet high. The wind prevailed between W.S.W. and W.N.W. with foggy and clear weather alternately. At noon we observed in latitude 64° 15′, and our longitude by chronometers was 30° 46′. The variation by azimuth in the forenoon was 8° 19′ easterly.

At 10 o'clock at night, the weather being foggy, we narrowly escaped striking an ice island in passing. We hailed our consort, but she was so close to our stern that she passed also very near to it. The temperature of air at 8 o'clock in the evening was 34°, that of water 36°. In the afternoon of the 9th, the fog clearing away, we saw an appearance of land in the N.W.; but, after the usual practice of pursuing all such appearances, we discovered it to be one of our delusive attendants, the fog banks. The wind now shifted to south and blew strong, accompanied with snow squalls.

At daylight in the morning of the 10th the chief mate reported land within sight, in the shape of a sugar loaf; as soon as I saw it I believed it to be a rock, and fully expected to find *terra firma* a short distance to the southward.

It was 2 o'clock in the afternoon before we reached it; and not till then, when passing within 300 yards, could we satisfy ourselves that it was not land, but black ice. We found an island of clear ice lying close, and detached above water, though connected below, which made a contrast of colour that had favoured or rather completed the deception. In short, its north side was so thickly incorporated with black earth, that hardly any person at a distance would have hesitated to pronounce it a rock. This was a new disappointment, and seriously felt by several of our crew, whose hopes of having an immediate reward for their patience and perseverance were again frustrated.

The wind was at south and blowing a fresh gale, with which we might have gone rapidly to the northward; but the circumstance of having seen this ice island so loaded with earth, encouraged me to expect that it had disengaged itself from land possessing a considerable quantity of soil; and that our arrival at that very desirable object might, perhaps, not be very distant. These impressions induced me to keep our wind, and we stood to the S.W.

I may here remark that many of the doubtful rocks laid down in the chart of the North Atlantic have been probably objects similar to what I have described; and still remain unascertained, to the great annoyance of all cautious navigators. Our latitude at noon was by account 66° 26′, and our longitude by chronometers 32° 32′. The temperature of air was 35° 30′, that of water 34°.

On the 11th in the morning the wind shifted to S.W. by S., and we stood to the S.E. At noon our latitude by observation was 65° 32′, that of account 65° 53′; and the chronometers giving 44 miles more westing than the log. We had in 3 days experienced a current running N. 64° W. 48 miles: the difficulty, however, of keeping a correct reckoning, from the many changes made in the course and quantity of sail, must subject the error to a suspicion of arising more from bad observation than from a real current. We had evidently been set to the northward and westward, which is contrary to what is generally the case, as the current almost constantly sets to the eastward. In the afternoon I found the variation by azimuth 12° 2′ east.

During the 12th and 13th we had the wind from S.S.W., and we stood to the S.E. Ice islands were numerous, and on the 14th at noon our latitude by account was 68° 28′, and longitude by chronometers 29° 43′ 15″. In the afternoon, with the ship's head S.S.W. the variation by azimuth was 8° 5′ east. At 4 o'clock ice islands were so numerous as almost to prevent our passing; sixty-six were counted around us, and for about 50 miles to the south we had seldom fewer in sight.

On the 15th at noon our latitude observed was 68° 44′, by account 69°; this difference of 16 miles in the latitude with easting given by chronometers, makes a current in 4 days of N. 53° E. 27 miles. In the forenoon, with the ship's head S. by W., I took a set of azimuths, which to my great astonishment gave the variation but 1° 20′ east; in the afternoon I took a second set, which gave 4° 58′. As I had taken great pains in making the observations, and the instruments were good, however unaccountable this great difference was, I could not do otherwise than abide by the result.

On the 16th at noon our latitude by account was 70° 26′, and longitude by chronometers 29° 58′; the wind was moderate from the westward, and the sea tolerably smooth. Ice islands had almost disappeared, and the weather became very pleasant. Through the afternoon we had the wind fresh from the N.E., and we steered S.W. by W.

In the morning of the 17th the water appearing discoloured, we hove a cast of the lead, but found no bottom. A great number of birds of the blue peterel kind were about us, and many hump and finned back whales.

In the morning I took an amplitude, which gave variation 12° 24′ east. The wind had shifted to the S.E. and became light. Our latitude at noon by account was 71° 34′, and longitude by chronometers 30° 12′. As the weather was now more settled, our consort sailed wide, in order to extend our view.

On the 18th the weather was remarkably fine, and the wind in the S.E. Having unfortunately broken my two thermometers, I could not exactly ascertain the temperature, but it was certainly not colder than we had found it in December (summer) in the latitude of 61°. With the ship's head S.W. by S. at about 8ʰ 30′ in the morning I took a set of azimuths, which gave variation 13° 23′ east. At noon our latitude by observation was 72° 38′, by account 72° 14′; hence, with chronometer difference of longitude, we had been set in three days S. 62° W., distance 30 miles. In the afternoon I took a long set of azimuths, which gave variation 19° 58′. This increase in so short a distance seemed unsatisfactory; on which account I neglected no opportunity of making observations in order to reconcile these irregularities. I had all the compasses brought upon deck, and I found them to agree, but rather inactive in traversing.

In the evening we had many whales about the ship, and the sea was literally covered with birds of the blue peterel kind. NOT A PARTICLE OF ICE OF ANY DESCRIPTION WAS TO BE SEEN. The evening was mild and serene, and had it not been for the reflection that probably we should have obstacles to contend with in our passage northward, through the ice, our situation might have been envied. The wind was light and easterly during the night, and we carried all sail. The sun's amplitude in the morning of the 19th when the ship's head was S. by E. gave variation 15° 10′ east.

The weather being pleasant, our carpenter was employed in repairing a boat, and we were enabled to make several repairs on the sails and rigging. At noon our latitude by observation was 73° 17′, and longitude by chronometers 35° 54′ 45″. In the evening, by several sets of amplitudes, I found the variation to be but 5° 35′ east. About midnight it fell calm, but presently a breeze sprang up from the S.W. by W., and we hauled on a wind S. by E.

In the morning of the 20th the wind shifted to S. by W. and blew a fresh breeze, and seeing a clouded horizon, and a great number of birds in the S.E., we stood in that direction. At 10 o'clock in the forenoon, when the ship's head was E.S.E., I took a set of azimuths, which gave variation 11° 20′ east. The atmosphere now became very clear, and nothing like land was to

The POLAR PART of the NORTHERN HEMISPHERE,
Exhibiting a comparative View of LAND & SEA with that of the SOUTHERN.

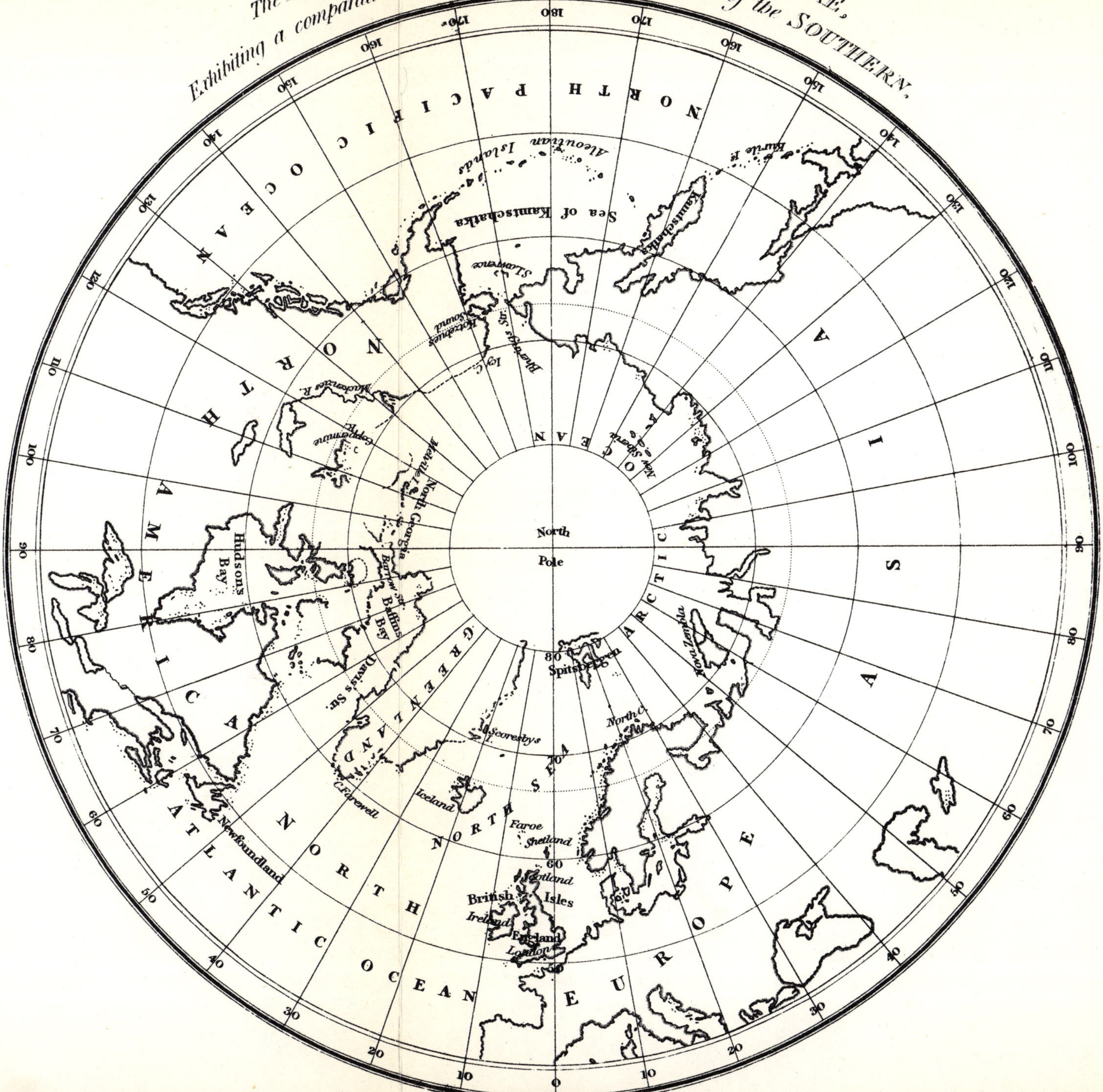

Sid.y Hall, sculp.t

The POLAR PART of the SOUTHERN HEMISPHERE, Exhibiting a comparative view of LAND & SEA with that of the NORTHERN.

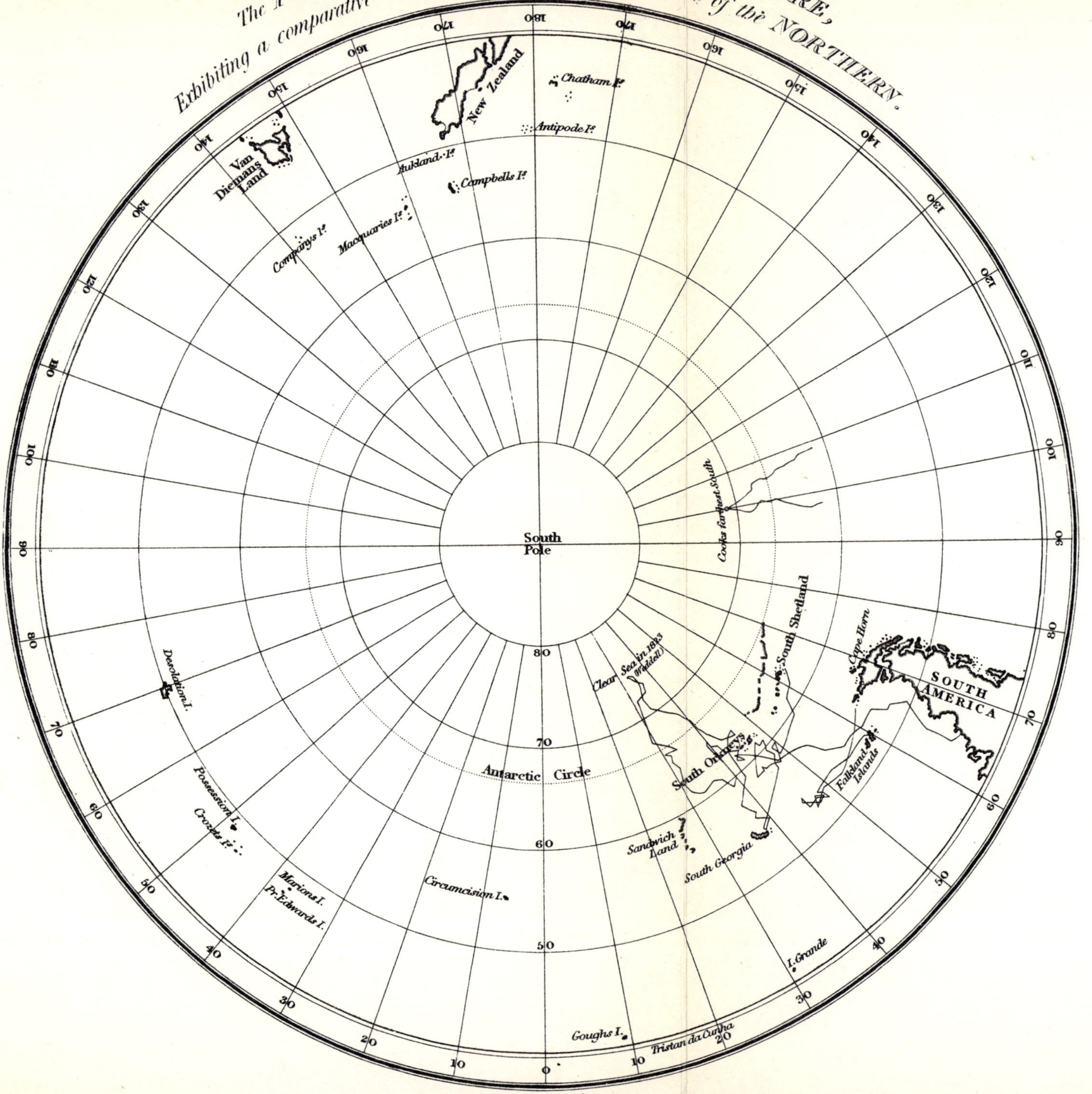

Sid. Hall, sculp.

Drawn by A. Masson from a Sketch by Cap. Weddell. Pub. by Longman, Hurst, Rees, Orme, Brown & Green, 1825. I. Clark sculp.

Brig Jane, & Cutter Beaufoy, in latitude 68° South, passing to the Southward through a chain of Ice Islands. Feb.y 1823.

Drawn by A. Masson, from a Sketch by Cap. Weddell. Pub. by Longman, Hurst, Rees, Orme, Brown & Green, 1825. I. Clark sculp.

Brig Jane, and Cutter Beaufoy, in the latitude of 74°. 15 South, returning Northward, 20th Feby 1823.

be seen. Three ice islands were in sight from the deck, and one other from the mast-head. On one we perceived a great number of penguins roosted. Our latitude at this time, 20th February, 1822, was 74° 15′, and longitude 34° 16′ 45″; the wind blowing fresh at south, prevented, what I most desired, our making farther progress in that direction. I would willingly have explored the S.W. quarter, but taking into consideration the lateness of the season, and that we had to pass homewards through 1000 miles of sea strewed with ice islands, with long nights, and probably attended with fogs, I could not determine otherwise than to take advantage of this favourable wind for returning.

I much regretted that circumstances had not allowed me to proceed to the southward, when in the latitude of 65°, on the 27th of January, as I should then have had sufficient time to examine this sea to my satisfaction.

Situated however as I actually was, my attention was naturally roused to observe any phenomena which might be considered interesting to science. I was well aware that the making of scientific observations in this unfrequented part of the globe was a very desirable object, and consequently the more lamented my not being well supplied with the instruments with which ships fitted out for discovery are generally provided.

As the exact longitude of the ship and of harbours, &c. is of the first consideration, I had expended 240*l.* in the purchase of three chronometers; all of these performed remarkably well, and in particular, one of eight days, (No. 820.) Murray, London, continued regular in its daily rate of gaining through an unparalleled trial by repeated shocks, which the vessel (but slightly built) sustained during a month among field ice. Such perfection in this most useful machine, cannot be too much appreciated by commanders of ships, who, by assistance of so precise a nature, can easily avoid embarrassment in critical situations, where many lives and much valuable property frequently depend on a true knowledge of the ship's place.

The laws to which the compass seems to be subject in regard to its variation, have lately undergone such accurate investigation by eminent individuals, that the phenomena attending it are now, in a great degree, ascertained.

My own actual observations with regard to the variation, are inserted at the end of the volume.

Those which I made about the latitude of 60 degrees, are collected for local attraction from the table of experiments made with Mr. Barlow's plate, in H. M. S. Conway, by Captain Basil Hall, and by Mr. Foster; but the observations arrived at about the latitude of 70 degrees cannot be reconciled, as to quantity of local attraction, with the theory adopted on the subject: I therefore let them remain at the observed results. I found a difference of from 3 to 5 degrees between the variation taken at the binnacle and that on the main hatches; and I have found as great a difference when the observations were made, even on the same spot, an hour apart. In fact, it appeared evident that the magnetic energy of the earth upon the needle was much diminished when far to the southward; partly arising, no doubt, from the increased dip or diminution of horizontal action on the needle, which must be attracted in an increased degree by objects immediately about it. This, however, cannot be altogether decided till a more satisfactory theory in respect to the emanation of the magnetic influence has been demonstrated.

The Aurora Australis, which Mr. Foster saw in his voyage round the world with Captain Cook in the year 1773, I particularly looked for during the time the sun was beneath the horizon, which was more than six hours, but nothing of the kind was observable. As the twilight, however, was never out of the sky, that might be the cause of its not being visible.

The remarkable and distorted appearances which objects and the horizon itself assume by refraction in high northern latitudes, occurred here but little more than in an ordinary way. The water spouted by whales half an hour after sunrise in the morning of the 19th exhibited an increased refraction, but it soon disappeared.

The reason of this phenomenon not existing as singularly in the south as it does in corresponding northern latitudes, may be attributed to this sea being clear of field ice.

It distinctly appears to me, that the conjecture of Captain Cook, that field ice is formed and proceeds from land, and is not formed in the open sea, is true. He latterly, however, changes his opinion from having found ice solid in field in the latitude of 70 degrees to the northward of Bhering's Straits. But I think it likely that the ice he fell in with there proceeded from land in the north, not more distant, perhaps, than 150 miles. No person can doubt the probability of my conjecture, when it is remembered, that in the latitude of 74° 15′ south (which, according to the received opinion of former navigators, that the southern hemisphere is proportionably colder by 10 degrees of latitude than the northern, would be equal to 84° 15′ north,) I found a sea perfectly clear of field ice; whereas in the latitude of 61° 30′, about 100 miles from the land, I was beset in heavy packed ice. As in that situation we could not see the land, had I not known of the existence of South Shetland, I might have fallen into the commonly received error, that this ice proceeded continuously from the South Pole. If, therefore, no land exist to the south of the latitude at which I arrived, *viz.* seventy-four degrees, fifteen minutes, — being three degrees and five minutes, or 214 geographical miles farther south than Captain Cook, or any preceding navigator reached, how is it possible that the South Pole should not be more attainable than the North, about which we know there lies a great deal of land?

The excessive cold of the southern hemisphere has been variously accounted for, every philosopher adopting that theory which best suited his own hydrographical system. Saint Pierre supposes it to proceed from a cupola of ice surrounding the South Pole, and stretching far northward. We have now better *data* to go upon; for though great exertions were used in the years 1773 and 1774 to discover the *terra australis incognita* without success, yet we find there is a range of land lying as far north as the latitude of 61 degrees. We may also conjecture, without much fear of being in the wrong, that the land with which we are acquainted lying in latitude of 61 degrees, and in longitude 54° 30′, namely, the east end of

South Shetland, stretches to the W.S.W., beyond the longitude in which Captain Cook penetrated to the latitude of 71° 10′. It is this land which, no doubt, ought to be looked upon as the source from which proceeds the excessive cold of these regions. The temperature of air and water in the latitude of 60 and 61 degrees, I have mentioned to be but little above the freezing point. The cold earthless land, and its immense ice islands, which are continually separating in the summer, and are made, by prevailing westerly winds, almost to girdle the earth, is evidently the cause of the very low temperature which prevails.

The part of the country which I have seen is without soil, reared in columns of impenetrable rock, inclosing and producing large masses of ice, even in the low latitude of 60° 45′.

It is certain that ice islands are formed only in openings or recesses of land; and field ice, I think, is not readily formed in a deep sea.

On soundings, the water is soon cooled down to the freezing point; hence field ice is found at the distance of many miles from any shore. These considerations induce me to conclude, that from having but three ice islands in sight, in latitude 74 degrees, the range of land, of which I have spoken, does not extend more southerly than the 73d degree. If this be true, and if there be no more land to the southward, the antarctic polar sea may be found less icy than is imagined, and a clear field of discovery, even to the South Pole, may therefore be anticipated.

CHAP. III.

RETURN TO THE NORTHWARD. — NO SOUTH ICELAND IN THE LATITUDE LAID DOWN IN COMMON CHARTS. — SEPARATION OF THE VESSELS. — PASSAGE THROUGH ICE ISLANDS. — ARRIVAL OF BOTH SHIPS AT SOUTH GEORGIA. — SOUTH GEORGIA. — PENGUINS, AND OTHER OBJECTS OF NATURAL HISTORY. — SAIL AGAIN. — THE AURORA ISLAND. — ARRIVE AT THE FALKLAND ISLES.

HAVING now determined on returning, I made the signal to our consort to bear up and steer N.W., and we made all possible sail.

Our crews were naturally much disappointed at our ill success in not finding a southern land, as their interest in the voyage was to be a proportion of the cargo procured. In order, therefore, to reanimate them by acknowledging their pamerit, I expressed my approbation of their patient and orderly behaviour, and informed them that they were now to the southward of the latitude to which any former navigator had penetrated. Our colours were hoisted, and a gun was fired, and both crews gave three cheers. These indulgences, with an allowance of grog, dispelled their gloom, and infused a hope that fortune might yet be favourable.

In honour of our most gracious Sovereign, the name of King George the Fourth's sea was given to this hitherto unvisited part of the ocean.

The wind continued from south till midnight, when it fell calm. In the morning of the 21st a breeze sprang up from the westward. We continued steering N.W., under as much canvass as our consort's slower rate of sailing would admit, and on the 23d at noon, we had returned to the latitude of 71° 25′ by observation, and 71° 38′ by account; hence we had experienced a northerly current of nearly thirteen miles in two days. This northerly set favours the theory of St. Pierre, who supposes such a current to be caused by the fusion of the Polar ices; but if it exist at all, (since it may have been merely an error of reckoning,) it is certainly too small to effect the flux and reflux of the ocean. In order to give a chance of ascertaining the general current in these seas, I secured a bottle well with the cork, and threw it overboard with a notice inclosed of the state of the sea in latitude 74°, &c. The water again being discoloured, we sounded with 240 fathoms of line, but got no bottom, though I am of opinion it would have been obtained at a greater length of line; but as we had no more, nor a lead sufficiently heavy, we could not be so experimental as I wished. Ice islands now became more numerous, and our consort took on board a quantity of fallen ice for water for present use. In the afternoon it became calm, and I tried the current by mooring the boat in the usual way, and found it setting to the N.E. one-sixth of a mile per hour. At 6 P. M. a breeze sprang up from N.N.E., and we made sail to the westward. The winds continued northerly, sometimes blowing strong with snow, till the evening of the 20th, when we had another calm. Our latitude at noon by observation was 67° 33′, and longitude by chronometers 40° 2′. In the afternoon I took a set of azimuths, which at the binnacle, when the ship's head was west, gave variation 15° 58′ easterly. In the forenoon I observed the froth of the sea to lie S.E. and N.W., which, by the observation for latitude and longitude, indicated a current setting to the S.E. about one-eighth of a mile per hour; at ten at night a breeze sprang up from the S.E., and we made sail. The 27th, being fine in the forenoon, I took a set of azimuths in mid-ships, when the ship's head was N.W., which gave variation 22° 8′.

In the afternoon, when the ship's head was N.W., a second set gave only 11° 00′ easterly. This last observation was taken at the binnacle, but the ship's local attraction was not sufficient to account for the great difference in the results. In the night of the 27th the wind freshened at south with snow squalls, and we steered N.N.W., carrying as much sail as we could safely navigate with among ice islands. On the 28th at noon our latitude by observation was 65° 2′, and longitude by chronometers 40° 45′. We had now little ice in sight, in comparison with what appeared when in nearly the same latitude on the 27th of January. In the evening we hauled up N.W. by W. to look into the longitude of 45°. The first of *March* being fine, I took several sets of azimuths, all of which produced nearly the same result. Having used the same instruments, and the observers being the same as when in the latitude of 67° and upwards, I was persuaded that the former differences did not arise from inaccuracies of observation, but rather from the inactivity or insufficiency of the needle. The mean of azimuths gave variation 16° 31′. Our latitude at noon by observation was 63° 29′, and longitude 42° 41′. On the 2d in the morning it blew a strong breeze from N.W. and the weather was foggy; in the afternoon it cleared up, and we saw an appearance of land in the S.E. but it presently vanished. At midnight the wind shifted to north, and blew a gale with snow squalls. In reaching to the westward we fell in with many small ice islands, and we wore ship to the N.E.: the weather continued foggy with strong gales till the 4th in the morning, when it moderated, and at noon we had clear weather. Our latitude by observation being 63° 21′, and longitude by chronometers 45° 22′, we were in a situation to have seen what is represented on the South Atlantic chart in common use, as South Iceland, but, alas! no such place exists.

It is much to be regretted that any men should be so ill-advised as to propagate hydrographical falsehoods; and I pity those who, when they meet with an appearance that is likely to throw some light on the state of the globe, are led through pusillanimity to forego the examination of it. But the extreme reluctance I have to excite painful feelings any where, restrains me from dealing that just censure which is due to many of my fellow seamen, who, by negligence, narrow views of pecuniary interest, or timidity, have omitted many practicable investigations, the want of which continues to be felt by the nation, and more especially by merchants and ship-owners.

During the night of the 5th, the weather being foggy, we lost sight of the Beaufoy, and though we made several tacks we were then unable to regain sight of her. In the night of the 6th, the wind shifted suddenly from N.N.W. to S.W., and left a most distressing sea, which obliged us to heave to: at daylight, not seeing any thing of the Beaufoy, I concluded that she was making the best of her way to South Georgia, the place of rendezvous. I was uneasy at our separation, for although I had full confidence in the care and ability of Mr. Brisbane, I still wished to have continued my attentions, more particularly on account of our being among ice islands. In the morning of the 7th it blew a gale from S.W. and this being a favorable wind we steered N. by E. under a close-reefed main topsail, reefed fore-sail, and reefed fore-top-mast staysail, with which in squalls we ran at the rate of 10 miles per hour. At 6 A.M. we were under the necessity of working through a cluster of ice islands which having much fallen ice about them, the passage was rendered very dangerous: I was, according to the best practice, attempting to steer to windward of most of them; but the sea running too high, we were obliged to keep before the wind. The chief mate was stationed in the foretop to look out for low ice in the hollow of the sea; and it was only by strict regard to the helm, and the sails, that we happily got through without an accident. With a free side wind an ice island should be passed on the windward side, as by this means the loose ice, which always drifts farthest, is avoided.

Though this gale was so violent as to produce a sea which cleared the decks of almost every movable, it was from so favorable a quarter for sailing homeward, that we could not afford to lay to through the night on account of ice; but kept all the people of the watch looking out a-head; and thus we passed several ice islands without danger.

On the 9th, in the morning, the wind moderated and shifted into the N.N.W. We had made during the last gale 349 miles of distance, and at noon our latitude by observation, was 55° 21′, and longitude by chronometers, 38° 55′ by D. R. 49° 12′. We were now far enough north to be relieved from the fear of falling in with ice, and the navigation became comparatively easy.

Up to the 12th we had variable winds from the northward and westward accompanied with thick fog; and at 8 o'clock in the morning, the weather becoming clear, to our great joy we discovered our little consort in the N.W., and soon after we communicated and found all well. With the wind blowing strong at west, we steered to the northward in company; and at 10 A.M. we saw the island of South Georgia, bearing N. by W. distant about 9 or 10 miles. Notwithstanding the forbidding appearance of this land, every one, I believe, in the two vessels, feasted his eyes upon it; and at 3 in the afternoon both ships came to anchor in Adventure Bay, (S.W. part of Georgia,) in 7 fathoms water, over a bottom of strong clay.

Our arrival here, though it was not a country the most indulgent, we considered to be a very happy event. Our sailors had suffered much from cold fogs and wet during the two months they had been navigating the south; and as we had been nearly 5 months under sail, the appearance of scurvy (that disease so fatally attendant on long voyages) was to be dreaded. Our vessels, too, were so much weather-beaten, that they greatly needed refitting; so that taking into account our many pressing wants, this island, though inhospitable, was capable of affording us great relief.

Our crews here fed plenteously on greens which, although bitter, are very salutary, being an excellent antiscorbutic: with regard to meat, we were supplied with young albatrosses, that is to say, about a year old: the flesh of these is sweet, but not sufficiently firm to be compared with that of any domestic fowl.

Our harbour duties, and a search upon the island for animals for our cargo, were immediately commenced and carried on with zeal, although we experienced frequent interruptions from heavy gales which were now prevalent; it being near the time of the autumnal equinox of this hemisphere.

I took opportunities of making various observations on shore, and found the head of the bay to lie in latitude 54° 2′ 48″, and in longitude, by the mean of two of the best of my chronometers,

38° 8′ 4″. The variation of the compass at the same place by azimuth, was 11° 15′ east. The head of this bay being surrounded with mountains, I ascended the top of one of them for the purpose of taking the altitude of the sun when at some distance from the meridian, but after planting my artificial horizon, I was surprised to find, that although there was not a breath of wind, and every thing around perfectly still, yet the mercury had so tremulous a motion, that I could not get an observation. The ground was evidently agitated internally; though it was only by means of the quicksilver that I could detect it.

On the 17th of April, our harbour business being completed, both vessels put to sea, and with the wind at east, we directed our course towards the Falkland Islands.

South Georgia, it appears, was discovered by a Monsieur La Roche, in the year 1675. It was visited by a vessel called the Lyon in 1756; but was not explored till Captain Cook did so in the Resolution, in the year 1771.

I need not remind the reader of the great advantages navigation, and geography in general, have acquired from the discoveries and investigations of that able navigator; but the public may not be aware of the great extent to which his researches in the South, in particular, have been beneficial to Great Britain.

His official report regarding the island of South Georgia, in which he gave an account of the great number of sea-elephants (called by him sea-lions), and fur seals, found on the shores, induced several enterprising merchants to fit out vessels to take them; the elephants for their oil, and the seals for their skins. These animals are now almost extinct; but I have been credibly informed that, since the year in which they were known to be so abundant, not less than 20,000 tons of the sea-elephant oil has been procured for the London market. A quantity of fur seal-skins were usually brought along with a cargo of oil; but formerly the furriers in England had not the method of dressing them, on which account they were of so little value, as to be almost neglected.

At the same time, however, the Americans were carrying from Georgia cargoes of these skins to China, where they frequently obtained a price of from 5 to 6 dollars a-piece. It is generally known that the English did not enjoy the same privilege; by which means the Americans took entirely out of our hands this valuable article of trade.

The number of skins brought from off Georgia by ourselves and foreigners cannot be estimated at fewer than 1,200,000. I may here also remark, that the Island of Desolation, which Captain Cook likewise visited, and first made known, has been a source of scarcely less profit than the island of Georgia. Hence it may be presumed, that during the time these two islands have been resorted to for the purpose of trade, more than 2000 tons of shipping, and from two to three hundred seamen have been employed annually in this traffic.

Having thus given an idea of the value of what has already been discovered in the South Seas, I shall say something of the island of Georgia as to its extent and peculiarities.

The island is about 96 miles long, and its mean breadth about 10. It is so indented with bays, that in several places, where they are on opposite sides, they are so deep as to make the distance from the one side to the other very small. Near the west end in particular, there is a neck of this kind, about half a mile broad, over which boats are frequently transported.

Dalrymple, in a very old chart, represents this island as having a channel quite through it; which may probably have been the case, since, near the middle, there is an ice-berg, which seems to run from side to side.

The tops of the mountains are lofty, and perpetually covered with snow; but in the valleys, during the summer season, vegetation is rather abundant. Almost the only natural production of the soil is a strong bladed grass, the length of which is in general about two feet; it grows in tufts on mounds three or four feet from the ground.

No land quadrupeds are found here; birds and amphibious animals are the only inhabitants:—of the bird tribe, the king penguin is the most worthy of notice. The penguins (or, as they ought properly to be called, pinguins, the name being evidently derived from the Latin word *pinguedo*, on account of its fatness,) are of a very gregarious nature. They go in large flocks along the shore, erect, and with a waddling gait. When seen through a hazy atmosphere, they may be not inaptly mistaken for a body of men; and, indeed, Sir John Narborough has whimsically likened them to "little children standing up in white aprons." Those which he describes, however, were a very diminutive species in comparison with the king penguin, the bird to which I refer.

In pride, these birds are perhaps not surpassed even by the peacock, to which in beauty of plumage they are indeed very little inferior,—as may be seen in our principal museums. During the time of moulting, they seem to repel each other with disgust, on account of the ragged state of their coats; but as they arrive at the maximum of splendour they re-assemble, and no one who has not completed his plumage is allowed to enter the community. Their frequently looking down their front and sides in order to contemplate the perfection of their exterior brilliancy, and to remove any speck which might sully it, is truly amusing to an observer.

About the beginning of January they pair, and lay their eggs. During the time of hatching, the male is remarkably assiduous, so that when the hen has occasion to go off to feed and wash, the egg is transported to him, which is done by placing their toes together, and rolling it from the one to the other, using their beaks to place it properly. As they have no nest, it is to be remarked, that the egg is carried between the tail and legs, where the female, in particular, has a cavity for the purpose.

The hen keeps charge of her young nearly a twelvemonth, during which time they change and complete their plumage; and in teaching them to swim, the mother has frequently to use some artifice; for when the young one refuses to take the water, she entices it to the side of a rock, and cunningly pushes it in, and this is repeated until it takes the sea of its own accord. There are three other kinds of penguins, all of them nearly of the same size, but little more than half the bigness of that which I have described. Their plumage is not near so fine, but they walk erect, and are of the same form with the king penguin. The names by which they are distinguished are, the macaroni, the jack-ass, and the stone-cracker penguin. The macaroni is so called from its having been likened to a fop or macaroni, though I must confess I do not see the similitude. The next has its name from the noise it makes, which resembles the braying of an ass. And the third is denominated from its pecking or cracking stones when irritated. All these birds have a practice of cunningly stealing from one another, during the time of nest-building, the materials of which they are constructed. They differ from the king penguin in these particulars, and also in having nests, which are sometimcs in the sides of tussac mounds, but generally on the side of a hill, and are composed of a few sticks and stones. They remain with their young but four months, viz. from January to April, at which time they take them off shore for several successive days to the distance of four or five miles, in order to accustom them to the water; and when they can endure it, they go off to sea.

The Albatross (the Diomedia of ornithology) is a bird which has been often seen by navigators off the Cape of Good Hope, and in southern latitudes, and has been frequently described; but as the species abounds in the island of Georgia, I shall record some observations I have made in regard to their domestic habits, &c. A full grown albatross sometimes measures 16 or 17 feet from the tip of one wing to the tip of the other when expanded; but more commonly they average about 12 feet. These birds are so abundantly covered with feathers that, when plucked, they appear not above one half the original size, and our astonishment at their apparent magnitude immediately vanishes. I have found them when cleaned, to weigh from 12 to 25 lb.

There is something humorously remarkable in their way of mating; the couple approach one another with great apparent ceremony, bringing their beaks repeatedly together, swinging their heads, and contemplating each other with very deliberate attention. Sometimes this will continue for two hours together, and to a person inclined to be amused the whole transaction would appear not unlike one of our own formal courtships in pantomime. They have great power in their beaks, and, when on the nest, I have observed them defend themselves for half an hour against an active dog. Their feet are webbed and remarkably large, so that when the water is smooth they can walk on the surface with hardly any assistance from their wings, and the noise of their tread is heard at a considerable distance. Their eggs are inferior to those of geese, but they have less yolk, and more white in proportion to their size, and weigh generally one pound and three quarters. All birds of the albatross and gull kind lay their eggs in October, and, when new laid, they are a great source of refreshment.

The bird next in size found here, is called by sailors a Nelly; it is of the peterel kind, and of a mixed grey and brown colour, having an unpleasing appearance, and being extremely voracious. Their fondness for blubber often induces them to eat so much that they are unable to fly. A flock of perhaps five or six hundred has been known to devour 10 tons of the sea-elephant fat in six or eight hours. From this appetite for oily food, their flesh is uneatable, nor are their eggs so good as those of the other birds I have mentioned.

The smaller oceanic birds of the southern hemisphere have, for the most part, a residence in this island; but as they are well known it is unnecessary to enumerate them.

I fear that in the description of these animals I have been tedious, since by some readers, such remarks may be considered as of little importance; but the hints which the peculiar instincts of these creatures furnished, I have preferred to a minute detail of their dimensions and colours, with which the public are already well acquainted.

Having given an idea of the value of Southern Discoveries to Great Britain, and said all that is necessary of the animals fallen in with, I shall return to the journal of our voyage.

At 2 o'clock on the 17th of April, the east end of Georgia bore N.E. ½ N. distant about 14 miles. The wind freshened at south, and produced a cross and disagreeable sea: on the 18th the wind was southerly, and the weather foggy, which prevented my getting sight of the shag rocks as I had intended. They are represented as situated in the latitude 53° 48′, and longitude 43° 25′, and are said to be even with the water, which I believe not to be the case, as I have been credibly informed, that they appear in three pinnacles, or in the shape of sugar loaves 60 or 70 feet high, with a reef running round them. These reefs, I presume, have given rise to the supposed existence of the Aurora Islands. The Atrevida Spanish man of war having been sent, in 1796, to survey what are called the Auroras, probably saw these rocks, and by a confused concurrence of circumstances, the commander supposed he had discovered three islands, which were accordingly officially reported to the Spanish government. These islands have since found a place in our charts with the track of the Atrevida round them; giving credit to which every body has been led to believe in their existence: consequently as they lie in the track of ships bound round Cape Horn, the notion must be a great hinderance to navigation.

An instance of this appeared in the case of a friend of mine, who informed me that once having had to lay to for daylight with a fair wind on account of these islands, his passage round the Cape was much protracted.

But as we are now near the place where this supposed Spanish discovery was made, it may not be improper to give an account of a search I myself made for these islands in my first voyage in the year 1820. But to shew how undisputed the authority is for their existence, I shall first insert a translation of official reports from the Spanish, relating to this matter. It is as follows:

Extracts translated from the Publications of the Royal Hydrographical Society of Madrid, published by Authority in 1809. *Memoria segunda, tomo* 1°. *p.* 51, 52.

"THE AURORA ISLANDS.

"We do not learn that they ever were seen before the year 1762, in which they were discovered by the ship Aurora, which gave them her name. In 1790 they were likewise seen again by the ship Princess belonging to the Royal Philippine Company, Captain Manuel de Oyarvido, who shewed us his journal in Lima, and gave us some information with regard to their situation. In 1794, the corvette Atrevida went purposely to *situate* them, having practised in their immediate vicinity from the 21st to 27th of January all the necessary observations, and measured by chronometers the difference of longitude between these islands and the port of Soledad in the Maluinas (or Falkland Isles). The islands are three: they are very nearly in the same meridian: the centre one is rather low, and the other two may be seen at nine leagues' distance.

"Their latitudes and longitudes are as follows:

	° ′ ″		° ′ ″
Latitude of the most southern island.			53 15 22 S.
Longitude west of Cadiz.	41 40 00	W. Gr.	
Long. Cadiz and Gr.	6 17 15		
			47 57 15
Latitude of the second island or the low one.			53 2 40
Longitude west of Cadiz.	41 38 00	W. Gr.	47 55 15
Latitude of the third island which has hitherto been undiscovered, and therefore called New Island.			52 37 24 S.
Longitude from Cadiz.	41 26 00	W. Gr.	
Reduced to Gr. long.	6 17 15		
			47 43 15 W.

"The captain of the Princess says, that to E.S.E. of the island, most to the south, at the distance of 11 miles, there is a bank or shoal, but the corvette Atrevida, which made various efforts to find it, could not discover it, and only saw different banks of snow, which, at some distance, appeared like banks or shoals."

The above is given as the conclusive testimony of all the surveys; here follow certain particulars less known: —

Appendix to the above-mentioned Work, vol. 1. p. 213. Number IV.

"An Account of the Campaign or Cruize of the Corvette Atrevida from the Time of her leaving the Maluinas in *January*, 1794, in search of the Islands Aurora, until her Arrival at Montevideo on the 15th *February* following.

"Having finished with all possible exactness the observations we had to make in Port Soledad, and having embarked the instruments and whatever belonged to the corvettes, it was determined on the 10th of *January* to weigh anchor and make sail. The wind had been fresh all day from S.W., but it calmed towards evening; and on endeavouring to raise the anchor in that point it was found so tenaciously embedded that the launch suffered much. From midnight the necessary labour was continued, and at daylight we got under weigh, the boats having been first taken in.

" The wind at the time was west, and we improved it under all sail to the E.S.E. This cruise (or campaign) had for its only object to search for *the Aurora Islands* (whose position was considered as uncertain), from 12′ to 15′ of latitude, and 7° of longitude, according to the different reckonings of the navigators who had given information concerning them. We took advantage of the winds sometimes favourable, sometimes contrary to our course, keeping in the parallel of 53½°, and with prudent precaution determined to lie by at nights. On the 15th our observations and the sight of gulls and other birds gave us indications of being near the islands. In these lyings to, we suffered the double martyrdom of losing precious time, and encountering rollings and a cold that were insufferable even to those who had just experienced the intemperance of Cape Horn.

" At day-break on the 16th, we saw two large banks of snow or ice distance 5 miles to the N.E. The pyramidal figure would not have failed to have flattered our hopes if their proximity had not destroyed the illusion; latitude 53° 40′ the parallel of the islands prevented us advancing a mile, without a clear horizon.

"Until the 18th, in the morning, continued a fog: the wind was not much, but the sea was still very cross. The observation of mid-day was 54° 11′ S. of latitude, half a degree south of the parallel established for our investigations. We luffed immediately, to gain what we had lost, with every possible sail. In the evening we discovered a large hummock in the form of a sugar-loaf, which we took for a bank of snow. All the next day and night the fog continued, so that we could not distinguish objects at half a mile's distance.

"On the 20th in the evening, after some hours of calm, and variable winds, it blew from the S. S. E., and somewhat cleared away. We steered east, and on the 21st, at mid-day, found ourselves in latitude 53° 40′ S., and longitude 42° W. Cadiz (equal to longitude 48° 17′ 15″ W. Greenwich.)

"At 5½ P. M. we perceived to the northward, at a great distance, a dark lump, which appeared to all of us like a mountain of ice. Notwithstanding, we bore away for it under a press of sail; and when we were near it, we saw distinctly a great mountain in the form of a pavilion (or tent) divided vertically into two parts; the eastern extremity *white*, and the western very *dark*; on which latter side was a snowy band: —and we also noticed some breaks in the dark streak.

"We all agreed that this was *the* island; but we saw no other, and none of the circumstances agreed with those reported of the Auroras.*

* Extracts from some of those voyages. "In 1762, the ship Aurora, on her return from Lima, saw two islands, 35 leagues to the W. of the Maluinas, according to account, running N. E. and S. W., distant 2½ to 3 leagues. The eastern was the smallest, and had a reef which extended towards the other; leaving, however, a clear channel, through which that ship passed. The western had 5 to 6 miles in extent, from N. to S. On their inaccessible sides, they could not perceive any bays. One mile to the north, no soundings with 120 fathoms. The observations of the same day placed *it* in 53° 15′ S., and in 325° 22′ of longitude from the meridian of Teneriffe, corrected to the sight of making Ascension."

"In 1769, the ship San Miguel being in the lat. of 53° 27′ S., and long. 318° 36′ from Teneriffe, saw six hummocks of land of different sizes; and thinking them to be the islands Beauchene, to the southward of the Maluinas, corrected their reckoning, and afterwards made to the island of Ascension in 8°, when they thought themselves in the meridian of Trinidad, or Ascension of America. So enormous a difference of 16½° made them suspect that they had been the Auroras."

"In 1774, the ship Aurora saw one evening a-head several hummocks, which they thought to be banks of snow. They continued during the night lying-to, and next morning saw them again. The green water continuing, and several birds which they had seen two days before, they approached it,

"We passed within one mile of the island, coasting it on the western side; and, from that point, it presented us the view of a sharp rock, trending from north to south. The southern part, constantly exposed to the freezing winds from that quarter, was covered with snow; and being cut perpendicularly on the north-west side, with winds much more temperate and moist, the land was there perfectly discoverable. From thence, steering S. W. we lay off and on during the night, to see whether the observations of the next day could be made under happier circumstances.

"At daylight, we saw another island at a great distance, also covered with snow, but not so high as the former one. At 6^h we might be distant 10 miles, to the N. $\frac{1}{4}$ N. E. (N. b. E.), and the first was seen to the S. E., distant about 8 miles. At 9^h we lost sight of it; and although

---

and saw that it was an island stretching from N. W. to S. E., about 3 leagues in length; and, being in its parallel, they observed, in 53° 38′ of latitude, and by estimation in longitude 326° 10′ from Teneriffe. To the E. S. E. from this island, at three or four leagues' distance, they saw another, which shewed a heavy surf, and which they estimated to be in 53° 42′ latitude, and 326° 33′ longitude from Teneriffe. Two other vessels, the Pearl in 1779, and the Dolores in 1790, saw these islands also, but without noticing their position."

the wind freshened from the N.W. we went round it without effect; because the clouds not having dissipated, we could not get the latitude at meridian. We, nevertheless, waited; and at one o'clock had an altitude, and another at three o'clock, by which we concluded the latitude which referred to the islands we had seen, and the longitude calculated by the chronometers: the first was determined to be in latitude 53° 15′ 22″ S., and longitude 41° 4′ 0″ W. of Cadiz. The wind was now at S.W., and we hauled to the southward, seeking in higher latitudes more favourable winds to get to the westward, and make the coast of Patagonia.

"On the 24th at mid-day, we were in 55° 28′ latitude S.; and as we did not meet better winds, but rougher seas and most intense colds, it was resolved to lessen the latitude, in search of more favourable weather. We stood to the northward, on the larboard tack, with all sail; and on the 26th, at evening, discovered to the E. ¼ N. E. a white lump, which at first appeared to us a field of ice; but its immobility soon convinced us that it was an island. It is a large rock, making in sharp pinnacles, but formed like a saddle-hill. The N. E. was covered with snow, but the southern part, being perpendicular, would not retain it. At a mile from this last point, there extended several breakers, terminating in small islands. We coasted along this great rock at a regular distance, and sounded frequently, without finding bottom. On the 27th, in the morning, we had good observations of latitude and longitude; which, referred to the said island, placed it in 52° 37′ 24″ S. latitude, and 41° 26′ longitude west of Cadiz."

In consequence of the credibility of these documents, I was induced to make a strict search for these islands; and shall now, for the benefit of navigation, relate the circumstances of the investigation.

Having examined the daily rates of my chronometers in the harbour of St. John's in Staten Land, and taken on board a supply of wood and water, we weighed anchor on the 27th of January, 1820, and made sail to the eastward. At eight o'clock P. M. the east end of Staten Land bore S.W. by W., distant five leagues. During the 28th and 29th, the wind was from W. N. W. with hazy weather; at noon our latitude was 53° 17′, and longitude 55° 22′. We continued under a press of sail, keeping the latitude of 53° 15′, and on the 31st we had fine weather with the wind from the northward. In the forenoon we passed some kelp, and had several birds about the ship, which gave me hopes that we were approaching the islands.

Our latitude, at noon, by observation was 52° 47′ S., and longitude by chronometers 48° 47′ W., and by D. R. 48° 38′. In the evening I observed the variation of the compass to be 16° 11′. At seven in the evening we had passed over the (laid down) latitude and longitude of these islands, without observing the least appearance of land. We *obtained* and continued in the parallel of latitude, running through the place assigned to them till we arrived in the longitude of 46°. I considered this allowance for error in longitude to be pretty ample; particularly since the Atrevida sailed from Port Soledad in the Falkland Islands; from which, to the place for our investigation, was but about three days' sail: hence her common reckoning could not have erred much, and she had chronometers which should have been nearly exact. These considerations produced in my mind a degree of surprise; and I could not, at that moment, reconcile my experience with the facts which had been asserted. I was resolved, however, not to abandon the object of my pursuit, without being fully satisfied of the truth or falsity of this geographical problem. It was now remarkably clear; and, from the mast-head, land of common height might have been seen at the distance of eight leagues; but still, nothing of the kind was observed. We next steered S. S. E. into the latitude of 53° 17′, and then W. by S., in order to get sight of the southern island; but in vain — not the smallest indication of land appeared. On the 2d, it blew a strong gale from the N. N. W. with thick weather; and we hove to, under a close-reefed main-topsail, sent down the top-gallant yards, and struck the masts. At noon the weather cleared up, and we got the meridian altitude of the sun, which gave latitude 52° 58′, and our longitude by chronometers was 48° 6′, our latitude by D. R. being 53° 20′. We had experienced a northerly current of 22 miles, part of which must be attributed to error of reckoning.

The situation for the middle island bore now S. 33° E., distant eight miles. We had a clear view of 6 or 7 leagues, but nothing like land was to be seen. The only chance now left us for finding these Auroras, I conceived, was by making various courses between the latitudes of 53° 15′ and 52° 37′; and this we did, till we reached the longitude by chronometers of 46° 29′. Having all this time seen nothing resembling land, except fog-banks which had often given us severe disappointment, we returned westward; and, on the 5th, our latitude at noon was 52° 44′, and longitude by chronometers 48° 33′. We had thus again passed over the site of these islands to no purpose. On the 6th, our latitude by observation was 53° 24′, and longitude by chronometers 49° 49′. We continued to stand to the westward under easy sail, with the wind northerly; and on the 7th, our latitude by observation was 53° 33′, and longitude by chronometers 51° 5′. Having thus diligently searched through the supposed situation of the Auroras, I concluded that the discoverers must have been misled by appearances; I therefore considered any further cruize to be an improvident waste of time; and, to the gratification of my officers and crew, directed our course to the Falkland Islands.

From the apparent validity of the printed documents setting forth the existence of the Auroras, I was naturally led to consider in what way those Spanish officers could have fallen into so great a mistake. There are two ways in which it might be accounted for, (with men unaccustomed to traversing cold and tempestuous seas, encumbered with ice,) and into which they might easily fall in their conclusions. The reports of voyagers previous to the cruize of the Atrevida are, from their imperfect knowledge of the science of navigation, not much deserving of attention. The investigation performed by the Atrevida, however, is certainly a matter of some consequence, from their having been particularly instructed to ascertain the situation of these islands; and it was to be expected, therefore, that this hydrographical point should have been left undoubted.

They sailed from Port Soledad on the 14th of January, having chronometers on board, a circumstance which ought to have insured accuracy, and proceeded into the vicinity of the place pointed out for their research. On the 21st, they saw an island; which, as they express it, appeared like a great mountain, in the form of a pavilion or tent divided vertically into two parts. This may possibly have been the Shag Rocks, which lie nearly in the same latitude, but differ six degrees in longitude. About this time, much ice was found drifting from the southward, and it is probable that it had formed round the base of these rocks; and the peaks appearing above, clear of snow, and black, would leave no doubt of that part being land. The ice formed on the south side, and probably forced on this reef of rocks, might be taken for a range of land covered with snow; and upon the same data it may be presumed that what they describe as the second island was an ice-berg; and the third, which is described as having been seen on the 27th, was, perhaps, the same as that which was seen on the 21st, *viz.* the Shag Rocks, with the appearance of the base altered by the ice having shifted its position. The difference of longitude between the Shag Rocks and the place assigned to the Auroras seems hardly to admit of my conjecture of their being the same; but it is well known, that the longitude of places, in many instances, has been egregiously misrepresented, from assuming different meridians, as also from typographical and various other mistakes resulting from ignorance.

The only other way in which a reason can be advanced to account for the fallacy of this discovery is, that what they saw were all ice-islands, incorporated with earth, similar to the one which I have mentioned having seen far to the southward.

Having thus brought to a conclusion, what I consider a subject of interest to hydrographical science, *viz.* the ascertaining the non-existence of these islands, I now return to our own position, when by reason of foggy weather we were unable to get sight of the Shag Rocks.

We proceeded to the westward under as much sail as we could carry; but the wind was so continually shifting between S.W. and N.W. that we made but little progress: and our only advantage was obtained by tacking as the wind shifted, for however short a time. The fore-topsail was almost constantly close-reefed, and frequently furled. Our consort continued in company, and we neglected no opportunity of making westing. On the 22d of April, our latitude by observation was 54° 15′, and longitude by chronometers 46° 49′, by D. R. 47° 11′.

During the 23d and 24th, we had the wind from east to south; but at noon of the 24th it shifted into the S.W. The weather continued to be very unsettled; and the wind often shifting, and continuing to blow hard, produced a sea so irregular, that several of our shrouds and backstays were carried away; and but for the precaution I had taken, of having equal to three additional shrouds on a side, to the lower masts, we certainly should have lost them. Sailing in the neighbourhood of the supposed Auroras, with long nights and heavy gales, would have caused great anxiety had we not been previously satisfied of their non-existence; and I certainly felt gratified at deriving this benefit from the pains I had formerly taken to ascertain that circumstance.

On the 3d, at noon, it blew a heavy gale at W. S. W. and we lay to. In the afternoon our consort lost her bowsprit, by a heavy sea passing over it, though only a small part of it was then without the bows. We fortunately had a spar, with which we supplied her, when the weather became moderate.

On the 2d of *May*, at noon, our latitude by

observation was 53° 44′, and longitude by chronometers 59° 27′, and by D. R. 61° 6′. The weather was still boisterous; but every interval, during which sail could be made, was gladly embraced; and the following day, at 11 o'clock, we saw the island of Beauchene, bearing N.W., by W. distant 5 leagues. We proceeded to the westward, along the south side of the Falklands, and, owing to a succession of adverse gales, and a strong easterly current, we did not get into harbour till the 11th of May, when we came to anchor in New Island, at the west end of the Falklands.

CHAP. IV.

DEATH OF A SEAMAN; SUPERSTITIONS. — FALKLAND ISLANDS. — CAPTAIN BARNARD'S NARRATIVE OF HIS SOLITARY RESIDENCE ON NEW ISLAND. — LOSS OF THE CORVETTE L'URANIE. — MUTINY ON BOARD THE HEROIND. — FALKLAND ISLANDS TAKEN POSSESSION OF BY CAPTAIN JEWITT, FOR THE PATRIOT GOVERNMENT OF BUENOS AYRES.

My intention being to winter here, I chose an anchorage in Quaker Harbour, in Swan Island, for our winter quarters, struck the brig's topmasts, and made her secure in all respects against the heavy gales which might be expected. The cutter I kept efficient, for the purpose of pursuing our business.

It would be tedious to narrate minutely our daily proceedings, I shall therefore mention only what particularly occupied my attention.

Our cooper and carpenters constructed establishments on shore for carrying on their respective duties, and our general harbour arrangements were made. I was particular in observing the winds and weather, as I was quite aware that few people are acquainted with the nature of this climate. An abstract of these observations I shall give in another place.

In order to avoid the necessity of shortening the voyage, on account of provisions, I reduced each man's allowance, in both vessels, to half a pound of salt meat per day; four pounds of bread, one pint of flour, three half pints of oatmeal, and the same of peas, for each man, per week. The want of flesh meat was made up with what a hunting party could procure, together with the geese found on the shores; which, though excessively fishy, were well relished with a keen appetite.

On the 18th of June, on returning to the brig, from a cruize in the Beaufoy, I received the distressing information of a man having died in my absence. His name was Francisco Antonio: he was a native of Terciera, one of the western islands. It appeared that John Atkinson, the carpenter, had done every thing for him which his incompetent skill in physic, though prompted by a feeling heart, could suggest; but without avail. The deceased had been several months in a consumption, and was likewise subject to cramp in the bowels; of which it appeared he had died. By the time I arrived, he had been dead three days, and the carpenter had prepared a coffin. The ceremony of interment now only remained, which we immediately performed in Swan Island. I read the funeral service of the English church over the body; and, to mark out the spot, we placed a board at the head of the grave.

The death of this man made such a melancholy impression on the mind of the cooper in particular, that his health was a good deal impaired. He had been about the deceased during his illness, and was present at his death; and, having only the company of the carpenter and a boy, in an uninhabited country, with no variety which might have diverted his attention from the contemplation of so mournful an event, a weakness of mind was the consequence. Such feelings, when they produce mental imbecility, certainly should be discouraged; but they are generally preferable to a careless and callous disregard of the fate of others, and the solemn consideration of futurity. Our dog, too, was observed to jump into the sleeping-cabin of the deceased, and to exhibit actions which were considered as bearing a very mysterious signification. Sailors are generally believed to be superstitious; and certainly it is surprising that those men, who feel undaunted amidst the slaughter of a hard-fought battle, should tremble with the opposite extreme of cowardice at the idea of a ghost or hobgoblin. These impressions, no doubt, take their rise from the practice of sailors amusing one another with frightful stories on their still and dark night-watches.

During the latter end of *July*, and the months of *August* and *September*, we had several heavy gales from the southward, with snow; but it seldom remained longer on the ground than twenty-four hours, except on the tops of the highest mountains.

Finding that our cargoes could not be completed here, I resolved on going to South Shetland; and accordingly, in *September*, we refitted both vessels, and moved them westward 12 miles, to New Island.

On the 7th of *October*, having prepared, but with scanty means, for a southern navigation, we weighed the anchors, and proceeded towards South Shetland.

Having spent two winters among the Falkland Islands, and visited nearly all their harbours, I may venture to speak of them with the expectation of advancing something that may be useful to strangers.

This uninhabited group, which is now generally known by the name of the Falkland Islands, consists of nearly ninety islands, lying between the latitude of 51° and 52° 45′ S., and between longitude 57° 20′ and 61° 40′ W. Two of them are of considerable extent, and these (the two main islands, from which the others take their name,) are properly called the East and West Falklands. The western island is by much the largest; but is so indented, that its exact size cannot be easily ascertained. Its greatest length, from N. E. to

S.W. is nearly 100 miles, and its greatest breadth about 50. The eastern island, the length of which from N.E. to S.W. is about 78 miles, and its greatest breadth 47, is also so indented, that in one place two bays nearly meet.

Between the two main islands the sound is from 7 to 12 miles broad; and many of the smaller islands are situated in it. This channel is navigable for ships of any size, and by attending to the best chart, which is that of Lieutenant Edgar, it may be passed through with safety, as all the dangers are there laid down. I cannot omit this opportunity of bearing my strongest testimony to the accuracy with which Lieutenant Edgar has delineated the coast of the western main island, and the surrounding small ones of this group.

Not being personally acquainted with the author, I am induced to recommend his chart entirely by the experience I have had of its great utility, during the many dark and stormy nights which I have passed among these islands. The harbours in this sound I have anchored in, and have found them commodious, and, indeed, equal to any in the world. On the northern coast of the western island there are many entrances; the principal one is that leading to Port Egmont, and which may be seen from some distance at sea.

By keeping the opening about S.E. by S. (by compass), it may be sailed into without risk.

About 9 miles N.N.W. from the entrance lie two islets; by passing within half a mile of the western side of these the course will be about S.S.E. ½ E.

The English settlement was made at this port, but certainly the site was ill chosen. The ruins of part of the town still remain, and stand on the south side of a mountain not less than 600 feet high. The settlers had extended their gardens seemingly to the westward of this mountain, but during the winter the solar rays must have been almost lost to them throughout the greater part of the day. How such a bleak and unpropitious situation could have been their choice, I am at a loss to understand, unless it were on account of the anchorage.

The harbour is spacious even to a fault; for its enormous size, during strong winds, renders the communication with the shore inconvenient. The best anchorage is immediately off the creek at the foot of the ruins bearing N.N.W., in 9 fathoms water, about three fourths of a mile from the shore. Off the east point of the creek runs a reef which is marked out by the kelp. The bottom here is so tough, that, after having broke many blocks and handspokes, I was obliged to heave the vessel close down at low water, and wait for the tide to flow the anchor out of the ground.

The best watering place is at the head of the creek, and the most expeditious and convenient method of obtaining water is to fill the casks at low water mark, and raft them off to the vessel. Fuel, the next necessary article, may be obtained by digging peat, about a hundred yards above the top of the creek; but it requires drying, and is not so good as is to be found at some other places.

The tide flows here at 10 minutes past 7 o'clock on the full and change of the moon, and rises about 9 feet. A few years ago refreshments were plentiful in this port, as there were many hogs, which had been left by the settlers, running wild on Saunders' Island; but they are now nearly extinct. Upland geese, which a few years ago were very numerous, are now scarcely to be found; so that the only supplies which may be expected are ducks and geese which feed on fishy substances on the shores, and thus very soon become nauseous to the taste. It is proper thus to mention what the islands are capable of affording now, for the reports of several years ago do not apply to the present time. An instance of this occurred in the case of a French ship which arrived at Port Egmont in the year 1820, for a cargo of seal skins and oil. The captain was a lieutenant in the French navy, and his ship was elegantly and expensively fitted out. It appeared that the voyage was projected upon the foundation of his father having, forty-two years before, been at this port, and at that time found the beaches lined with sea elephants and seals. The son expected the same to be still the case; but as none were to be found, he abandoned the voyage, with great loss, no doubt, to his employers.

The mistake of Commodore Byron as to the fecundity of the seal might be easily fallen into. He says, (vide Byron's Voyage,) "We were not surprized at meeting with such a great number of seals, when we afterwards found that they had sometimes 18 or more at a litter. Sea lions of a prodigious size are also found on the coast. We had many battles with this amphibious animal, the killing one of which was frequently an hour's work for six men."

The seal, as is now known, brings forth ordinarily not more than one at a time; and I may remark a circumstance which might cause the Commodore to fall into error in his conclusions on this subject. The disproportion between the large male and female seal is nearly as great as between a cow and her calf. One large male, like the grand seignor, has frequently when on the beach from 15 to 20 females under his immediate dominion. These, from their comparative smallness, might by the Commodore be easily taken for the young, and the male for the mother.

With regard to the killing of the sea lion (properly the sea elephant), it is now to one man, acquainted with the practice, the work of three minutes; but without stabbing it in the heart, or breaking its brain, the feat is so difficult that probably as long a time would be requisite as that mentioned by Byron.

The next principal anchorage to Port Egmont is West Point Harbour, which lies at the western extremity of the south land of Berkeley's Sound. The chart accurately exhibits two passages to this anchorage; one by the north, the other by the south. The Jason Islands lie to the N.W., and are much in the way of the southern approach. Strangers should be careful to avoid these islands in the night-time, or in unsettled weather, as the tide runs so strong and irregular through them as to render a ship almost unmanageable. The south passage to West Point Harbour is easily made by being careful when coming from the westward to haul close round West Point Island, so as to enter the gut or channel: by neglecting this precaution, with the wind from the westward, you may fall to leeward of the passage, and find it difficult to work out of the lee bays, into which there is frequently a heavy westerly swell rolling. The latitude of the anchorage is 51° 24′ 15″, and the longitude by a number of deductions from celestial observations and chronometers 60° 36′ 30″. The best anchorage is abreast of a small cove on the south side of the harbour in five fathoms, over a bottom of sand and mud. The velocity of the tide is scarcely perceptible in this situation, though it rises about 9 feet by the shore, and it flows on the full and change of the moon at 30 minutes past 7 in the morning. Water may be procured at the top of the cove; and at the head of the harbour there is also a water run, in which mullets may be caught by building a fish wire. This kind of refreshment is abundant during the spring and autumn of this hemisphere, both here and at Beaver Island, as also at Little Port Egmont, a bay in the west side of the passage to Port Egmont. Rock ord have been likewise caught on the north shore of Swan Island, but they are very scarce. West Point Island has a cove, in which we lay during two winter months in 1820; but it is not large enough for general convenience. At the west end of the island is a rookery (if I may call it so) of the small albatross, which in October affords a good supply of eggs. Some brush-wood grows around the cove, but it is too small to be of use, even as fuel. In coming through the gut from the southward with the ebb tide, which runs to the N.E. with great rapidity, the great harbour when opened must be hastily entered to avoid being swept to the northward by the tide.

From the south entrance of the gut, North Island lies S. 25° W. distant 22 miles. New Island I consider the most easy of access of any in the western quarter. Ship Harbour, which is commodious, lies in latitude 51° 42′ 36″, and longitude 61° 9′. Though by difference of time from Cape Horn, the longitude of which I make by lunar observations and time-keepers 67° 13′ 45″, it will be 61° 15′. The mean 61° 9′ may, however, be nearer the truth. In coming from the westward in the latitude of 51° 42′, New Island may be easily distinguished by its being the most northerly large island of that cluster, and by two small islands lying at the north end, called Saddle Island and North Island: between these, and the north end of New Island, is a clear passage; but in strong winds the tide ripples violently, which, however, I have passed through without accident.

Ship Harbour being the anchorage in this island the most to be recommended, I shall observe that in proceeding to it with a strong westerly wind, as rounding the north end of the island, the sail on the ship should be particularly attended to, as the gusts of wind off the high land blow with great violence. With the wind at S.W. the south passage may be chosen. A cluster, called Seal Rocks, lie off the south end of New Island, between which and the rocks is the best passage, and by keeping without the edge off the kelp, which lies off a short distance from the end of the island, there is no danger. The small round islands, on the eastern side of New Island, have good channels within, and between them Ship Harbour is the third bay from the south, and may be easily recognised, by having a small island, which I called Ship Island, in it. Behind this is the best anchorage in seven fathoms water, in a bottom of stiff clay; with the south point of Ship Island bearing S.E., covering the S.E. point of the bay. The anchorage is perfectly land-locked.

The want of wood on these islands would be a great inconveniency, were it not that good peat is very abundant. On Ship Island it is inexhaustible: I have burnt many tons, and found it an excellent substitute for coal. In order to get it dry, it is necessary to pull it from the sides of the pit, not very deep; and as there are several peat holes, by working them alternately the material may be procured in a state fit for use.

Good water may be obtained at a sandy beach abreast of the anchorage; but the well from which the water is generally taken is so near the beach that high tides render it brackish. Owing to this circumstance we found, when at sea, that several of our casks of water were undrinkable. The well or pool might with little trouble be made eight or ten yards higher on the bank, and the water be passed to the casks with buckets.

This island is mountainous, and its western side presents a range of frightful precipices, one of which is 550 feet above the sea, which in westerly storms beats against its base with extraordinary violence. The eastern side, on the contrary, falls sloping into points forming bays. The length of the island is, from north to south, about seven miles, and the mean breadth about two and a half.

New Island is remarkable for having been for two years the solitary residence of a Captain J. Barnard, an American, whose vessel was run away with in the year 1814, by the crew of an English ship, which, on her passage from Port Jackson, had been wrecked on the south side of these islands. I met with Captain Barnard in 1821, at the place of his exile, and his conversation naturally turned to that subject, which, being interesting, "I greedily devoured." A particular account of this residence on an uninhabited island would not fail of being considered almost as wonderful as the celebrated fiction of Robinson Crusoe, since there was a great similarity in their situations. The principal incidents attendant upon this event were as follows: Captain Barnard was at New Island with his vessel in the performance of a voyage for seal furs, and when on the south side of the islands, he met with the crew of the wrecked English ship. Their number might be about 30, including several passengers, some of whom were ladies. He kindly took them to his vessel, and treated them with all the hospitality which their destitute situation required. Captain Barnard was from America, with which England was then at war, and this circumstance created doubts as to the sincerity of their friendly intentions to one another, though he had promised to land them on his passage home at some port in the Brazils.

Owing to the additional number of people, hunting parties were frequently sent out to procure supplies, and when the Captain, with four of his people, were on an excursion of this kind, the wrecked crew cut the cable, and in defiance of the Americans, who were on board, ran away with the ship to Rio Janeiro; whence they proceeded to North America.

On Captain Barnard's return to New Island, he was struck with astonishment at finding his ship carried off, as he had never suspected any design of the kind. On reflection, however, he soon guessed the cause; as it was quite apparent that the fear of being taken to America, where they would become prisoners of war, had been the motive to the commission of this action, which was a bad return for the asylum Captain Barnard had afforded the perpetrators of it. His conduct towards them, certainly, did not justify their entertaining such a suspicion; but it seems they chose rather to act dishonourably than trust to his protestations, that he would land them in the Brazils.

Nothing in the way of supplies having been left for poor Barnard and his four companions, of which even the captors of his ship ought to have thought, he was forced to consider how they were to subsist; and recollecting that he had planted a few potatoes, they directed their attention to them, and, in the course of the second season, obtained a serviceable supply. They had a dog which now and then caught a pig; and the eggs of the albatross, which were stored at the proper season, with potatoes, formed a substitute for bread, and the skins of the seals for clothes. They built a house of stone, still remaining on the island, which was strong enough to withstand the storms of winter, and they might have been comparatively happy, but that they were cut off from their relations and friends, without any immediate prospect of being removed from the island.

To add to the misfortunes of Captain Barnard in being separated from his wife and children, his companions, over whom he exercised no authority, but merely dictated what he considered was for their mutual advantage, became impatient even of this mild controul, took an opportunity to steal the boat, and he was left on the island alone. After being thus entirely abandoned, he spent the time in preparing clothes from the skin of the seal, and in collecting food for winter. Once or twice a day he used to ascend a hill, from which there was a wide prospect of the ocean, to see if any vessel approached; but always returned disappointed and forlorn, — no ship was to be observed. The four sailors, in the meanwhile, having experienced their own inability to provide properly for themselves, returned to him after an absence of some months. He still found much difficulty in preserving peace among his companions; indeed one of them had planned his death, but fortunately it was discovered in time to be prevented. He placed this man alone with some provisions on a small island in

Quaker Harbour, and in the course of three weeks so great a change was made on his mind, that when Captain Barnard took him off, he was worn down with reflection on his crimes, and truly penitent.

They were now attentive to the advice of their commander, and the above-mentioned offender became truly religious and exemplary in his behaviour. In this way they continued to live, occasionally visiting the neighbouring island in search of provisions, till the end of two years, when they were taken off in the month of December, 1815, by an English whaler bound for the Pacific. Captain Barnard informed me, that a British man of war had been sent expressly from Rio Janeiro to take them off, but by some accident the vessel, though at the islands, did not fall in with them.

I have already made such observations on the navigation of this division of the islands, as I considered essentially necessary for the direction of strangers, as well as for general information, and I shall now say something in regard to the eastern main island. The principal port has many names, but that by which it is generally known is Port Louis, at the head of Berkeley's Sound. It is situated at the eastern extremity of the island, and the anchorage is off the ruins of Saint Louis, 12 miles from the entrance of the sound. The remains of about 30 houses, which had been well built, are still standing. They appear to have been erected by French emigrants from St. Maloes, about the year 1764. These industrious and enterprising people, after having made considerable progress in fertilising the ground, were displaced by the Spaniards, who claimed the islands. They, however, partly through political motives, that it might not be of consequence enough to become a bone of contention and involve them with other powers, or probably on account of their having vast possessions in other parts of the globe, neglected the improvement of the country, and latterly entirely abandoned it. It is matter of regret that these French emigrants were not allowed to remain, as a settlement at this point of the South Atlantic would evidently afford great facilities to navigation. The extensive tracts of ground, well clothed with grass, and the quantity of fine cattle running wild on the island, are sufficient proofs of its being a country that might be settled to advantage. The winters are mild, the temperature being seldom so low as the freezing point. Several of my crew, indeed, went without stockings during the greater part of the winters we spent there. The south wind, however, is cold and stormy, but it is not frequent: the prevailing winds are between S.W. and N.W., which, blowing from the coast of Patagonia, are comfortably temperate.

This climate appears to be in general much more temperative now than it was forty years ago, the cause of which may probably be, that immense bodies of ice were then annually found in the latitude of 50°. This ice, passing to the northward, between the Falkland Islands and South Georgia, would necessarily lower the temperature of both air and water, and consequently an unfavourable opinion of the climate was produced.

During the three voyages which I have made in these seas, I have never seen southern ice drifting to the northward of South Georgia. Great changes must, therefore, have taken place in the south polar ice; but this I leave for conjecture, upon the data which the appearance of the sea at the utmost southern limit of my voyage affords.

The harbour of Port Louis lies in latitude 51° 32′, and longitude 58° 3′ 30″. The entrance of the bay, which is formed on one side by the N.E. point of the main island, is immediately seen on approaching within a few miles; and to Hog Island, about seven miles up the bay, the passage is quite open. On drawing near this island, two large beds of kelp will be observed, between which is a passage running about W. by N. I have sounded among this kelp, and found from seven to ten fathoms; but as there may be rocks interspersed, it should not be passed through with a ship. The channel to the anchorage off the ruins may be seen, by referring to the plan which I took, with as much accuracy as my peculiar circumstances would allow.

Off the N.E. point of the bay there is a ledge above water, called the Volunteer Rocks, and N.E. by E., about three quarters of a mile from the point, lies a sunken rock, upon which a French frigate was lost in February, 1820. As I was among the islands at the time, and on the spct soon after it happened, I had an opportunity of ascertaining the circumstances attending this disaster, which were these:—

Commodore Freycenet had performed a voyage of science almost round the world, and after having spent nearly three years, was returning home when this distressing accident happened. It appeared that the abruptness of the coast had inspired them with confidence in approaching it; and they had incautiously hauled within three quarters of a mile of a point called the Volunteer Rocks, where there is always a strong ripple of the tide. Being near high water at the time, the break over the rock was not visible, and the

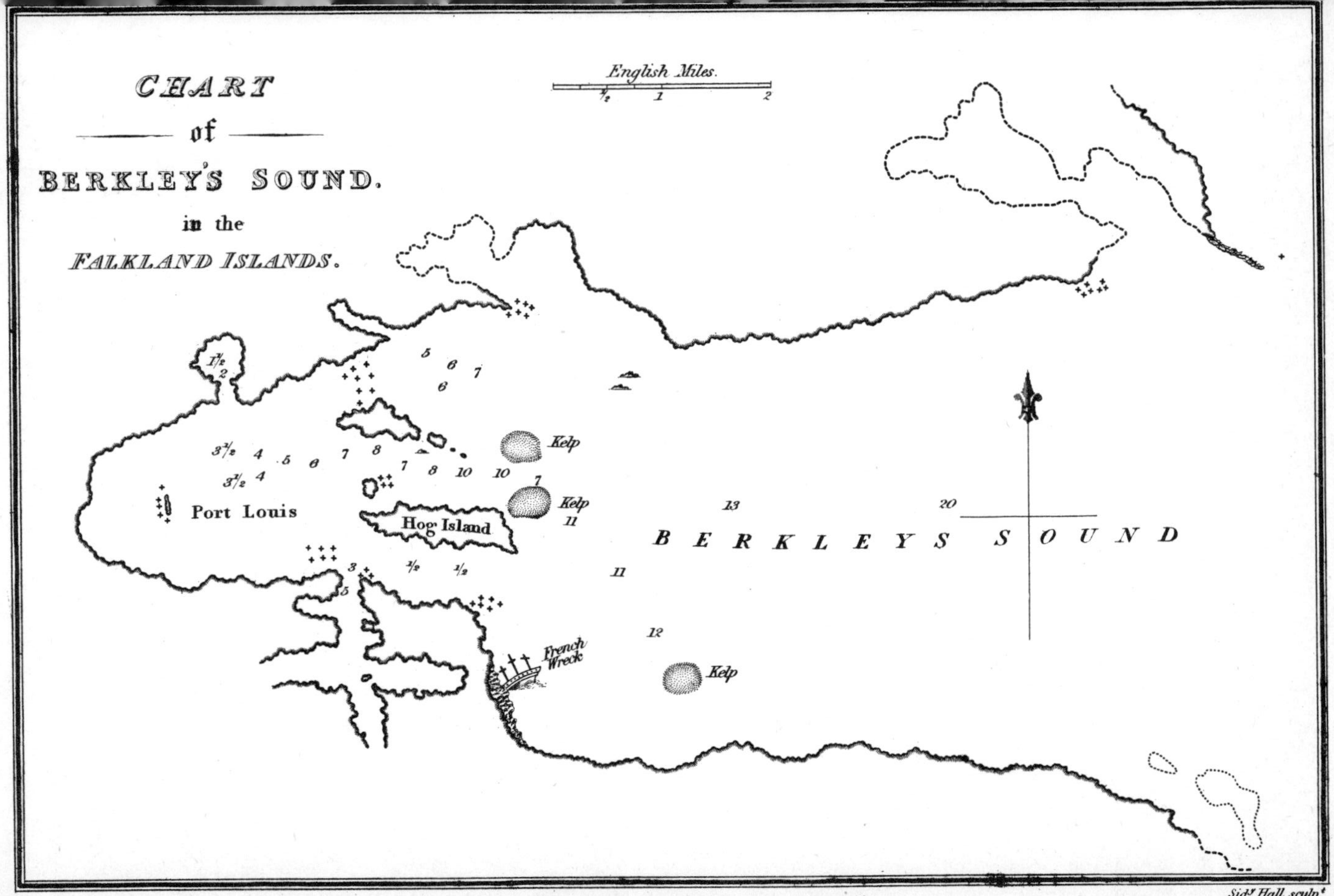

London, Published by Longman & Co. Paternoster Row, Augt. 1825.

Sidy. Hall, sculpt.

ship struck upon this point, and soon beat a hole in her bottom. She, however, presently slid off into deep water, and the pumps were necessarily set in motion, but were not sufficient to keep her free. The Commodore hoped to save his vessel by laying her on the ground well up the bay, and had actually reached a sandy beach, about ten miles from where she had struck; but the water having gained over the mess-deck, and the tide being down, she took the ground in such deep water, that the mess deck was constantly covered, which cut off all prospects of recovering her. He had prudently secured a quantity of provisions, while sailing up the bay; and with these, and every other useful movable, the crew got safe to land. It was several weeks before they knew of any ship being at the island; and in the mean time they had commenced building a small vessel out of the wreck.

As they had saved but about two months' provisions, these were reserved for their passage to the main; and their present support was derived from hunting only. Fortunately, it is on this maloon or island that bullocks and horses are found running wild. Of both these they shot many; but as there were 160 people to feed, the difficulty of taking a sufficient number, owing to their fleetness, caused so scanty a supply, that latterly the crew was reduced to feed on the sea elephant, penguins, and other fishy meats, extremely offensive to a delicate stomach. They were at length relieved from their distressed situation by an American sloop, which, in passing, saw them, and went to their assistance. The ship to which this sloop was a tender, lay at West Point harbour, and I, at the same time, lay with my vessel at Port Egmont. The French commodore not knowing that any other vessel was in the islands, sent an officer in the sloop to the ship at West Point, to treat with the captain for a passage in his vessel to the main. The sloop, on her way, passed through, and anchored in Port Egmont, and the master, who was the chief mate of the ship, came on board, but did not mention the wreck, or that he had a French officer along with him: on the contrary, he cunningly prevented this officer from calling upon me, evidently for the purpose of avoiding competition in getting the passage-freight of these unfortunate people. A few days afterwards I moved the Jane up to West Point harbour, where the General Knox lay, and soon learnt the particulars of the stranded ship. A schooner, also attached to the General Knox, arriving from the wreck, brought the news of a patriot ship, and a South seaman, homeward bound, having arrived at Port Louis; and as secrecy could no longer be preserved, and the schooner was to return to Port Louis, I immediately procured a passage for the purpose of purchasing provisions from the homeward-bound whaler. On my arrival at Port Louis, I found the two ships at anchor; the patriot ship was named the Mercury; the whaler, the Sir Andrew Hammond, commanded by Captain W. Hales — with this gentleman I took up my quarters. I was soon informed that the French commodore had negociated a passage with the captain of the Mercury to take them to Buenos Ayres. What the sum was I never learned; but Captain Orne, of the American ship, had for himself named 20,000 dollars, a large sum from people in distress. I do not, however, suspect Captain Orne of a want of sympathy in the sufferings of others, for I respect him much for many virtues he possesses, and rather attribute his apparent extortion to an idea of the ability of the owners to be liberal.

As the Commodore was now informed of my vessel being in the islands, in order to remove any impression he might have received of my indifference as to his situation, in not having appeared in the competition for his relief, I addressed a letter to him, explaining how very lately I had come to the knowledge of his situation, and how much I regretted not having had it in my power to offer my services much earlier. He sent me the following answer, which I annex, in order to show that my backwardness arose, not from inattention, but from ignorance of his misfortune: —

"*Malouines Islands*, 24*th April*, 1820.

"SIR,

"The obliging, but unfortunately too late offer, which you vouchsafed to make me, by your letter of this day, causes me to regret, most sensibly, the not having had sooner an understanding with you. I would have desired above all things to have negociated with the captain of an English vessel, where my situation required that attention to which others, less friends of loyalty and science, could not be sensible. I wish not to know why you have been but so lately informed of the disaster which befell the corvette l'Uranie; probably, Sir, you may discover, without much difficulty, what sordid avarice could devise to keep you in this ignorance. In short, Sir, I am on the point of sailing, and it is proper that I should follow the course which fortune has been pleased to mark out.

"I wish, Sir, that you may realise every expectation that you have formed, and procure those advantages which you should of right attain. Accept, I beg of you, with all devotion, those assurances of distinguished consideration, with which I have the honour to be,

"Sir,
"Your very humble
"And very obliged Servant,
"(Signed) L. DE FREYCENET."

I afterwards had a conversation with Captain Freycenet, in his state-room, and from his conversation, which was in English, I perceived that he was much affected by his late misfortunes; his health, no doubt, had been impaired by the inconveniences with which he had to struggle, and the aggravation of having been cast on shore after a long and fatiguing voyage; but he enjoyed the sympathising consolation of his lady, who was young and very agreeable. I dined in company with them, and the extreme vivacity of Madame F. seemed well to accord with the character of the French fair: it was reported, that in the midst of the greatest danger and confusion, she retained a most surprising firmness and composure of mind; resembling in this, according to all accounts, the unexampled fortitude of many French ladies luring that murderous period of the French Revolution, when their dearest friends and relations were torn from them by merciless assassins.

The Commodore generously presented me

with a small vessel which he had made here from the ship's launch, with a bill of gift. Captain Hales supplied them with bread, and several other articles they required, for which, however, the purser wished to pay him with the old stores of the wreck; but he warmly refused any recompence, and wrote the commander a letter, stating, that he would consider his acceptance of such an offer to be an act of meanness, and observing that his owners, he was sure, would highly approve of any assistance he might render, without exacting payment.

At length, final and honourable arrangements were made, and Commodore Freycenet sailed with his officers and men to the river Plate, where they arrived in safety.

To return to our remarks on these islands.

The settlers, when they abandoned the eastern island, left behind them several horses and horned cattle, which have increased so much that on going a few miles into the country droves of both animals may be seen. I have taken several of the bullocks by shooting them. They are generally ferocious, and will attack a single person; and thus those who hunt them are enabled to get within pistol-shot of them by the following stratagem: four or five men advance in a line upon the animal, and by appearing only as one person, it stands ready to attack, till within

100 yards, when the hunters spread themselves, and fire, endeavouring to shoot the bullock either in the head or in the fore-shoulder. The horses will also attack a single person, and their mode of doing so, is by forming a circle round him, and prancing upon him; but by means of a musket they may be readily dispersed.

Port St. Salvador is situated about half way on the northern side of the eastern main island; but as it is difficult of access, I shall not particularise nor recommend it as a place of anchorage for strangers.

While lying in this port in 1820, I had a letter brought me from the commander of a patriot national frigate of 30 guns, then at anchor in Port Louis; and to convey an idea of the kind of claim made by the South Americans to these islands, I shall subjoin his letter, with some account of his proceedings: —

National Frigate Heroind at Port Soledad,
" *November* 2. 1820.

" Sir,

" I have the honour to inform you of the circumstance of my arrival at this port, commissioned by the supreme government of the United Provinces of South America to take possession of these islands in the name of the country to which they naturally appertain.

" In the performance of this duty, it is my

desire to act towards all friendly flags with the most distinguished justice and politeness.

"A principal object is to prevent the wanton destruction of the sources of supply to those whose necessities compel or invite them to visit the islands, and to aid and assist such as require it to obtain a supply with the least trouble and expense.

"As your views do not enter into contravention or competition with these orders, and as I think mutual advantage may result from a personal interview, I invite you to pay me a visit on board my ship, where I shall be happy to accommodate you during your pleasure.

"I would also beg you, so far as comes within your sphere, to communicate this information to other British subjects in this vicinity. I have the honour to be,

"Sir,

"Your most obedient humble Servant,

"(Signed) JEWITT,

"Colonel of the marine of the United Provinces of South America, and commander of the frigate Heroind."

The following morning I walked over a distance of 7 or 8 miles to Port Louis, where the frigate lay; and finding a boat on shore, obtained a passage on board. Captain Jewitt received me with great politeness, and notwithstanding the mutilated and worn out state of his ship and crew, he assumed an air of power and authority beyond my expectation. He told me his business was to take possession of the Falkland Islands for his government, and that every thing necessary for an establishment would be procured from Buenos Ayres so soon as he could purchase a cutter, of which there were several among the islands. It evidently appeared, however, that his principal business was to refresh his crew; for never, since the time of Lord Anson, perhaps, had an instance occurred where the scurvy had been so destructive to a ship's company. Though they had been at sea about eight months only, and had frequently during that time been supplied with vegetables from the Cape de Verds, this dreadful disease was making rapid progress among those unfortunate people. The patient was seized first about the knees, and the malady rapidly rising to the stomach, caused dissolution in 36 or 40 hours. During the first days of their arrival here, they died to the number of 5 or 6 in a day. I was glad to give any information in regard to the country, which might be the means of assisting in the recovery of these poor men; and by the use of fish, wild fowl, and indigenous and other vegetables, I had the pleasure of seeing them soon become convalescent. The sick were landed at the ruins of the town of St. Louis; and though there were no roofs to the houses, they found an immense oven in which they were well sheltered from the weather. The complement of men, when the ship sailed from Buenos Ayres eight months before, was 200: they had not now more than 30 seamen and 40 soldiers fit to do duty; 50 had been put on board a prize, so that about 80 were either sick or had died of the scurvy.

Understanding that I could conduct his ship up the sound, for he was then 6 miles below the proper anchorage, the commander begged the favour of me to move her: his extreme politeness required some return: but in addition to that consideration, I saw he was much in want of men, and conceived it possible that if I were unaccommodating, he might entice my crew, or perhaps force them into his service,—I therefore determined to make him my friend by exchanging civilities.

I chose the time for proceeding up the sound, and the anchors were weighed, but with difficulty, the officers being obliged to assist at the capstan. I at length brought the frigate to a safe anchorage off the ruins of St. Louis. The day being too far spent to reach my own ship before dark, Captain Jewitt invited me to remain on board during the night. I accepted his invitation; and during the course of the evening he gave me an account of a mutiny which had happened about three months before, when they were a few degrees to the north of the equator.

The circumstances which I considered interesting he related nearly as follows:—The necessity for having an effective crew, and the impossibility of getting men all of good characters, had induced him to take some out of the common prison. Among these was a man who had attempted the capture of a small vessel with specie on board, lying at anchor at the river Plata; but the night being dark, he had, fortunately for the owner of the money, mistaken the vessel, and got on board a national schooner, where he was seized and committed to gaol. Captain Jewitt saw that this man was a bold, fearless character, but persuaded himself, that, under judicious direction, he might be made useful; and he therefore determined to take him as a petty officer, though the governor remonstrated with him on the subject, and impressed on his mind that the prisoner was a person of the most abandoned principles. Captain Jewitt replied, he would take the risk; and should he be guilty of mutiny, he would shoot him. The governor's anticipation turned out to be correct, as will appear in the sequel. They had been at sea some time without any dissatisfaction appearing among the crew: every indulgence the service would allow of was granted to them; and the officer taken from prison the captain had promoted from time to time till now he held the rank of lieutenant. From the day of his obtaining this promotion, the commencement of the mutiny might be dated. This villain, by being in closer intercourse with the officers, contaminated the minds of some, and thus propagated a spirit of insubordination among the seamen; so that a plan for the execution of the most horrid murder was formed, which was prevented by a very fortuitous circumstance.

On the night of the 19th of August, Captain Jewitt was lying in his cot ruminating on the variety of characters he had on board, when his mind became, as it were, providentially excited to the necessity of being vigilant in observing the conduct of his crew. He immediately got up, put on a dark-coloured cloak, and, unobserved, reached the fore part of the gun-deck on the larboard side. Here the lights had been extinguished for the purpose of concealing the proceedings of the conspirators: — from the opposite side he overheard a party closely engaged in mutinous communications. He was thunderstruck at discovering the cruel and inhuman intentions of these wretches; but when he understood that at midnight, it being then 40 minutes past 11, the scene of murder was to commence, and that he was to be the first victim of their barbarity, by stabbing him in his cot, he waited to hear no more, but instantly hurried back without being perceived. He immediately sent for the captain of the troops, informed him of the state of the ship, and desired him to have the soldiers under arms as speedily as possible. As soon as they were reported ready, he ordered two of the officers, whom he suspected, to be put in confinement, and, at the same time, called the seamen on deck. The soldiers were drawn up on the quarter-deck, and all the officers, in whom he could place confidence, were under arms.

At so sudden a discovery of their horrid designs, and the vigilant appearance of the captain's party, the mutineers became panic-struck. They, however, came aft, and Captain J. accused them of their crime, desiring those who were not implicated immediately to cross over to the starboard side. A murmuring took place, as if they intended to oppose; but distrusting one another, they tacitly suffered the ringleaders to be seized and secured in irons. Thus, by the mere accident of Captain Jewitt's having gone forward, at that critical moment, and overhearing their villanous plot, a dreadful course of murder was prevented. Subordination having been restored, he made the necessary arrangements for holding courts-martial, according to the forms established by the patriots of Buenos Ayres, by which the commander of a ship of war is invested with the power of life and death. The evidence which was here adduced implicated so many unsuspected persons, that he found mercy incompatible with the safety of the ship, and the lives of the innocent. It appeared that their intention was to destroy all those who might be found inimical to their principal design, which was to hoist black colours, and scour the seas as pirates, making murder their principal means of safety.

At length, after the most deliberate examination of the evidence, by himself and the officers of the ship, Captain Jewitt was under the distressing necessity of pronouncing sentence of death on two officers and two seamen. One of the officers was the person he had taken out of prison, and had promoted. On the day appointed for execution, a stage was erected over the starboard cat-head, and these four unfortunate men met their death by being shot. I much lamented, said Captain Jewitt, that so severe an example was necessary, and had I been a disinterested spectator, I certainly would have called aloud for their pardon; but my peculiar situation would not allow the feelings of compassion to influence me. Here he finished his narration; and, presently, the death of his first lieutenant was reported, to which he replied, with great composure, being familiar with death in every form, "Very well: secure his effects." This deceased officer, he told me, was passively concerned in the mutiny; but he spared him from trial on account of his sickness.

Captain Jewitt, with great politeness, ordered a cot to be slung for me on the larboard side of his sleeping cabin; and when we retired, I remarked that he slept in his trowsers, with a dirk belted round him, and a pair of pistols over his head. As I was not provided with any such weapons of defence, I had only to trust for safety to a strict observance of neutrality; but the ship remained in peace, and I slept undisturbed.

In a few days, he took formal possession of these islands for the patriot government of Buenos Ayres, read a declaration under their colours, planted on a port in ruins, and fired a salute of twenty-one guns. On this occasion the officers were all in full uniform, being exactly that of our navy, which but ill accorded with the dilapidated state of the ship; but he was wise enough to calculate the effect of such parade, upon the minds of the masters of ships who were in the islands, and as he had laid claim to the wreck of the French ship before mentioned, to the entire exclusion of several vessels which had arrived, bound to New Shetland, he was aware that an authoritative appearance was necessary. In fact, he struck such a terror on the minds of some ship-masters, lest they should be captured or robbed, that one of them proposed taking up arms against him; but on my pointing out to him how groundless were his fears, and introducing him to Captain Jewitt, he confessed his mistake, and his fears subsided.—On the 20th of November I sailed from Port Louis, and left Captain Jewitt completing his repairs. I have since learned that he took the ship to the river Plata, and that he is now in the Brazilian service.

CHAP. V.

SAIL FROM THE FALKLANDS: VOYAGE, ICE ISLANDS, CURRENTS. — DIFFICULT NAVIGATION. — STORM AND DANGERS. — DIFFERENCE BETWEEN THE ICE IN THE NORTHERN AND SOUTHERN HEMISPHERES. — SPERM WHALE SEEN. — SOUTH SHETLANDS.

HAVING said as much as the field of my observation allows me, in the description of these islands, and of the incidents which have of late years taken place in their vicinity, I shall now return to our having sailed from the Falklands on the 7th of October, bound to South Shetland.

At 6 P. M. we had obtained an offing, and Rodney's Bluff bore N.E. distance about seven leagues. The wind continued blowing fresh from the north, with haze till the morning of the 11th, when it shifted suddenly into the S.W. and brought clear weather. Our latitude at noon by observation was 57° 27′, and longitude by chronometers 65° by D.R. 66° 1′; in the afternoon the wind shifted to S.S.E., and we put about to the S.W.

At day-light of the 12th, the wind had shifted into the S. W. and blew a strong gale: at daylight of the 13th, the gale moderated, leaving a heavy swell from the westward; and at noon we saw an ice-berg in the S. W.

On the 14th, the wind was westerly; and our latitude at noon was 58° 6′, longitude by chronometers 62° 46′, and by account 65° 24′: our consort kept her station, and we occasionally communicated.

On the 15th, the wind was easterly, and blew lightly at noon. We were in latitude by observation 59° 7′, by D. R. 59° 16′, and longitude by chronometers was 63° 28′, and by account 66° 42′. At eight A.M., of the 16th, we passed an ice island, which we estimated to be about two miles in length, and, during the night, we passed seven others. I was much surprised at falling in with these, as in my two former passages to Shetland we had not seen one. At noon the weather was hazy, and in the afternoon, with the wind northerly, a thick fog set in. At 3h 30′ P.M. we were astonished to find ourselves upon the edge of field-ice, and close to a large ice island. We had barely room to avoid it, the cutter hauling one way, and the brig the opposite, by which means we escaped the danger. Our latitude was now 61° 21′, and longitude by chronometers 64° 15′; hence, the outer edge of the ice was ninety-five miles from the land. As I thought it might possibly be only a patch, we ran along the edge to the

E.N.E. in search of an opening; but after running twenty miles, and finding the ice every where quite compact, at 10 P.M. we hauled off to the N.N.W.

At day-light of the 17th, we sailed to the southward, and in making the ice again, we discovered an opening, into which we entered. We passed through several heavy patches, and found our latitude at noon 61° 49′, and longitude by chronometers 61° 53′, by D.R. 66° 38′, producing a difference or error in reckoning of 165 miles in ten days; which, after allowing one-fourth for error, gives an easterly current of half a mile per hour during the time specified: but it had not run equally. As the current was evidently setting strong to the eastward, I thought that the western edge of the ice might not be far from the part we first fell in with, as at that time it was so foggy that we could not see farther than a quarter of a mile. We accordingly made the appropriate signal to the Beaufoy, and plied the vessels to the westward.

During the 18th and 19th, we had strong and moderate breezes, alternately, from the westward. In the morning of the 20th the wind turned into the S.W., and blew a fresh gale, which brought us under close-reefed topsails; we continued to pass along the edge of the ice, but could find no opening.

On the 21st the wind was moderate, and observing the ice to have slackened considerably, I was hopeful that the last strong wind from the south-west had driven it from the land, leaving clear water, which could we attain, I judged we might reach an anchorage. I was mistaken in my conjecture, for we had not penetrated far when we found the ice too heavy for our weak barks to displace, and we were obliged to use our endeavour to return to clear water again. At noon we saw James Island, the western island of the group bearing S. by E. by which with the difference of latitude, the distance was estimated to be 70 miles. The weather was remarkably clear, and the island being covered with snow, appeared like a white cloud in the horizon, with some dark streaks running vertically where the snow had been melted.

Through the night of the 21st, not being able to find a passage to clear water, we were under the necessity of tacking about in a pool till daylight. The extent of this pool was about a mile and a half, which as the wind was strong and the night very dark, we found small enough. The ice about us was what is called packed, *i. e.* broken into large masses in contact with each other; and some pieces were so heavy as to make our running against them as dangerous as striking upon a rock. We frequently had it close on board before we could perceive it, so that, in fact, it would have been safer to have entered the ice the preceding evening, and have lain in it, but that I was afraid its rolling motion would break away our guard-boards. At day-light we coasted the pool for an opening, without success, and we had only the choice of remaining, or of forcing a passage, which latter we immediately set about, under all sail, and by keeping the vessels' heads to the northward, in the afternoon we reached clear water.

At noon our latitude by observation was 61° 30′, and longitude by chronometers 61° 7′. By our having made easting since noon of the day before, notwithstanding we had made 20 miles of westing by the log, it appeared that while lying in the pool during the night, we had been carried with the ice rapidly to the eastward. I was not sorry at finding this to be the case, as it afforded the prospect of reaching an anchorage to the westward of the ice. The wind continued westward, and we searched the ice for an opening, occasionally passing through extensive heavy patches.

In the morning of the 26th the wind shifted to north, and the weather became foggy. We had now got to the westward of the main ice, and at 8 A.M. the fog clearing away, we saw James Island, bearing E. by S. ½ S. distant 12 leagues. We immediately hauled towards an opening in the western part of the group which I had named Boyd Straits, in honour of Captain David Boyd, of the Royal Navy. We soon, however, found ourselves impeded by heavy compact ice, and the wind freshened from N.W. to such a degree as to oblige us to take in the foretop-sail, and it was with difficulty we obtained an offing.

On the 27th the winds were light, and the weather foggy, and as we had much heavy ice around, with a great westerly swell, our situation was hazardous. At midnight the wind freshened to a gale at west, and we lay to with the ship's head to the N.N.W. In this drift we fell in with many ice islands, some of which, by the heaviness of the sea around us, were rolling with the noise of an earthquake.

At 8 in the morning of the 28th, the wind shifted suddenly into the S.W., and increased to a complete hurricane. I was glad to see the Beaufoy was prepared for the worst, and by the advantage which a cutter possesses over a square-rigged vessel, in having fore and aft sails, with comparative little bulk aloft, she seemed to lie much easier than we did. Our main topsail was storm-reefed, which requiring the sheets to be eased off several feet, reduced the sail to the size of a mere napkin. The cold was intense, and in consequence of the wind having shifted, the sea ranged on board on the leeside, sweeping every thing before it. A whale-boat, and every thing moveable was washed off deck, and an accumulated mass of ice was ultimately left in their place. To this latter circumstance, alarming as it appeared at the time, may perhaps be attributed, in some measure, our preservation, as our vessel was no doubt greatly assisted by this binding of ice to withstand the shocks of an irregularly violent sea. This I concluded to arise from the cohesive nature of ice, which by almost enveloping the vessel, prevented the fastenings from being distressed. The gale continued with great violence from the S.W. by S., and by midnight the sea had become more regular. So much ice had formed in the head, and on the fore-castle, that the vessel rose to the sea but sluggishly, and the fear of falling in with ice, kept us constantly on the alarm. In still water, little, or no ice can be formed upon the hull; but as it was with us in this instance, there was no part six feet above the deck where the sea water did not reach, and which had not a quantity of ice upon it.

The rudder was frozen fast in the trunk, and but for the little sail we had aloft, which kept the vessel steady, and fortunately was new, we should in all probability soon have been a wreck. The Beaufoy had not been seen for several hours; and indeed we could have rendered no assistance one to another, although we had been together, and the occasion ever so distressing. We had only therefore to wait with patience for the approach of day-light, and to confide in a merciful Providence for our preservation.

On the morning of the 29th, the gale moderated, and we were rejoiced to see from the mast-head, the Beaufoy in the S. S. W. Many of our crew were hurt in the early part of the gale, by being thrown down, and nearly all of them were frost-bitten. They had been above a twelvemonth from home, and consequently their clothes were nearly worn out. Several of them had not a second pair of stockings or a shirt to change with; and I had parted with every rag I could spare to remedy these inconveniences. Blankets were cut up to make stockings, and the pump leather had been used to mend shoes. I never, during my experience at sea, have seen an equal degree of patience and firmness as was exhibited by these seamen. No dastardly request to reach a better climate was ever hinted at, but they continued in the strictest obedience and determination to make light of difficulties.

In the course of the forenoon we closed with the Beaufoy, and I was glad to hear that they had suffered no particular damage; the decks had been full of water, but she had shipped much less than the brig had done. At noon, James Island bore S. ½ E., distant about sixty miles.

Owing to not having found ice here in any considerable quantity, on either of my two former voyages, I was led to hope that it would speedily clear away; and was, therefore, determined not to relinquish an object, when, perhaps, we were on the point of attaining it.

We retained an offing, in order to repair damages, sustained in the late hurricane, and to clear the ship of ice; which, however, we could not effectually do, as the wind continued at south-south-west, producing keen frost, and, on the 30th, we had a fresh gale. It was the 1st of November before we stood in again for the edge of the ice; and, though I fully expected that the heavy southerly winds had driven it from the shore, I soon had the mortifying prospect of finding it as compact as before, though the edge had wasted so that we could approach several miles nearer land.

We continued about this situation till the 5th, in the morning, when we were roused by striking against a small island of ice. Many of these were strewed around us, and we had been sailing among them, during the night, without difficulty; but on my going below for a few minutes, the man at the helm, in passing one, became confused, or misunderstood the directions of the officer of the deck, and put the helm the wrong way, by which the ship struck her larboard bow against the mass, with so much violence, as to throw the people out of their cabins. I was on deck in an instant, and directed the carpenter to sound the pump well; and in not more than two minutes after striking, he reported three feet water in the hold. I ordered him to sound a second time, while I prepared to make a signal to the Beaufoy, and to ply the pumps. Before, however, the signal could be made, he confessed that he had been mistaken in his first soundings, by the line having been wet, and that we had only the usual quantity of water. The carpenter insisted on the vessel having struck the ice somewhere forward below water; but as there was no additional leakage, I passed the event into the list of defects, and gave it no farther consideration. The effects of this blow afterwards appeared to have been of serious concern, for, on docking the vessel in London, a plank was found driven between two timbers in the larboard bilge.

On the 7th, we attained within the distance of eight leagues of James Island, and here found the ice so heavy and compact, as far to the southward as the eye could reach, that we were obliged to stand again to the northward. Having, in the course of our endeavours to obtain a passage through the ice, struck against several masses with great violence, I took advantage of this comparatively fine day to lower the boat, and examine the extent of the damage we had sustained. We found the bends considerably injured, and the outer part of the stem broken. The swell of the sea did not permit us to do any thing by way of repairing at this time, and, as we made but little more than the usual quantity of water, we felt no alarm at our situation.

Towards evening, the wind freshened from the N.E., and put the outer part of the ice in motion towards the west; we, therefore, stood to the N.N.W. under easy sail, to prevent our being taken by it.

During the 8th and 9th, we made various efforts to open a passage to the land, but without success.

At 3 A.M. of the 10th, James Island bore S. ½ E. distant about 40 miles. At 1^h 30′ P. M. I took eleven sights of distance between the sun and moon, and then deduced the longitude of the east end of James Island to be 62° 16′. On the 11th, as the ice appeared somewhat thinner towards the E.S.E., I thought it possible that we might reach the anchorage of New Plymouth

Harbour; and we accordingly made the attempt, but without success, as we had not penetrated more than seven or eight miles before both vessels became immoveable. The cutter having come up among the loose ice we had displaced, ranged alongside. We had now forty ice islands around us, and most of them were in motion from under currents. As it was as much out of our power to return as to go forward, we furled the sails. My attention was principally directed to the movements of these masses, as some of them were going westerly to windward, and the packed ice in which we were beset had an easterly motion. The wind was strong from the S.W. during the night, but it made no apparent change in the disposition of the ice. In the morning of the 12th we had closed with a large ice island, and in spite of all our endeavours to avoid it, we continued approaching.

At 10 o'clock, it was within two ships' length, and, from its peculiar shape, threatened to overwhelm us; for the upper part of the side nearest to us, which was about 180 feet high, projected so much as would have admitted the brig's masts coming in contact with it underneath, and this overhanging part was cracked from the top down to the water-line. From both vessels being unavoidably together, both were likely to suffer by the same accident. All our attempts to heave the vessels out of the course of this danger were in vain, but they had the good effect of occupying the crews, and thus withdrawing their attention from their perilous situation. Within half an hour, I had the appalling sight of the overhanging mass immediately over our quarter-deck; with the fearful sensation that, if our masts came in contact with it, the projecting part would fall upon us, and sink both vessels. Our escape was caused solely by our having a large floe piece of ice between us and the ice island, which prevented our masts from touching it. The packed ice separated to each side, and we passed round the north corner. The rolling of this island in its passage had produced a slackness in the other ice, of which I was determined to take advantage for returning, and so cast off the cutter. We made all possible sail, with the wind at S.W.; and continued making progress in a N.E. direction till the evening, when both vessels became again unmoveable. The cutter was now about one mile astern, and, indeed, I saw that it was necessary for our safety to be at a short distance from each other, that we might not both be subject to the same accident, as would have been the case when under the ice island before mentioned.

On the 13th, the wind was light from the W.N.W., and we were consequently unable to make any way; but on the morning of the 14th, it freshened, and for our safety we made all sail to the northward.

At 4 A. M., we saw rocks astern bearing S.S.E. distant about ten miles, which we judged to be about Cape Sheriff. In the afternoon we were set into ice of the most dangerous description. Many pieces which appeared to be the bottoms of ice islands were about from 80 to 100 feet in superficial extent; and as they were 10 feet above water, they must have been at least 40 feet in depth, as from the specific gravity of such sort of blue and solid ice, we judged that about 30 feet must be under water. The rolling motion of several of these pieces was so great, that had one of them taken the side of the ship fairly in its descent, her destruction must have been inevitable.

Among them there were narrow openings, through which we endeavoured to navigate; but in passing one piece, it struck us, though only with a corner, on the starboard side, and tore down our bulwarks and main-guard board. We repaired the wreck, and passed through two or three miles of this kind of ice. As there were occasionally small ponds, in which the vessel acquired considerable velocity, the evolutions we had to perform kept our men constantly at the braces to back and fill the sails. About 5 P.M.

we had reached a pool about one mile in diameter, though with many heavy pieces of ice floating in it. The Beaufoy had been unavoidably sent four or five miles to the westward of us, and as we saw her distinctly, I determined to wait in this pool till she should reach us.

During the 15th, the water being smooth here, I further examined the vessel's bows and found three of the binds broken, and the stem much damaged as before mentioned. We made repairs by nailing lead and plank over tarred canvass on the holes and cracks which, though they did not materially strengthen the vessel, prevented leakage in the meantime. In the evening, having observed the cutter to be fast approaching, we entered the nearest northern patch of ice, and at half past four of the morning of the 16th we reached clear water, and hove to under the edge of the ice for the arrival of the Beaufoy.

I was much rejoiced at having one vessel out of the ice, considering all dangers in an open sea as of no moment compared with those we were subject to in such weak vessels, having only two and a half inch plank in the bottom, among large rolling masses of ice.

As I have been in the Greenland seas, and am well acquainted with the nature and danger of that navigation, I may remark that sailing among

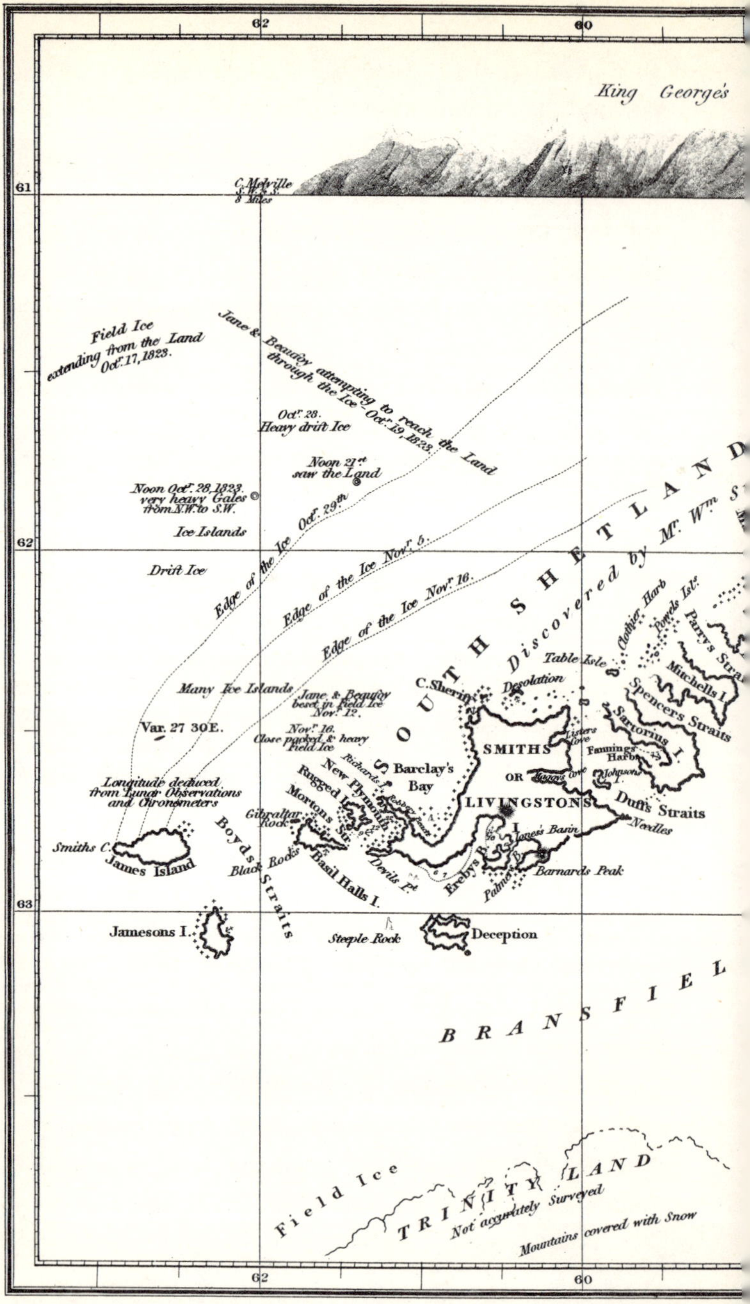

London, Published by

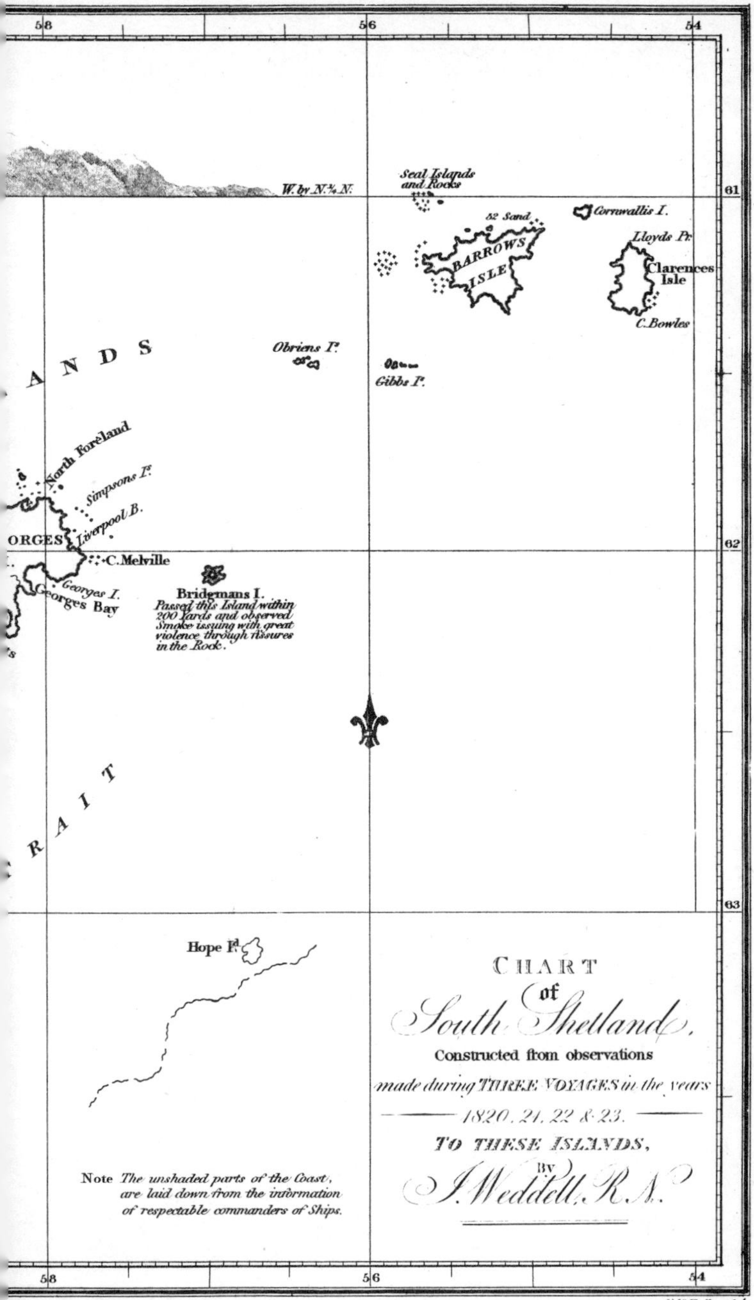

noster Row, Augt 1825.
Sidy Hall, sculpt

ice in these southern latitudes is attended with much greater risk. This is occasioned by a heavy westerly swell which keeps the ice in motion, and seldom entirely subsides. The vast expanse of ocean to the westward of Shetland acted upon by winds prevailing between S.W. and N.W. is the cause of this almost constant swell, and as the heaviest gales come from between these points, it is sometimes of a mountainous description.

At two in the afternoon, the Beaufoy having joined company, we stood to the westward, and at 4 o'clock we saw a sperm whale, which confirms Mr. Smith's report of such sort of whales being found on this coast, as stated by him in his account of South Shetland.

The weather being now more settled, we lowered our boats, and set out in pursuit of the whale, but did not succeed. It was supposed that the fish having seen the copper of the vessel, had become what is technically called *gallied*, and disappeared.

At 9 P. M. on the 16th, James Island bore S.E. by E. distant 16 or 17 miles, but as I found the ice still heavy and compact, I saw no prospect of obtaining anchorage in time for procuring sea elephants, and therefore communicated with the Beaufoy, and with the wind at N.N.E.

we stood to the N.W. on our passage to Cape Horn.

As the South Shetlands are not yet generally known, and I have had an opportunity of ascertaining some particulars in regard to them during three voyages, a short account may here be useful for general information; and for the convenience of navigators, I have annexed a chart, constructed from observations made during my survey of these islands.

The discovery of this archipelago, as already mentioned, was made by Mr. William Smith, commander of the brig William, on a passage from Monte Video to Valparaiso in 1819, as is stated in the following extract from that vessel's-log book.

"After taking our departure from Monte Video, nothing material occurred until I got into the latitude of Cape Horn, with a fair wind to go to the westward, and steering S.S.E. with an intention to make the island again, and continuing this course for a few days, I, to my great satisfaction, discovered land. On the 15th October, at 6 P.M., in latitude 62° 30′ S., and longitude 60° W., by chronometers, bearing S.E. by E. about three leagues, hazy weather, bore up and sailed towards it. At four miles' distance sounded in 40 fathoms, fine black sand. Island bearing E. by S. to S.E. by E., sounded in 60 fathoms, same bottom. Hauled off during the night to the northward. At daylight stood in for the land again, at three leagues' distance from the body of islands. Sounded again 95 fathoms, fine sand.

"*October* 18th. Weather clear and pleasant, saw the main land bearing S.S.E., distance from the island about three leagues; having ran as far as the Cape, we found the land trend off to the N.E., coasting to the eastward; I sounded, found it similar to the former, fine sand. The point called North Foreland E. by S.; hauled in for it; got the island to bear W.N.W. distance half a league; sounded regular from 20 to 35 fathoms, good bottom, sand and gravel. Finding the weather favourable, we lowered down the boat, and succeeded in landing; found it barren and covered with snow; seals in abundance. The boat having returned, and being secured, we made sail off shore the ensuing night. In the morning, altered the course so as to reach the land to the southward in view. At 11 A. M. the North Foreland bore S.E. by E. five leagues; the land then took a south-easterly direction, varying to the eastward; weather thick and squally, with snow.

"I thought proper, having property on board,

and perhaps deviating from the insurance, to haul off to the westward on my intended voyage. Stormy, variable winds; made Cape Millan; could perceive some high land to the westward of the Cape, stretching in a south-west direction; the weather becoming thick and squally, made sail to the westward. Having sailed 150 miles on W.S.W., the weather moderating, saw another head-land bearing E.N.E., distance 10 leagues; very high; observed, latitude 62° 52′ south, longitude, by chronometers, 63° 40′ west; named this South Cape; found the land to extend from the Cape in a southerly direction. Shaped my course for Valparaiso, where I arrived on the 24th November after a passage of 60 days from Monte Video.

(Signed) "Wm. Smith." *

The northern range of South Shetland islands lie between latitude 61° and 63°, and longitude 54° and 63°, and consist of 12 main islands and innumerable rocks above water, as shown in the accompanying chart. Their extent was first ascertained by Mr. Edward Barnsfield, then master of the frigate Andromache, who was sent out for the express purpose by Captain Sheriff, com-

* Accounts of this discovery were originally made known to the British public in the Literary Gazette.

mander of the vessel, and commodore on the western coast of America.

Mr. Edward Barnsfield acted with great boldness in obtaining a knowledge of this land; but circumstances did not admit of his extending or pursuing his observations, so as to give a particular account of it. To his valuable remarks, however, as far as they go, I have added my own, which corroborate them, together with a particular delineation of the coast.

The names which he gave the different headlands, &c., in obedience to official authority, I have retained; and, in a more extended survey, I have added to some parts names from peculiarities of appearance in the land, and to others, the names of gentlemen of talent and enterprise. I began my observations in 1820, being the first vessel fitted out from England which anchored in these parts; and have been happy, since that time, in imparting the knowledge I possessed to persons who required information for the safety of their ships and lives of their crews. From having done so, I have seen many of my communications in print, which, however, I do not regret, though it may detract from their entire novelty now, when published by myself.

The appearance which these islands would assume, were they divested of ice, would be very different from what they at present exhibit. In Smith's Island, an ice-berg runs through from north to south; indeed, almost all of them are so interspersed and intersected with ice-bergs, that the earthy, or rather rocky, parts of the country are much smaller in bulk than would be supposed from a distant view.

The highest, and most forbidding in aspect, is the western island, which, in 1820, I named James Island, as I was the first who landed upon it. The highest part of it I estimated to be nearly 2500 feet above the level of the sea. The whole island is almost inaccessible, and constantly covered with snow, excepting some perpendicular rocks which will not retain it.

None of the islands afford any vegetation, save a short straggling grass, which is found in very small patches, in places where there happens to be a little soil. This, together with a moss, similar to that which is found in Iceland, appears in the middle of January, at which time the islands are partially clear of snow.

To the eastward of Cape Melville is Bridgman's Island, which is evidently volcanic, as in passing it in the year 1821, within 200 yards, I observed smoke issuing through the fissures of the rock, and apparently with much force. The figure of this island is nearly round; and it is about one-eighth of a mile in diameter, and

400 feet high, partaking of the form of a sugar-loaf. There are several good harbours in these islands, as may be seen by referring to the chart.

The composition of the rock, which forms the Shetland Islands, appears to consist of quartz, with disseminated iron pyrites; and of quartz in prismatic concretions, copper green, and copper pyrites.

From the almost total want of vegetation to subsist upon, there cannot be a single terrestrial animal in these islands; but of amphibious creatures, there are several. The sea-elephant was found in vast numbers. Of these, the crews, under my direction, killed upwards of 2000. The fur-seals, which appear to be found only in the South Seas, were still more numerous. Some sea-leopards have also been seen. As the peculiarities of these animals, and many of their instinctive habits, may be interesting, I shall describe them.

The largest is the sea-elephant. The male has a cartilaginous substance, extending forward from the nose, five or six inches, somewhat resembling the proboscis of the common elephant, and from this circumstance has obtained the name.

The largest of these animals which I have seen were males, not less than twenty-four feet long, and fourteen in circumference: the females are generally about one-third less. In form, they have much the appearance of the common seal, with which most people are acquainted, and, therefore, a particular description would be superfluous; but it may be necessary to mention those habits and peculiarities in which they differ.

The males come on shore about the end of August and beginning of September; and in this month, and the first part of October, they are followed by the females, which, being with young since the preceding season, choose the land at this time for the purpose of parturition and procreation. When the males first arrive, the fat of three or four of them will make a ton of oil; but the average of both male and female is about seven to the ton. As they live, while on shore, entirely without food, by the middle of December they have become very lean; and their young being at this age able to take the water, the whole of the breeding herd leave the shores.

A second herd come up about the middle of January, for the purpose of renewing their coat of hair; in March, a herd of full-grown males come up, for the same purpose; and, by the end of April, every kind of them has returned to the sea.

The circumstance of these animals living on shore for a period not less than two months, apparently without taking food of any description, may certainly be considered a remarkable phenomenon in natural economy. That they live by absorption is evident, — that is, by consuming the substance of their own bodies; because when they come first on shore, they are excessively fat, and when they return to the sea, they are very lean.

Their inactivity and extreme lethargy when on shore is astonishingly contrasted by their sagacity and agility when in the sea. They have been known to keep a boat from landing, by intercepting it in the water when the crew had no fire-arms; and frequently, when one is pricked with a lance, it will attack the boat with great ferocity.

It is curious to remark, that the sea-elephant, when lying on the shore, and threatened with death, will often make no effort to escape into the water, but lie still and shed tears, merely raising the head to look at the assailant; and, though very timid, will wait with composure the club or the lance which takes its life. In close contact, every human effort would be of little avail for the destruction of this animal, unwieldy as it is, were it to rush forward, and exert the power of its jaws; for this, indeed, is so enormous, that, in the agony of death, stones are ground to powder between its teeth.

If the skull be indented in the killing of a female with young, the indentation is found also upon the skull of the young. This sympathy, which has been denied with regard to the human species by some physiologists, evidently exists in the economy of this animal.

The species of seal, which inhabits these shores, is exclusively the fur-seal, or what is called, in zoology, Phoca Falklandica, the Falkland Island Seal. This species has been distinguished by naturalists for its peculiarity of shape; but the circumstance of its possessing a valuable fur, as well as the remarkable habits of the animal, have not been noticed in any description of the seal with which I have met.

The fur, from the almost general use to which it is applied in the manufacture of caps, must be well known; and it is therefore unnecessary to describe it further, than merely to observe, that after the hair which grows through and over it is extracted, its natural appearance is of a fine and curly brown.

Nothing in this class of animals, and more particularly in the fur-seal of Shetland, is more astonishing than the disproportion in the size of the male and female. A large grown male, from the tip of the nose to the extremity of the tail, is six feet nine inches, whilst the female is not more than three feet and a half. This class of males is not, however, the most numerous, but being physically the most powerful, they keep in their possession all the females, to the exclusion of the younger branches; hence, at the time of parturition, the males attending the females may be computed to be as one to twenty, which shows this to be, perhaps, the most polygamous of large animals.

They are in their nature completely gregarious; but they flock together, and assemble on the coast at different periods, and in distinct classes. The males of the largest size go on shore about the middle of *November*, to wait the arrival of the females, which of necessity must soon follow, for the purpose of bringing forth their young. These, in the early part of *December*, begin to land; and they are no sooner out of the water than they are taken possession of by the males, who have many serious battles with each other, in procuring their respective seraglios; and, by a peculiar instinct, they carefully protect the females under their charge during the whole period of gestation.

By the end of *December*, all the female seals have accomplished the purpose of their landing. The time of gestation may be considered twelve months, and they seldom have more than one at a time, which they suckle and rear apparently with great affection. By the middle of *February*, the young are able to take the water; and after being taught to swim by the mother, they abandon them on the shore, where they remain till their coats of fur and hair are completed. During the latter end of *February*, what are called the Dog-seals go on shore: these are the young seals of the two preceding years, and such males as, from their want of age and strength, are not allowed to attend the pregnant females.

These young seals come on shore for the purpose of renewing their annual coats, which being done by the end of *April*, they take to the water, and scarcely any are seen on shore again till the end of *June*, when some young males come up and go off alternately.

They continue to do this for six or seven weeks, and the shores are then again abandoned till the end of *August*, when a herd of small young seals of both sexes come on shore for about five or six weeks;—soon after, they retire to the water. The large male seals take up their places on shore, as has been before described, which completes the intercourse all classes have with the shore during the whole year.

The young are at first black, in a few weeks they become grey, and soon after obtain their coat of hair and fur. M. Buffon describes the longevity of the seal to be even so great as a hundred years. I have estimated the female seal to be in general at its full growth within four years, but possibly the male seal is much longer, very likely five or six years; and some, which I have contrasted with others of the same size, could not, from their very old appearance, be less than thirty years.

When these Shetland seals were first visited, they had no apprehension of danger, from meeting men; in fact, they would lie still while their neighbours were killed, and skinned; but latterly they had acquired habits for counteracting danger, by placing themselves on rocks, from which they could, in a moment, precipitate themselves into the water. The agility of these creatures is much greater than, from their appearance, an observer would anticipate. I have seen them, indeed, often escape from men running fast in pursuit to kill them. The absurd story, that seals in general defend themselves by throwing stones at their pursuers with their tails, may be explained in this way; that when the animal is chased on a stony beach, their mode of propelling themselves is by drawing their hinder flippers forward, thereby shortening the body, and projecting themselves from the tail, which, when relieved by the effort of the fore flippers, throws up a quantity of stones to the distance of some yards.

Their senses of smell and hearing are acute, and in instinct they are little inferior to the dog; that is, I judge their sagacity in the water much exceeds that which they exhibit on the shore; for though they are fitted to remain a certain time on land, their natural element is the water. In proof of their docility, I may mention that I have reared several young ones from three or four weeks old, to the age of two months, which were so tame as to eat out of the hand with considerable fondness; but by some accident they were allowed to fall or walk overboard.

These fur-seals may be distinguished from the hair-seals of this hemisphere by their being rather of a smaller size, and having the nose smaller and more pointed. In swimming they have a jumping motion like that of the porpoise.

The quantity of seals taken off these islands, by vessels from different parts, during the years 1821 and 1822, may be computed at 320,000, and the quantity of sea-elephant oil, at 940 tons. This valuable animal, the fur-seal, might, by a law similar to that which restrains fishermen in the size of the mesh of their net, have been spared to render annually 100,000 furs, for many years to come. This would have followed from not killing the mothers till the young were able to take the water; and even then, only those which appeared to be old, together with a proportion of the males, thereby diminishing their total number, but in slow progression. This system is practised at the river of Plata. The island of Lobos, in the mouth of that river, contains a quantity of seals, and is farmed by the Governor of Monte Video, under certain restrictions, that the hunters shall not take them but at stated periods, in order to prevent the animals from being exterminated. The system of extermination was practised, however, at Shetland; for whenever a seal reached the beach, of whatever denomination, he was immediately killed, and his skin taken; and by this means, at the end of the second year, the animals became nearly extinct; the young having lost their mothers when only three or four days old, of course all died, which, at the lowest calculation, exceeded 100,000.

I have mentioned that the only species of seal found on these islands is that possessing the fur; but a creature was reported to have been seen by one of my crew, which, according to his account of it, must have been a non-descript.

A boat's crew were employed on Hall Island, and the man who saw this animal was left on one side of the island to take care of some produce, while the officers and the rest of the crew were engaged on the other side.

The sailor had gone to bed, and about 10 o'clock he heard a noise resembling human cries, and as daylight, in these latitudes, never disappears at this season, he rose, and looked around, but on seeing no person, he returned to bed; presently he heard the noise again, and rose a second time, but still saw nothing. Conceiving however, the possibility of a boat being upset, and that some of the crew might be clinging to some detached rocks, he walked along the beach a few steps, and heard the noise more distinctly, but in a musical strain.

On searching around, he saw an object lying on a rock, a dozen yards from the shore, at which he was somewhat frightened. The face and shoulders appeared of human form, and of a reddish colour; over the shoulders hung long green hair; the tail resembled that of the seal, but the extremities of the arms he could not see distinctly. The creature continued to make a musical noise while he gazed about two minutes, and on perceiving him it disappeared in an instant. Immediately when the man saw his officer, he told this wild tale, the truth of which was, of course, doubted; but to add weight to his testimony (being a Catholic), he made a cross on the sand, which he kissed in form of making oath to the truth of his statement.

When the story was told me, I ridiculed it; but,

by way of diversion, I sent for the sailor, who saw this non-descript, into the cabin, and questioned him respecting it, he told me the story as I have related it, and in so clear and positive a manner, making oath as to the truth, that I concluded he must really have seen the animal he described, or that it must have been the effects of a disturbed imagination.

The small species of penguins are here abundant; and of sea-fowl, the following may be enumerated: aglets; Port Egmont hens; white pigeons; the grey peterel, called by sailors the Nelly; snow birds; and, on the coast, I have seen blue peterels.

Several pieces of wreck have been seen on the western islands, and apparently of the scantling of a 74 gun ship, which makes it too probable that these are the remains of a Spanish ship of war of that rate, which has been missing since the year 1818, when she was on her passage to Lima.

On a beach in the principal island, which I named Smith's Island, in honour of the discoverer, were found a quantity of seals' bones, which appeared to have been killed some years before, probably to sustain the life of some ship-wrecked crew; suggesting the melancholy reflection that some unfortunate human beings had ended their days on this coast. In the year 1820, the first time these islands were visited for their produce, four ships were totally lost. Part of the crews of these vessels remained during the winter of 1821, but notwithstanding every precaution they could take, with a strong house and ample supplies, they suffered severely. The range of land which lies 30 leagues to the south of the northern cluster, consists of islands, and has been visited for produce, but has not been accurately described. It can seldom be approached on account of ice, and the mountains are constantly covered with snow.

No farther circumstances worthy of remark having fallen within the sphere of my observation on these inhospitable shores, I shall now return to the situation of the ship on the evening of the 16th of *November*, when we had taken our departure from these islands, bound to Tierra del Fuego.

CHAP. VI.

VOYAGE TO TIERRA DEL FUEGO. — CAPE HORN. — THE NATIVES; THEIR VISIT, MANNERS, &c. — PUNISHMENT OF A THIEF, AND ITS GOOD EFFECT. — NATIVE DOGS. — THE HABITS, BEHAVIOUR, &c. OF THE FUEGIANS. — ISLANDS OF ST. FRANCIS. — CHANGE OF ANCHORAGE. — OTHER TRIBES. — CANOE. — STATE OF SOCIETY, &c. — ISLANDS OF DIEGO RAMIREZ. — LANGUAGE OF THE FUEGIANS AND CURIOUS HEBREW ANALOGIES. — MUSIC AND ITS EFFECTS. — NEW CLAY CLOTHING. — NECKLACES, BASKETS, BOWS. — ARRIVAL OF THE BEAUFOY. — FUEGIAN SETTLEMENT. — VESSELS SEPARATE. — FACE OF THE COUNTRY. — EFFECT OF CLIMATE ON THE FUEGIAN CHARACTER.

THE wind was moderate and easterly till the 18th in the afternoon, when it shifted into the S.W. Our latitude at noon by observation was 58° 44′, and longitude by chronometers 66° 1′, by D.R. 67° 27′, the variation at 4 P.M. was 27° 30′. On the 20th the wind shifted into the N.W. quarter, and we stood to the W.S.W. On the 21st, in the morning, the wind again shifting to S.W. we tacked to the northward, and about four in the afternoon we saw Cape Horn, bearing N. by W. about ten leagues; in this position the Cape appears conspicuous, with the hills of Hermit's Island just above the horizon. See Views of Land, 19. Cape Horn is remarkable for its truly imposing figure and situation, terminating the greatest north and south extension of land on the globe. The many disasters which have befallen ships off this cape, the difficulty of getting round it to the westward, and above all, the sufferings of the fleet under Lord Anson, and in the expeditions of Pizarro, induce people to consider this promontory with more than common interest.

The weather proved squally and unsettled through the night of the 23d, and we retained an offing. At daylight the wind blew strong from S.S.W., and we bore up for the bay of St. Francis, which we reached by two o'clock in the afternoon, and anchored in Wigwam or St. Martin's Cove, in 16 fathoms water, over a bottom of sand and mud.

On the 25th we were employed in wooding and watering the vessels, and during the day I made observations, for latitude, longitude, and variation. On the south side of the harbour is a small cavity in the rock, in which I placed the compass for taking a set of azimuths, but on observing the sun to bear N. 29 W. at noon, I suspected the rock to be magnetic, and took a portion of it on board to ascertain the fact. I stripped the card off the needle in order to make it more susceptible, and found it, as I expected, slightly acted upon by the rock. I next fixed the place for observation at the head of the harbour, where there was probably no local attraction, and found the variation to be 23° 4′ east: the latitude in the same situation was 55° 53′ 37″, and the longitude by chronometers was 67° 29′ 45″.

We took the opportunity of being in port to repair farther the damage the vessels had sustained by the ice, though we were not at leisure to lighten the brig as much as was required for making effectual repairs.

On the 26th the weather was remarkably fine, and the wind blew lightly between S.S.W. (by west), and N.N.W. In the afternoon the Beaufoy sailed, to examine some neighbouring islands for seal-furs. She had not passed out of sight, when to my astonishment I saw two native canoes paddling towards us: several of the brig's crew were on board the Beaufoy; but as I considered, that if properly treated, nothing hostile need be feared from the strangers, in whatever numbers they might appear, I did not recall them.

It was not long before the Fuegians arrived within hearing; and soon made themselves known by a singing noise, accompanied with a variety of gestures, which as I afterwards learned were symbols of friendship. They presently paddled within eight or ten yards of the ship, and I desired our men to make friendly signs to them in return, conveying a wish for them to come on board; but they would not approach. Amazement was apparent in all their actions; and they seemed so agitated that, for a full quarter of an hour, they continued gabbling without the smallest intermission. At length their wonder at our persons having in some degree subsided, they paddled fore and aft about the ship, and were to all appearance undecided whether the vessel was dead or alive; for never having seen a ship before, it could not be expected that they should at once reason from the analogy which their canoes afforded. Finally, having acquired more confidence, they came on the starboard side, and two of the men ventured on board. From their very miserable appearance, I thought the best office I could do them, would be to give them something to eat and drink. I therefore had beef, bread, and wine brought, and helped them plentifully. Of the beef they eat a little, but neither the good Madeira wine nor the bread was acceptable.

I soon saw that they were particular in keeping their women in their canoes, at which I was not sorry, as from the jealous disposition of savages in general, it was advisable for us to avoid any intercourse with their wives. I did not, however, neglect helping the ladies to a little wine, which I gave them in a japanned cup; and this utensil appeared so marvellously fine in their eyes, that they spilled the wine in examining it, and cunningly retained it. I did not attempt to recover the cup, as I thought they were certainly in want of it for drinking with; but on the following day I saw it in about a dozen stripes suspended at the women's necks.

The men seemed astonished at all they saw, and every kind of iron work attracted their attention more than any thing else—a cast iron pot of 200 gallons surprised them so much, that they were even afraid to approach it. Perceiving their fondness for this metal, and having a quantity of hoops on board, I gave each of them a piece, with which they were quite delighted; and soon after receiving the present they left us, and repaired to their wigwams, which were situated at the head of the harbour.

On the following morning, the 27th, by sunrise, they were lying off, making a great shouting, expressive of their anxiety to see us, and to get on board. I had given orders that they should not be admitted till our crew were called on deck in the morning, which was usually at four o'clock. In the course of a little time a third canoe was seen approaching, which our first visitors met at some distance from the ship; and by their coming immediately on board all together, it was evident that the latter had been informed by their countrymen of the friendly reception they had met with. The number of our present visitors was twenty-two men, women and children, and now that they had acquired confidence in our amicable intentions, they became interesting and amusing. I gave them all in turns a sight of the cabin; and the bright stove, and the looking-glass, were objects that pleased them greatly. The monkey trick of looking behind the mirror for the reflected object was frequently practised; and though they had no doubt often seen themselves reflected in the water, yet having never before observed so sudden and distinct an appearance, their intuitive judgment was not sufficiently acute to satisfy them of the similarity.

Knowing the propensity Indians generally have to stealing, a watch was kept over them; but on the boatswain returning from the head of the harbour, he informed me that they had stripped a barrel of the hoops. An adept in the art of pilfering had also displayed no mean talent in stealing an iron belaying pin, notwithstanding the strictness of the look-out.

I judged it proper to impress them with an idea of the offence of stealing; and accordingly placed this criminal in the main rigging, and gave him a smart lash with a cat of nine tails, making him understand that it was a punishment for the crime of which he had been guilty. This gentle chastisement had the desired effect, for they were ever after afraid even to lift a piece of iron without permission.

On the 27th the weather was fine with a fresh breeze from the S.W. Our carpenters were employed felling trees, and sawing them into boards. The operation of sawing amused our friends, the Fuegians, greatly; and their attachment to the saw would no doubt have led to the stealing of it, had we not always brought it on board at night. This day only men and boys came on board: the cause of leaving their women behind I could not learn, but they were probably employed in some domestic concerns.

Among this tribe was a fine grown boy of about the age of fourteen, whom I would have liked much to remain with us, but as soon as he understood my desire he returned to his canoe, and I never afterwards could persuade him to come on board.

On the 28th the wind was variable, having gone completely round the compass, and blowing fresh. This morning all the Fuegians came along side, and in a different dress, or rather *colouring*, for the women had changed the hue of their countenances from red to jet black, and the men were decorated with red and white streaks running horizontially across the face. Their appearance altogether was as grotesque as can well be imagined; though in their estimation it was, no doubt, considered the perfection of fashion. In the early part of our acquaintance, whenever I expressed a desire for any of their small articles they gave me them without any return; but now they had acquired an idea of barter, and in exchange for any of their articles of simple manufacture, they demanded something bright, such as buttons, &c.; but bits of iron hoops were particularly objects of esteem; and I have no doubt, but in this trifle they conceived our riches to consist.

A youth of engaging features whom I had on board, was the most successful in this traffic: the women seemed much interested with him, though I am at a loss to know whether they were right in their idea of his sex, as with them the females do all the work, and this youth was here kept in constant employment. I procured a young dog from them, which was remarkable for its cunning: they have only one kind of this animal, and it partakes much of the nature of the fox, resembling it a good deal about the head, and being nearly the size of the terrier. They are remarkably fond of their dogs; and if they have any object to which they ascribe supernatural power, it may possibly be to them, since their attention to them, and dependence on them for safety, is greater than could be expected.

On the 29th, the weather was fine, and the wind from W.S.W. Early in the morning, the Beaufoy arrived; and this was not unobserved by the Fuegians, who immediately went on board, where they were kindly received by the crew. Curiosity was mutual, and the sailors took great delight in friendly intercourse with them. They committed several petty thefts on board the Beaufoy; and one in particular is worth mentioning, as it exhibits in a remarkable degree their powers of imitation.

A sailor had given a Fuegian a tin pot full of coffee, which he drank, and was using all his art to steal the pot. The sailor, however, recollecting, after a while, that the pot had not been returned, applied for it, but whatever words he made use of were always repeated in imitation by the Fuegian. At length, he became enraged at hearing his requests reiterated, and placing himself in a threatening attitude, in an angry tone, he said, "You copper-coloured rascal, where is my tin pot?" The Fuegian, assuming the same attitude, with his eyes fixed on the sailor, called out, "You copper-coloured rascal, where is my tin pot?" The imitation was so perfect, that every one laughed, except the sailor, who proceeded to search him, and under his arm he found the article missing. For this audacious theft, he would have punished the mimic, but Mr. Brisbane interposing, sent him into his canoe, and forbade his being allowed to come on board again.

On the 2d of *December*, about mid-day, the Fuegians were seen close to the shore, paddling their canoes out of harbour, without having previously shown any intention of leaving the place. This they were, no doubt, considering as a fortunate escape, for notwithstanding a strict watch had been kept over them, during their stay with us, I had reason to suspect that they had stolen several small articles, and were now thinking to get clear off with their booty. Instead of the roar which they generally kept up, not a voice was to be heard amongst them, and the canoes were so close to the shore, that we could scarcely discern them. I immediately ordered the boat to be manned, and put off. The Fuegians were now paddling with all their strength to get beyond our reach, but in vain: we soon overtook them; and they looked as if they expected to be searched for stolen goods; but they were not a little surprised when, instead of this, I presented each of the men with a piece of hoop, and each of the women, by way of a medal, with a brightened halfpenny, with a hole punched for a string, for suspending it to the neck.

They were very grateful for these trifles; and I took farewell of them with a hearty shake of the hand. Being now at ease, they commenced their usual roar and paddled off.

Having related these incidents as they occurred, I may, with propriety, say something of the impressions I received as to the character of this tribe.

I would willingly, for the honour of human nature, raise these neglected people somewhat higher in the scale of intellectual estimation than they have reached; but I must acknowledge their condition to be that of the lowest of mankind. At this age of the world, it appears almost incredible, and certainly disgraceful, that there should still exist such a tractable people in almost pristine ignorance.

As I found nothing of foreign manufacture among the Fuegians, it may be reasonably concluded that we were their first visitors, at least of the present generation. The savage custom of the women doing all the work prevails here: they paddle the canoes, while the men sit at their ease; they gather the shell-fish food, rear the children, build the wigwams, and, in short, perform every duty that requires exertion, though in return, however, the men show a good deal of affection for their wives, and are careful of their offspring. An instance of their parental affection appeared on occasion of my visiting their wigwams one morning unexpectedly, when, supposing that I had come on shore to steal their children, they infolded them in their arms, and all the signs of amity I could express, were insufficient to induce them to let them go.

The stature of these Fuegians is low. I measured two of their ordinary sized men, and found one of them five feet four inches, and the other five feet five. The contour of their faces, and the form of their heads, as exhibited in the annexed plate, are those which are found to be peculiar to most Indians: they have flat noses, small eyes, full and well formed chests, small arms; — their legs are small and ill shaped, which arises, no doubt, from the custom of sitting on their calves, in which situation their appearance is truly awkward.

The women are better featured than the men: many of their faces are interesting, and, in my opinion, they have a more lively sense of what passes. The only clothing the males wear, is a skin over their shoulders, reaching little more than half way down the back; some have not even this sorry garment. The women have generally a larger skin over their shoulders, and are, in other respects, clothed as decency requires; and even the youngest of their female children have the same covering, which evinces a degree of modesty seldom found amongst untutored people.

By the account I have given of this tribe, the reader will be able to form a general idea in regard to these remote Australians, but a particular relation of our further communications with them will be necessary to assist him in forming just conclusions; and as a single glance is not sufficient to enable an observer to decide accurately, I shall describe minutely their behaviour and inclinations, by which alone a true estimate of their character is to be obtained.

On the 2d of December, the weather being fine, Captain Brisbane accompanied me in a whale-boat up the bay, and assisted me in making observations on its navigation. From a considerable height, we perceived several channels running through the supposed termination, forming a cluster of islands, which, being separated from the main islands of Tierra del Fuego, by a navigable strait, may, with some propriety, be called the Islands of St. Francis, after the name of the sound, which appears to have been first entered in the year 1714.

Having sounded a safe anchorage, in very smooth water, which the accompanying chart exhibits, we returned on board.

At 10 in the morning of the 3d, we weighed,

and both vessels proceeded with a moderate breeze from N.E. towards the islands of Ildefonsos. At 6 P.M., Cape Horn bore E. ½ S. distance six leagues. In the morning of the 4th, we were within two and a half miles of the Ildefonsos, and each vessel sent a boat on shore. We continued off these islands, with pleasant weather till the 7th, when I stood over, with the Jane, to Tierra del Fuego, a distance of sixteen miles, to search for an anchorage. The principal officers being absent, I sent the boatswain, with a whale-boat, among some islands which were likely to afford what I sought. He presently returned with a report, of having found a cove, round a point, which I called Turn Point, with good bottom, in which several vessels might anchor. On this we made all sail back to the Ildefonsos, and after having received our boats on board, with a quantity of fur-seal skins, both vessels made sail to Turn Point. It was 12 o'clock before we reached the cove in which we were to bring up; and it being dark, I desired the boatswain to inform me when he thought we were within a proper distance to drop the anchor, as we could see the land but imperfectly; but through his indistinct recollection of the place we were close to the surf on the beach before he gave any intimation; and it was only by dropping the anchor, at the instant our situation was discerned, though with the topsail at the masthead, that we were prevented from going on the rocks. Fortunately the wind was light; and after the sails were taken in, by means of a stream-anchor laid out, we moved the vessel into safety. I was angry with the boatswain for his mismanagement; and that he might improve his judgment, by being reminded of his mistake, I called this place Blunder Cove. In justice to this person, however, I must say, he was a good seaman, and well disposed: his error in judgment arose, from having formed an opinion of the capacity of the anchorage from a boat;—for instead of being large enough for several vessels, there was scarcely room for one. The altitude of the eye above the horizon is frequently very delusive in the estimation of space, if the angle under which objects are seen be not particularly attended to. The Beaufoy had anchored a little to the outside of us; and the following morning, having determined on sending her again to Shetland, arrangements were made for that purpose. I fully expected that the coast would be clear of ice, by the time she would arrive, which would be within a few days of midsummer.

As I did not consider this anchorage convenient, I went in a whale-boat in search of one more commodious; and little more than a mile to the eastward, I found one with a clear bottom of sand and mud beneath in twenty fathoms water, within three cables' length of the shore. We were taking the depth of water with the lead, when among the kelp we saw four canoes of Fuegians.. They were a little startled at first observing us; but, according to the Fuegian mode of salutation, they soon commenced shouting, and making ludicrous attitudes expressive of joy. We rowed within twelve or fourteen yards of them, and held up some pieces of iron hoop, which caught their attention. Like our former visitors, jealousy, or particular care of their women, seemed a principal consideration; for the men all shifted into two canoes, and came to us, leaving the women behind. We soon inspired them with confidence, and pointed out the vessels, making signs to them to follow us, which they hurriedly did, bringing their women with them; and as the men on this occasion assisted to paddle the canoes, they were almost able to keep pace with our whale-boat against a head-sea. This tribe being strangers, and of better stature than those we had formerly met with, new interest was created in our intercourse with them. From the astonishment they exhibited, and from their not having the smallest article of any thing foreign with them, I am inclined to think that, like the others, they had never seen strangers before. They possessed a variety of articles of their own manufacture, for which we gave in exchange some things almost useless to us, but very interesting to them.

Though I was anxious to give them all the things we could spare, which might be of value to them, bits of iron hoop I knew were the most useful, as the only material for cutting which they possessed was the muscle-shell. I have no doubt that the articles they received from us will, for many years to come, bear testimony to future visitors of our friendly intercourse.

As in consequence of the separation of the Beaufoy we should be left with but two boats, I considered that, in the event of their being absent, one of the Fuegian canoes might be useful, and I, therefore, set about purchasing a new one from them. As it appeared to have cost them much labour in the construction, I could not but be liberal in my offer, and I presented them with two full barrel hoops, at which they shouted for joy, and in less than five minutes the family, with all their utensils, were shifted into another canoe, and the purchased one was ready for delivery. I ordered it to be hoisted in, and was surprised to find it heavy; but in getting it on deck, I found a platform of clay, the whole length of the bottom, about six inches deep: this was intended as ballast, and to preserve the bottom against the fire, which they constantly keep in the clay. The length of this canoe was twelve feet four inches, and at the broadest part two feet two inches: it was built of a strong birch bark, which appeared broader than the trees of this neighbourhood afforded, and was probably procured from the interior. Three pieces composed the whole vessel, one piece formed the bottom, and two the sides; all sewed together with tough twigs. The ribs or timbers were of a semicircular form, and placed with their flat sides downwards, and in contact with each other, in a vertical form; so that, with the cement of clay, the canoe is rendered strong, and capable of going against the wind at a quick rate. The internal arrangement of compartments seems orderly. The fishing utensils occupy the first division; in the next sits the female, who uses the foremost paddle; the third division is occupied as the fire-place; the fourth is the baling well, where the water is collected to be thrown out; and next follows the place where the men sit; in the fifth division sits the female, who uses the after paddle; and last of all is the after-locker, in which they keep all their valuables. Their spear poles are generally placed projecting over the stern.

Having secured the canoe and the paddles, I returned to the contemplation of the sellers, who, I was glad to see, were quite merry, and seemingly happy in the possession of the hoops with which I had paid them.

Hunger now beginning to pinch them, they turned their attention to some of the crew, who were employed in splitting whale-bone blades for making brooms; and perceiving the gum upon the bone, as it was still in the state in which it was taken from the whale, they seized this mucilaginous substance, and eat it most ravenously. I thought this an instance of depraved appetite, but in another part of the ship was one still more disgusting. They were here gobbling up some dirty rancid seal fat, which had been lying about for several days. I was willing that they should get something to satisfy the cravings of hunger, but this way of doing it was intolerable, and I obliged them to desist. I then gave them some young seal, and some bread, which they put away in their canoe for a future occasion.

As we had no spirits on board, I offered them wine, and pressed them to take some, but, like their countrymen at Cape Horn, they merely sipped a little, seeming not to like it.

The common missile weapon of the Fuegians is the sling, which is made of the skin of the seal or otter. It is generally about three feet long, and of the common form: the strings are sometimes made of small gut, handsomely plaited, and terminated by knots of ingenious workmanship. Having procured some of these weapons, I prevailed on one of the most intelligent natives to show us their method of using them, which turned out to be exactly like our own; for Mr. Brisbane, who well understood the art, used the sling with as much effect as the Fuegians, at which they were a good deal astonished.

Their principal spear-heads are entirely constructed of hard bone, and are about seven inches long, finely pointed, with a barb on one side four inches from the point. They have another kind, with one side filled with small barbs, made very sharp. These are fixed on a wooden pole, straight and smoothly finished, about ten feet long. To the bone is attached a string of hide of various lengths, and this weapon they use in the capture of almost every thing they pursue. In using the spear, they hold it nearly by the middle, and with the right eye cast along it, they dart it with great precision.

After dinner our people, before they went to duty, sought a little amusement with the strangers; and one merry fellow of our crew commenced singing and dancing, at which the Fuegians formed a circle round him, and imitated his song and dance most minutely. The circular movement, however, presently turned into a sort of play, in which a sailor and Fuegian were endeavouring to throw each other. I at first fully expected to see the Fuegian fall, but I was mistaken: he stood so firm, that it appeared more probable that our sailor, who was a stout athletic young man of twenty-three, would ultimately be thrown. The Fuegian was evidently as skilful as his adversary, but several of the natives, thinking their countryman in danger, flew to his assistance, and I was then obliged to interfere to bring them to order. The Fuegian seemed to enjoy a triumph, at which I was a little mortified, as their obtaining an idea of having equal strength and activity might prove dangerous to us. I could not avoid being angry with our sailor for his inactivity, and desired him in future never to contend with them in that way.

I was anxious to discover if they had any object of divine worship, and accordingly called them together about me, and read a chapter in the Bible; not that they were expected to understand what was read, but it was proper to show them the Bible, and to read it, in connection with making signs of death, resurrection, and supplication to heaven. They manifested no understanding of my meaning; but as I read and made signs, they imitated me, following me with a gabble when reading, raising and lowering their voices as I did. During this time, however, they appeared perfectly attentive, looking me stedfastly in the face with evident marks of astonishment. One of them held his ear down to the book, believing that it spoke, and another wished to put it into his canoe: in short, they were all interested in the book, and could they have made proper use of it I would willingly have given it them.

A thief, however, was not wanting in this party; for having brought the tinder-box on deck, for the purpose of ascertaining how they obtain a light, a Fuegian adept stole the steel. He was suspected, and on being searched it was found under his arm. I sent him to his canoe with threats of punishment, which he well understood.

They procure fire by rubbing iron pyrites and a flinty stone together, and catching the sparks in a dry substance resembling moss, which is quickly ignited.

Our sailors had given the Fuegians all the old clothes they could spare; and our visitors soon appeared in costume, one with only a jacket on, another with but a waistcoat, and a third in his shirt: they were all so clothed in patches that they made a most amusing appearance.

Nothing like a chief could be made out among them, nor did they seem to require one for the peace of their society; for their behaviour to one another was most affectionate, and all property seemed to be possessed in common, though each of them appeared strenuous to obtain it from us, without regarding his neighbour, probably for the honour attached to procuring any thing, or the novelty of first possession. The philanthropic principle which these people exhibit towards one another, and their inoffensive behaviour to strangers, surely entitles them to this observation in their favour, that though they are the most distant from civilised life, owing principally to local circumstances, they are the most docile and tractable of any savages we are acquainted with, and no doubt might, therefore, be instructed in those arts which raise man above the brute.

On the 9th of *December*, about noon, we weighed, and stood to sea, with the wind at N.N.E. The Beaufoy proceeded to South Shetland, and we stood under the east side of the Ildefonsos. These are so small as scarcely to merit the name of islands, the largest being not more than a quarter of a mile long. They appear as two in a S.E. or N.W. bearing; but the northern one is merely a cluster of detached rocks: the southern island is the largest and highest, and contains a quantity of tussac on its top, and sea-gull rookeries. These islands have no beaches, and can only be landed on when the water is very smooth. Between them is a channel of a mile wide, which being rocky should not be passed through. At various opportunities I ascertained the longitude of the southern islands by lunar observations and chronometers to be 69° 16′ 50″, and the latitude 55° 50′ 38″, and the variation at five miles' distance 26° 42′ easterly. The rock of which they are composed is trap porphyry, with porphyritic lava, and they wear a rugged and varied form, as may be seen by the annexed view.

In the night of the 9th we stood towards the islands Diego Ramirez, and at two o'clock in the afternoon of the 10th we sent two boats on shore. These islands extend N.W. and S.E. for a space of about four miles, in which are three principal islands, and a great many rocks above water. The middle island is the largest, and has tussac and sea-gulls upon it, but no water. The latitude observed places the south point in 56° 32′ 15″, and by chronometers in longitude 68° 24′ 15″. The composition of the rock is porphyritic lava. Specimens were deposited by me in the Edinburgh College Museum, and described by Professor Jamieson, which show that volcanic action has been present in the formation of these islands. — A distant view of them is annexed.

The weather continued fine, and the wind from the northward and eastward till eight A.M. on the 11th, when the wind freshened at S.E., and by the time we had taken our boats on board, it blew hard, and we bore up for Tierra del Fuego. On the 12th we came to anchor in Clear Bottom Bay, in 20 fathoms water, in coarse sand with mud underneath. During the 13th and 14th we had strong gales from S.W. to W., and we let go the sheet anchor, and rode a strain upon it. On the 16th we had heavy rain, and the wind abated. In consequence of the badness of the weather our Fuegian friends did not visit us; and having completed our harbour duties, on the 19th we weighed and proceeded to the Ildefonsos. We continued under sail pursuing our business at these islands with favourable weather, and the winds generally between W.S.W. and W.N.W. through the day, and northerly during the night. On the 25th in the afternoon I was surprised to see the Beaufoy approach us, as I fully anticipated that she would have obtained anchorage at South Shetland. Captain Brisbane informed me that the state of the ice on the coast of Shetland was nearly the same as when we left it on the 16th of November, although it was the 18th of December when he quitted the edge of the ice. He ran 40 miles along the coast, but could nowhere approach the land. The ice, too, he reported, was of that heavy blue description which was likely to require a long time to dissolve, and he therefore gave up the idea of waiting. He also informed me, that having split his sails the day before, on making this coast, he had put into a harbour which was very commodious, situated 11 miles up a sound, which I afterwards called New Year's Sound, having spent New Year's Day in it.

A smooth anchorage being necessary for examining the brig, and making repairs, we bore up for New Year's Sound, and at ten o'clock in the morning of the 26th we came to anchor in Indian Cove, so named from a tribe of Fuegians living near it.

Having moored the vessels in the south corner of the cove, we set about lightening the brig forward, in order to make repairs. I was not astonished when I found that the bows of the Jane were much damaged, as the shocks that she had received by unavoidably running against masses of ice were likely to have been even more destructive.

The two lower streaks of the wales*, on

* Strong planks that go round a ship, a little above her water line.

the bows, on the larboard side, and one on the starboard side, were found broken. The foremost piece of the stem was broken, and the plank that was stove under water was providentially jammed in between the timbers in such a way as, with the plank we had nailed over it on the coast of South Shetland, to have admitted very little water. The fore part of the vessel being sufficiently out of the water to effect the repairs, the carpenters were set to work.

The Fuegians had of course noticed the ships come in, as their settlement was on an island at the entrance of the cove; but as they had seen only the cutter before, they were cautious and slow in coming to the brig. They presently approached, however, in several canoes, shouting as usual, and spreading out their arms, apparently impressed with a sensation of fear and joy. I soon enticed them on board; for though we did not understand each others' language, yet intercourse with them afforded me, through their actions, a melancholy pleasure in observing the gradation of human understanding.

Among these I saw several with a cast of features differing from the general character of Fuegians, having high noses, and being somewhat taller than the rest.

It occurred to me that these differences of features might be faint traces of the Spaniards,

Drawn by A. Masson, from a Sketch by Cap. Weddell. Pub. by Longman, Hurst, Rees, Orme, Brown & Green, 1825. I. Clark sculp.

Brig Jane, and Cutter Beaufoy, in Indian Cove, Terra del Fuego.

who made a settlement in the straits of Magellan 244 years ago, but which lasted only seven years. The ancestors of these Fuegians might have been in intercourse with these Spaniards at that period; and those Fuegians I have mentioned as differing in features may have descended from that connection. This seems probable from their having two Spanish words *canoa*, canoe, and *perro*, a dog. My steward, who was a Spaniard, addressed them many times, but could never discover their having any other words of Spanish.

I found great difficulty in acquiring a slight knowledge of their language, from their continually repeating my words in imitation; so that I am not quite decided as to the meaning of many of their sounds, and shall therefore not attempt to describe them particularly.

Sayam	means	Water.
Abaish	——	Woman.
Shevoo	——	Approbation.
Nosh	——	Displeasure.

And in most of their words it may be observed that the sounds S and Sh predominate.

These words which I have mentioned are found to correspond pretty nearly with words of similar meaning in the Hebrew language. Thus I am informed that *yam* means sea or water, and *ausha*, woman, in Hebrew; and also that the sounds S and Sh occur perpetually in that language.

The words *canoa*, a canoe, and *perro*, a dog, which I have mentioned above as being derived from the Spanish, may also be ultimately referred to the same original; for in Hebrew, *canna* means a hollow reed or receptacle, a cane,—and *pera*, a wild animal, These and many other words, originally Hebrew, which are to be found in the Spanish language, can be easily accounted for, as having found their way into it through the Arabic, the language of the Moors; but how the Fuegians could get hold of Hebrew words is certainly a question of some interest to philologists.

On the 27th I sent the Beaufoy to the island of Diego Ramirez, with fourteen men additional from the brig. In the forenoon about forty Fuegians came on board, and amused themselves in various ways. A boy was kept constantly watching them, to prevent thieving; but from their spreading about the decks, though I had every valuable movable put below, he probably did not succeed in preventing stealth.

I had given the mass a present of some seal's fat, and young seal, killed when about three weeks old; but one of them, an old fellow about 60, was not satisfied with this donation, and stole a young seal from a sailor, who had cleaned it, intending it for his own dinner. It is the practice of the Fuegians to laugh at being detected in a theft; but this old man, on being discovered, was much alarmed, and went to his canoe, nor did he venture from the settlement until he understood, at my seeing him there, that he was taken into favour again.

This tribe were clothed in a similar way to those of their countrymen we had met with before: they had only a skin over their shoulders, and several of them were quite naked, unless red ochre may be considered a covering, for of that they wore a complete coat. We had few old clothes to spare, having been liberal to our first visitors; but in lieu of otter skins, which I purchased off their backs, I gave each of them a garment of some description. I had given one of them a white flannel shirt, which he slipped on, and skipped about among his companions in great ecstasy. This shirt being in high estimation, they wore it by turns for eight or ten minutes, and after being satisfied with it in this form, they tore it into ribbons, and divided it share and share alike. This was an instance of their holding property in common.

Having occasion to fill some casks with water in the after part of the ship, in order to raise her still more forward, I set the Fuegians to draw water; and after being shown the most convenient way, they performed it with as much expedition as our own people. I also employed them in pulling and hauling, when we required strength, and this they did with eagerness, but the noise of singing to each pull was deafening: after hearing one of our sailors *sing*, as is usual, they thought that it was to be imitated also, and all roared together in unison. The women and little children remained in the canoes close alongside, and they were kept amused by receiving small presents occasionally. I tried what effect music would have, and had the fiddle played to them. It seemed to please them, but the German flute still more, and vocal music more than either. The women, indeed, were in ecstasy at hearing a song given by a young man who had a fine voice. I showed them some sea paintings, which attracted their attention, though only for a moment; but I remarked those of the most glaring colours retained their admiration longest and most.

An opportunity offered our visitors of changing their dress. This was at a tub of dark clay, which we had brought from the Falkland Islands. They soon rubbed on a complete coat of it, and were highly pleased with their new costume. The women, too, were indulged with a slight rub; when the clay became dry, however, I fancy they found it unpleasant, as they all soon rubbed it off again.

Observing one of them with sore eyes, I made a liniment, and washed them. He evidently perceived my intention, and I believe expected that he was to be cured at once; which did not, of course, take place, but, by washing them twice or thrice a day, in three days they were nearly well. I had cut the hair from over the eyes of this man, because it irritated them; and his countrymen thought it improved the appearance, and came to me to have theirs cut in the same way. As it was a harmless request, I complied with their desire, and, to amuse them, powdered them with flour. The ladies were quite delighted with this head-dress, but I found it too expensive to be continued, not having an over-abundant supply of the article on board.

I had made them acquainted with the destructive effects of fire-arms, and at the report of a great gun, which we fired, the women shrieked, and the men were appalled, and looked at the engine with a vacant gaze.

I observed a bold and cunning fellow among this people, whom I judged to be the appointed thief of this tribe. This fellow, having found his way into the main-top, was trying to pull off the iron work about it. I made signs to him to come down, but he paid no attention. Having my pistols in my pocket, I pointed one at him, merely to frighten him into compliance, and he descended; but on reaching the deck, he put on a revengeful countenance, and threw a piece of rag in my face. As I was determined to check this insolence, I took up my fowlingpiece, which was at hand, and presented it; at which he fled to the forepart of the ship, and his companions with him, shouting for fear. The women joined in the howl of alarm; but peace was soon restored by my sending the offender into his canoe, and putting my fowlingpiece below. I intended, at a proper opportunity, to make this fellow sensible of his ill behaviour, but, in the meantime, I only forbade his coming on board. By this little misunderstanding their confidence in our friendly consideration for them was shaken, as they retired to their settlement much sooner than usual.

There being but eight of us in number on board, two of whom were boys, it became necessary, in case of any dangerously offensive behaviour of the Fuegians, that we should be armed, and I therefore required each person to have a cutlass, and a musket or pistol at hand.

In the morning of the 30th, about four o'clock, between forty and fifty Fuegians jumped on board, in defiance of those of our crew who were on deck. The second mate, Mr. Mathewson, taking an alarm, came to my state-room, saying that the natives intended to take possession of the vessel. His suspicions were rational, but his fears turned out to be groundless; for, on my going up with my pistols in my hand, some who were on the cabin stairs, trying to get below, flew up, and those on deck I brought immediately to order. It is not unlikely that a skirmish would have taken place had my people been allowed to strike them, for a little irritation would, most likely, have roused them at least to defence.

Their conduct in the morning had been irregular, but I took no further notice of it, after bringing them to their usual course of inoffensive behaviour.

In the middle of the day I assembled these people together, in order to ascertain if they had any idea of a future state. I practised the same mode of enquiry as I had done with the last tribe, by reading out of the Bible, and making signs to them. I certainly observed them to have a solemn feeling, which they exhibited by looking each other in the face, with a countenance expressive of extreme wonder, and speaking to one another in a low tone of voice; but, notwithstanding these appearances of a religious principle, I could discern nothing like a form of worship among them.

By making them small presents at various times, I procured a quantity of articles of their manufacture, such as necklaces, baskets, bows and arrows. These, which are their principal possessions, I shall shortly describe.

Their necklaces are very ingeniously put together, and consist of small shells of the turbinated genus, possessing a beautiful coloured enamel. They are perforated near the orifice, and are strung together on a cord made of gut, so neatly plaited, that, though it is only the thickness of small whip-cord, it contains no fewer than five strings, so exceedingly small that it creates some wonder how they can perform the plaiting by the hand.

Their baskets are made of strong grass, and exhibit considerable skill in the construction. The grass is put together after the manner of weaving, the blades being worked at right angles, and over the top is a handle equal to half the circumference of the basket.

Their bows are generally about three feet eight inches long, and are made of an elastic wood which is smooth and hard. The string is of seal-skin, and sometimes of gut plaited: the arrows are of hard wood, and finely polished; they are about twenty-five inches in length, with a sharp triangular flint for the point, fixed into a cleft in the wood. When the arrow has entered, the shaft may be drawn out, but the flint remains.

They have another weapon, consisting of a similar-shaped flint, inserted in a handle about nine inches long; and this they probably use as a stiletto.

I am not aware that these people are given to war, though I saw three of this tribe with scars on their bodies, which indicated their having received wounds.

On the 31st the Beaufoy arrived with a quantity of seal-skins, and came to anchor. Our carpenters had now completed their work on the bows of the brig, and we proceeded to stowing the hold, and bringing the vessel into her usual trim.

As I can duly appreciate the nature of a good shipwright, it is but justice to my carpenter, J. Aitkenson, to say that his skill and industry on this occasion, of repairing serious damages with few materials, gave me great satisfaction.

Our friends, the Fuegians, came again on board soon after the arrival of the Beaufoy, no doubt expecting a feast of seal's fat and flesh. They were not disappointed, for Mr. Brisbane had brought them a quantity, and it was shared out among them. Our people were busily employed in cutting blubber from the seal-skins, when the natives, enticed by the strippings of fat, expressed a desire to assist. I allowed them to do so, and they appeared clever at the business. It was soon noticed, however, that they had another intention besides that of dressing the skins; for one fellow, while at work, had hauled a skin, bit and bit, under his arm, in a most dexterous manner. But the second mate had observed the theft, and when the Fuegian was proceeding to leave the ship, made him deliver up his prize, at which he laughed most heartily, though on my approaching he retired to his canoe, quite aware that he had offended me.

Their knowledge of barter had evidently increased their spirit for thieving, so that they would now steal articles from the cutter, and endeavour to sell them at the brig for some things they liked better, and *vice versa*.

As we had now no fears of being overpowered by numbers, I had got the fellow on board, who had thrown the rag in my face, and made him understand that I had it in my power to punish him; his fears and humility, however, procured him his pardon, and he continued to behave himself properly.

In the afternoon Captain Brisbane accompanied me to the settlement. I had signified to the Fuegians that we intended to visit them, and they paddled home before us. We landed at a convenient place, and were met by a party, who conducted us to the town, which consisted of but a few wigwams, slightly constructed, and containing a population of about sixty.

The first circumstance that struck me was the absence of the women and little children: it was evident that on our approaching they had sent them into the woods, and had lighted fires almost all round the island. This appeared, in part, to be an effusion of joy at our visit; but it also seemed to be an invitation to other Fuegians, as two strange canoes came to us from the upper part of the sound. In one of the wigwams I saw a sea-gull, perfectly tame, and jumping about, which conveys an idea of their affection for the lower animals. I had used the precaution of having our boat at hand, and the crew armed, which enabled us to mix among them without fear. On my expressing a desire for muscles, they commenced roasting them for me, and vied with each other in bringing me the best. The old man whom I have mentioned as having stolen a young seal appeared here, and I gave him to understand that he was forgiven. To amuse and astonish them I killed two sea-gulls at one discharge of my fowlingpiece, at which they gazed with wonder, particularly the strangers; as I never allowed them to see me load the gun, but after firing always put the muzzle to my mouth, at which they generally fled back, believing that I loaded it by speaking into it. I thought it proper to hide from them the nature and management of fire-arms, as they are often found dangerous in the hands of barbarians.

Our people were mixing among them, singing and dancing, but on two of our crew wishing to go into the woods, the natives became uneasy for their wives, and I was obliged to interfere. This forbearance on our part did not, however, meet with a suitable return; for one of the Fuegians (mistaking the sex) behaved very strangely to a young man of our party, who with some difficulty made his escape to the boat.

Our curiosity being satisfied, we bade them farewell, and returned on board.

I saw no case of sickness among these people; none lame, except one man who had the palsy. As far as I had an opportunity to observe, the proportion of women is about two-thirds that of the men; and with respect to longevity, including the women, they may be said to contain four classes. The oldest, which were three men, by their wrinkled appearance I judged to be from 50 to 60 years of age; the second class were twenty-four individuals, about 40; the third, of which there were twenty-seven, were from 20 to 30; and the rest, being youths, girls, and children, were twenty-six; making the total number of this tribe to consist of about eighty persons.

On the 1st of *January* the Fuegians landed at the head of the cove and set fire to the woods. As the smoke, by the direction of the wind, came right upon us, I ordered a musket to be fired over their heads, to make them desist. They paid no attention to this, but continued kindling the woods, and as we were now almost enveloped in smoke I was determined to check them effectually, and therefore fired a great gun shotted in such a direction as to be perfectly clear of them, but so as to let them hear the whistle of the shot. On hearing this and the report of the gun, they ran precipitately to their canoes, and paddled home as fast as possible.

I was at a loss to know, in this instance, what they meant by setting fire to the woods, as they must have known that it would be troublesome to us, and I considered it always as a signal of friendship; in the present case, however, it was an actual annoyance, and was necessarily put a stop to.

The following morning the Fuegians came on board without taking the smallest notice of the guns that had been fired, and conducted themselves peaceably. The brig being ready for sea, at 10 we weighed, with the wind at west, and proceeded to the Diego Ramirez, leaving the Beaufoy at anchor. We continued under sail off these Islands, till the 4th in the morning, when we returned. The Fuegians, seeing us approach, calculated on receiving supplies, and hurried alongside. The vessel being under sail, I was much afraid some of their canoes would be upset, but they managed them surprisingly. We must have had nearly the whole settlement about us, together with some strangers, as I enumerated eleven canoes, each containing not fewer than seven individuals. I made a signal to the Beaufoy for a boat, and Captain Brisbane came on board. He informed me that the natives had behaved themselves in a very orderly manner, and that he had nothing to fear from being left alone with them. Our business requiring that the vessels should separate, I gave him his instructions, which were, to remain in the neighbourhood till the 20th, to proceed then to the Falkland Islands and South Georgia, and to rejoin me in the month of March, on the coast of Patagonia: but I particularly cautioned him not to remain among the natives longer than he found them friendly. Our final arrangements being made, we took a last farewell of the natives, who went to their canoes reluctantly, and we proceeded to the eastward for the coast of Patagonia. I was afterwards glad to learn from Captain Brisbane, that, during his stay, they behaved in a quiet, friendly manner.

The islands of Tierra del Fuego extend in length about 360 miles, from east to west, along the Straits of Magellan; and in extreme breadth, from north to south, about 160, from the straits to the extremity of Cape Horn.

This tract of country, as far as my information goes, contains a large population, particularly towards the shores of the Straits of Magellan.

Most of those islands are studded on the sides with a small beach tree, about twenty-four feet high, and eight or ten inches in diameter. They grow so crooked, that a straight trunk more than ten or twelve feet is rarely found. I built a boat of this wood, however, which when seasoned, answered the purpose very well.

In the interior of the country several mountain tops appear constantly covered with snow, though I do not consider the highest to be more than 3000 feet.

The great length of day in the summer season has an enlivening effect; and, when the weather is fine and the water smooth, the wildness of the scenery is quite romantic.

The volcano, which has been seen by several persons, in passing Cape Horn, was not at this time visible, but I picked up a quantity of vesicular flaggy lava, which, no doubt, had been ejected from it.

Captain Basil Hall saw it in flame during his passage round Cape Horn, in the year 1822, in His Majesty's ship Conway; and in 1820, when on our first voyage, in the month of January, I saw the sky much reddened over Tierra del Fuego, which I supposed at the time was produced by the volcano. The climate of this region has been differently described by persons who have passed through it, and I doubt not but they have been respectively correct, inasmuch as they have framed their report from the circumstances of weather at each particular time. The fact is, that much depends on the direction of the wind; since, in the middle of summer, when it blows strong at south, proceeding from the icy land of Shetland, the thermometer will often stand so low as 38°; and, with the wind from the opposite quarter, the weather is frequently almost as fine as that of summer in England.

I saw no quadrupeds, except dogs and otters, nor do I think there are any others to the south of the Straits of Magellan.

In conclusion of what I have to remark, regarding these Fuegians, I may say, I never saw men whose minds were so unimproved; and though they may possibly be defective in mental organisation, as has been asserted by some, yet there is little doubt, from their tractableness, that their condition might be easily alleviated. This would be the opinion of the philanthropic author of the following remark: "Any general character, from the best to the worst, from the most ignorant to the most enlightened, may be given to any community, even to the world at large, by the application of proper means, which means are to a great extent at the command, and under the control, of those who have influence in the affairs of men."

Few voyagers, who have had intercourse with these Fuegians, have been backward in pronouncing them to be the most miserable among men, and as not having mental capacity for instruction, but without explaining the circumstances which are, probably, the cause of their being so. I have had an opportunity of seeing, that their ignorance may be attributed principally to local causes.

It is not likely that any people, who have ever enjoyed the advantage of improvements for their better *subsistence*, will ever forget them. Hence, it may be presumed, that the ancestors of these tribes were in the same state of ignorant imbecility as the present race, unless we may suppose, that they were driven from the north of the Straits of Magellan, and coming into an unprolific country, which did not afford the means of continuing their acquired arts, they gradually ceased to remember them.

As few quadrupeds are found upon the islands of Tierra del Fuego, the natives cannot depend on hunting for their subsistence, and are consequently obliged to have recourse to fishing. This last occupation compels them to live on the sea coast, where the coldness and gloom of a protracted winter seems to check all mental improvement.

The inclemency of the climate, too, seems to produce upon these people a degree of inactivity, which, together with the inconveniency of moving from place to place, from the nature of the country, may produce their diminutive stature; for, if they originally migrated from the north of the Straits of Magellan, they must have been a more athletic race of men: the climate and the peculiarities of their situation have now, probably, exercised all their rigorous effects upon the inhabitants, and they have arrived at a stationary character. Had they been so circumstanced as to procure a subsistence by hunting, their bodies would, without doubt, have been more vigorous, and their minds, probably, not inferior to those of other savage tribes.

Nature has been bountiful in providing a most inexhaustible supply of shell-fish, upon which they principally live; and they are procured with so little trouble, that no ideas are required which can improve the reasoning faculties. No patience or perseverance is necessary, like that exercised by savages, who, in hunting, have to employ reason superior to the instinctive cunning of the animals they pursue. The Fuegians' food lies on the shores of different islands, and their journies are all performed in the canoe; so that being cramped in sitting, their legs are ill formed, and the females, who are the keepers of the canoe, from that circumstance, are worse shaped in the lower extremities than the men.

The rugged and mountainous country of Tierra del Fuego, which faces the south, offers no inducement to agriculture, nor indeed does it admit of it; but, towards the N.E. of these islands, the land is more inviting, and the climate better.

I have only now to recommend these people, in whom I have taken a lively interest, to the philanthropic part of the world, as presenting an untouched field for their exertions to ameliorate the condition of their fellow men.

True humane and religious charity is best bestowed on those who most need our help, and are willing to receive it; and this is certainly the case with these Fuegians, who, of all uncivilised tribes with whom we are acquainted, seem most destitute of every thing which tends to rouse the human mind to exertion.

CHAP. VII.

OFF CAPE HORN. — TIERRA DEL FUEGO. — TIDES: NATIVES. — THE RIVER GALLEGOS VISITED; AND THE SANTA CRUZ. — PRODUCE OF THE COAST. — SEA LIONS. — PATAGONIA. STRAITS OF MAGELLAN. — EARLY DISCOVERERS. — STATURE OF THE INHABITANTS; THEIR MANNERS, &C. — ATTEMPTS DURING THE REIGN OF CHARLES II. TO OPEN COMMUNICATIONS WITH THEM. — SOUTH AMERICAN COASTS. — MONTE VIDEO. — INHABITANTS. — SPANISH PUBLIC DINNER. — PRICES OF HORSES AND BULLOCKS. — HARBOUR DANGEROUS. — SAIL FOR ENGLAND. — ARRIVAL OFF FALMOUTH.

WE stood to the N.E. with the wind from S.E. by S., and on the 7th in the afternoon we were off Barnavelt's Island, near Cape Horn, and I sent a boat on shore. Nothing but a little grass grows on the island, and around it lie several small islets. The latitude from my observation at noon, when within five miles and a half of the island, gave for its centre 55° 48′ 16″, and longitude by chronometers 66° 39′. The wind continued from the S.E., and at day-light we saw the land in the N.N.W., but, by reason of the weather being foggy, we could not perceive the entrance of Straits Le Maire. We, however, stood on, and at nine A.M. the fog clearing away, I found we were actually in the straits, with the western point of Staten Land bearing E. by N. I have annexed a view of the land of Tierra del Fuego, on the western side of the straits, which, while that side only is seen, presents a gap or valley: which, being below the horizon, might be taken by a stranger for the southern entrance of the straits, thus creating a mistake, in foggy weather particularly, which would lead the vessel into danger.

In the forenoon we saw some whales close in shore, and the boats were sent in pursuit. We stood with the vessel within four or five miles off the shore of Tierra del Fuego, and sounded in a depth of 75 fathoms, over a bottom of fine sand. I had desired the chief mate, who was in one of the boats, to examine the state of the tide on the shore, and we remained lying to, with the wind at S.S.E. and S.E., from eleven o'clock till one, when the boats returned, without having succeeded in capturing any of the whales. We had, during this period, drifted to the southward against a fresh breeze, and the mate informed me, that the tide had been falling rapidly during the time they had been away, and that when they left the beach it was about low water. We stood into Success Bay, and about two o'clock the tide changed, and swept us violently to the northward, which must have been the tide of flood; and hence, by calculation, high-water, at the full and change of the moon, will take place at two o'clock.

The flood has always been supposed to run to the southward through the straits, but according to the circumstances I have described, I am led to believe it runs to the northward; though probably its continuing to run to the northward through the straits some time after high water by the shore, may have led to erroneous conclusions in that respect.

Before we got out of the bay, the Fuegians of these straits came down to the sea-side, and shouted at the full stretch of their lungs, inviting us to land; but as the wind was fair, and night approaching, we could not spare time to comply with their wish. I was sorry it was not convenient to have communication with this tribe, as it was in this bay, in the year 1769, that Captain Cook visited the inhabitants; and it would have been agreeable to have ascertained whether, from his intercourse with them, they had derived permanent improvement, though his stay amongst them was too short to produce any great result.

Off Cape Saint Diego is a heavy tide-rip when the wind is strong, and at those times it is better to avoid passing through it. We stood to the northward, across the entrance of the Straits of Magellan, and on the north side the land appears comparatively low, and fit for agriculture.

We coasted Patagonia to the northward, pursuing our business of examining the shores for fur seals, and taking black whales, as opportunities permitted; and on the 13th, having sought in vain for the river Gallegos, we came to an anchor in eight fathoms water, at the distance of about five miles from the land.

Being in the latitude in which this river is represented on the chart of Malespina, I landed to examine the shore, supposing that the entrance might be land-locked in such a way that it could not be seen at any distance from the shore. I had walked four or five miles along the beach to the southward, without discovering the object of my search, and was returning, when by accident looking over a bank, the situation of the sought-for river appeared, though with very little water in it. This mound was four or five feet above the level of the sea at high water. I have little doubt but the river was open at the time Malespina gave it a name, and must since that period, 1790, have been nearly dried up, by the waters having been diverted from the original course, and the sea having rolled in the bank into its entrance; or that at the time the river was discovered, there was in the mouth of it a bar or bank, which did not then appear above water; and that the sea has since receded on the eastern coast of Patagonia, leaving the bank

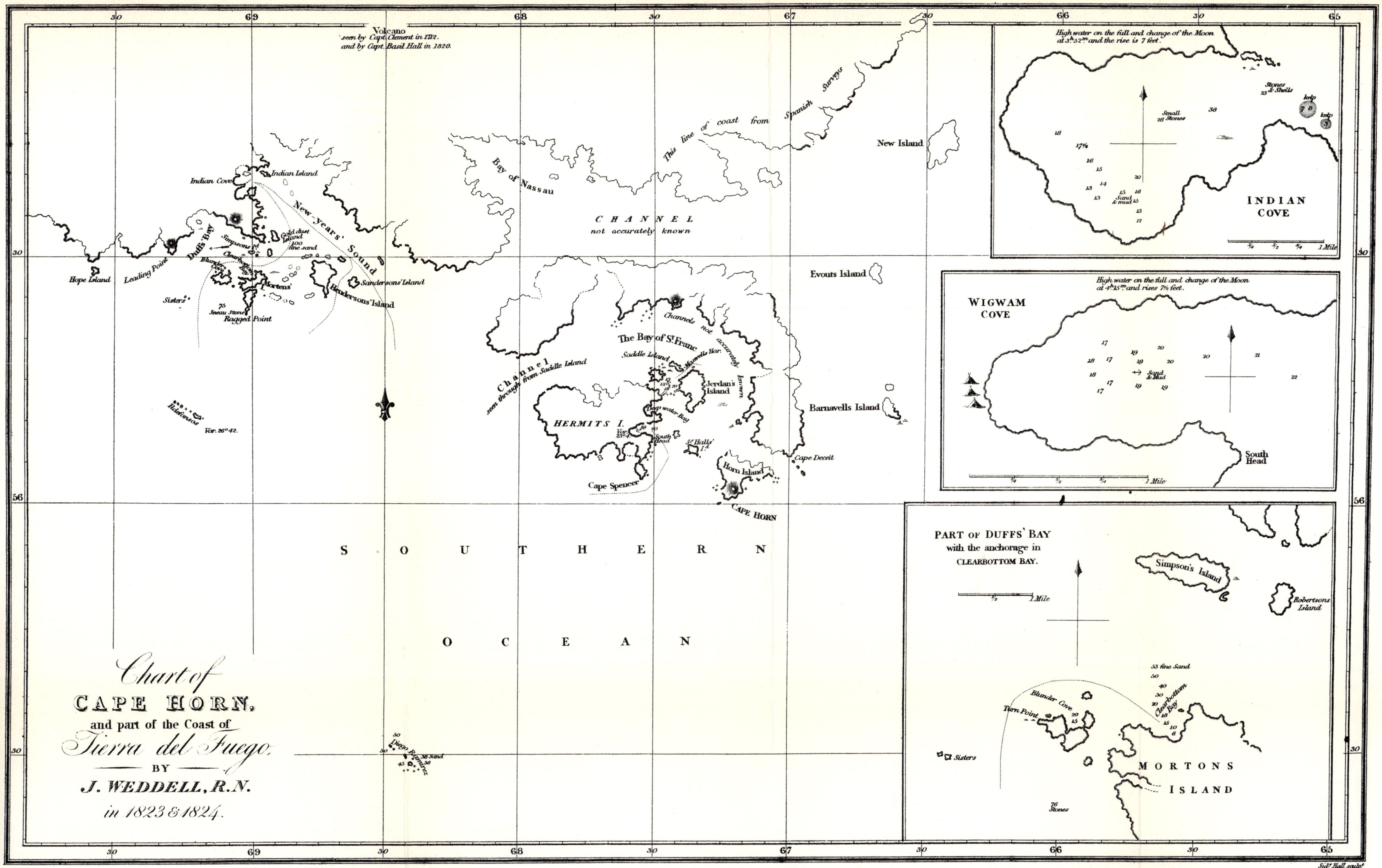

London, Published by Longman & Co. Paternoster Row, Augt. 1825.

Sidy. Hall, sculpt.

dry. Which of these may be the fact is not easy to decide; perhaps both the causes mentioned may have contributed to the change.

On the 14th, in the afternoon, the wind freshened to a brisk gale, and we allowed the vessel to drive with the anchor on the ground, nearly in the direction of the coast: at dark we hove the anchor up, and lay to. The weather proved tolerably fine, and the winds were variable, often light from the S.E., and we occasionally anchored to facilitate our operations.

On the 24th we put into the river of Santa Cruz, for the purpose of making some alteration on the hold, and converting some blubber into oil. The entrance of this river cannot be seen at a great distance, as the land which lies behind covers it. I have given a view of the coast, and a sketch of the river. The shore on the left side going in is high, whilst that on the right is quite low. The latitude of the entrance is 50° 12′ 16″ S., and longitude 68° 14′ 30″ W. Directions for sailing into it are added in the Appendix.

About seven miles from the entrance the Santa Cruz falls into two branches, the one running to the S.W., the other to the N.W. The northern, which is by much the smallest, I penetrated about twelve miles, which was very near its source, as the water was quite fresh, and the stream became a mere brook. That branch which runs to the

N.W. is, from its appearance, of some extent; and I should not wonder if it communicates with some branch from the Straits of Magellan, as the water at our anchorage, at the lowest tides, never ran fresh. The N.W. river being very shallow, the procuring of good water is attended with some delay, as it must be taken at the end of the ebb of the tide, when there is not depth enough to float a loaded boat, and you must therefore wait the following flood.

No large wood is found in the neighbourhood of this river. On the eastern shore are many bushes bearing a small black berry, little less than a sloe, which when ripe is pleasant to the taste, and highly beneficial as an antiscorbutic, of which we took advantage, and eat great quantities of them. I saw no traces of inhabitants where I landed, nor land animals, except guanacoes, of which there were many, but too timid to allow us to approach within musket-shot. Nearly in the middle of the main river is an island, which is called Sea Lion Island, from a number of those animals residing on it. This amphibious creature, of the seal genus, is most properly denominated the Sea Lion, from its similarity to that quadruped. The face is not unlike that of a lion; but in particular, a long mane, and the bold and fierce front which it presents, when standing on its fore flippers, bear a near resemblance to the appearance of that animal. A full grown sea lion measures eleven feet from the tip of the nose to the extremity of the tail, and eight feet in circumference; and differs from the ursine seal only in the peculiarities I have mentioned. They may, indeed, be considered as belonging to a class of monsters of the seal species. They resist their assailants with great ferocity, but their capture is easily accomplished by shooting them in the forehead.

The rise of the tide is so great in this river, being thirty-two feet, that the keel of the largest ship may be examined, by laying her on the ground; and there is sufficient water on the bar of the river at two-thirds flood of spring tides for a ship of the line. This circumstance might afford great convenience to a vessel requiring repairs in the bottom. The tide flows on the full and change of the moon at forty minutes past eight in the morning, and the ebb runs four miles an hour.

We had passed three times in and out of this river by the 17th of February, when we took our departure for the Falkland Islands.

Little is yet known of the portion of America south of the latitude of 42 degrees, generally described by the name of Patagonia. That part of the country which lies on the western side of the Andes, towards the Island of Chiloe, has been colonized by the Spaniards, and is better known.

As I have seen much of the coast of Patagonia, and have obtained some information from others concerning the country, and its inhabitants, I shall give a brief account of it.

The tract of country alluded to is bounded on the south by the Straits of Magellan, discovered in the year 1519, by Fernando Magalhaen, and called by us the Straits of Magellan, in the latitude of from 52 to 54 degrees south.

This passage to the Pacific Ocean was considered of great importance by the Spaniards, as they at first believed it to be the only way, sailing westward, to their valuable Peruvian possessions, and to the Phillippine Islands. These considerations induced them to make a settlement in the Straits, probably with a view of commanding the passage, to the exclusion of foreigners, and to facilitate the navigation to their own ships.

They chose, in 1581, a situation on the Patagonian side, about 120 miles from the eastern entrance of the Straits, and built a town, which they named Philippville, after the then reigning king of Spain.

The inviting riches of Peru, Mexico, and the West Indies, however, engrossed all spirit of enterprise, and all attention, so that the settlement of Phillippville became neglected, and in 1587, having existed but seven years, its inhabitants, who at the beginning were 400, were reduced by famine, to a single individual, of the name of Hernando.

The distinguished navigator, Cavendish, arrived at this place in the year 1587, and found this unhappy man, the only one reserved to tell the painful story of the fate of his unfortunate companions. Cavendish took him on board, and to perpetuate the melancholy history of the spot he called it Port Famine.

From the report given of the enchanting beauties of this place by Commodore Byron, we may suppose that there was a want of industry on the part of the inhabitants, as well as of neglect in the government of Spain, in not sending supplies till the lands could be cultivated, and grain brought to maturity.

Commodore Byron, having anchored in Port Famine in the year 1764, says, "The next day at noon, having had little wind, and calms, we anchored in Port Famine, close to the shore, and found our situation very safe and convenient; we had shelter from all winds except the south east, which seldom blows; and if a ship should be driven ashore in the bottom of the bay, she could receive no damage, for it is all fine soft ground. We found drift wood here, sufficient to have furnished a thousand sail, so that we had no need to take the trouble of cutting green.

The water of Ledger River is excellent, but the boats cannot get in till about two hours flood, because at low water, it is very shallow for about three quarters of a mile. I went up it about four miles in my boat, and the fallen trees then rendered it impossible to go farther; I found it, indeed, not only difficult, but dangerous, to get up thus far. The stream is very rapid, and many stumps of trees lie hidden under it; one of these made its way through the bottom of my boat, and in an instant she was full of water. We got on shore as well as we could; and afterwards, with great difficulty, hauled her upon the side of the river: here we contrived to stop the hole in her bottom, so as that we made a shift to get her down to the river's mouth, where she was soon properly repaired by the carpenter. On each side of this river there are the finest trees I ever saw, and I make no doubt but that they would supply the British navy with the finest masts in the world. Some of them are of a great height, and more than eight feet in diameter, which is proportionably more than eight yards in circumference, so that four men, joining hand in hand, could not compass them. Among others, we found the pepper tree, or winter's bark, in great plenty. Among these woods, notwithstanding the coldness of the climate, there are innumerable parrots, and other birds of the most beautiful plumage. I shot, every day, geese and ducks enough to serve my own table, and several others, and every body on board might have done the same: we had, indeed, great plenty of fresh provisions of all kinds, for we caught as much fish every day as served the companies of both ships. As I was much on shore here, I tracked many wild beasts in the sand, but never saw one: we also found many huts, or wigwams, but never met with an Indian. The country between this fort, and Cape Forward, which is distant about four leagues, is extremely fine; the soil appears to be very good, and there are no less than three pretty large rivers, besides several brooks."

The terminating point of this continent appears to have been discovered by two Hollanders, Jacob Maire, of Amsterdam, and Cornelius Schouten, of Hoorn, in the year 1516. The straits known by the name of Le Maire were called after the first mentioned navigator; and Horn, the present name of the Cape, is a corruption of Hoorn, the name of the city in Holland, of which Cornelius Schouten was a native. The discovery made by these intrepid men opened a new way into the Pacific, which took away much from the importance of the Straits of Magellan, and they have, in consequence, since that time been little frequented. The enormous stature of the Patagonians, as described by some navigators, who have passed through the Straits, is a matter worthy of consideration, since I find the subject spoken of by reputable authors with much uncertainty: this induces me to lay before the reader what information I have been able to obtain respecting this doubtful circumstance.

I have received particular accounts of the Patagonians residing in the Straits, from persons of veracity, who have lately passed through them; and the natives are described as being of ordinary stature, from five feet five inches (the stature of the Fuegians, from whom they are but little different), to six feet. From the circumstance of the land on the Patagonian side of the Straits being more temperate, and less mountainous than that of Tierra del Fuego, those who live on that side take more land exercise, and are somewhat more robust, better clothed, and live together in larger tribes.

These people, it should be remembered, are the inhabitants of the Straits only; in the interior of this country, which is of vast extent, there may be men of Goliah-like stature; but we can scarcely suppose them of the size described by a gentleman who was on shore with Commodore Byron, at his interview with the Patagonians, in the Straits of Magellan. (Vide Byron's Voyage, vol. ii. pages 826—7.) This officer says, that "when they were ten or twelve leagues within the Straits, they saw, through their glasses, many people on shore of a prodigious size, which extraordinary magnitude they thought to be a deception, occasioned by the haziness of the atmosphere, it being then somewhat foggy; but on coming near the land, they appeared of still greater bulk, and made amicable signs to our people to come on shore. That when the ship sailed on, to find a proper place of landing, they made lamentations, as if they were afraid our people were going off."

He also says, "there were near four hundred of them, and about one-third of the men on horses, not much larger than ours; and that they rode with their knees up the horses' withers, having no stirrups; that there were women, and many children, whom some of our people took up in their arms and kissed, which the Indians beheld with much seeming satisfaction. That by way of affection and esteem they took his hand between theirs, and patted it; and that some of those he saw were ten feet high, well proportioned, and well featured: their skins were of a warm copper colour, and they had neither offensive nor defensive weapons." He also says, that "they seemed particularly pleased with Lieut. Cumming, on account of his stature, he being six feet two inches high, and that some of them patted him on the shoulders, but their hands fell with such force that it affected his whole frame."

I have hinted in another place, that those with whom Commodore Byron communicated were probably chiefs; but it is more than probable that this tribe, of whatever size, were not inhabitants of the shore, but of the interior, and from the country farther to the northward, and of course seldom, perhaps never, on the shores of the Straits when any vessels touched there since that time.

Patagonians farther to the northward sometimes come down in the summer season, and have been seen by my officers, who described them to be generally about six feet high, well proportioned, and appearing, upon the whole, above the ordinary size. Unlike the Fuegians, they are fond of spirituous liquors; but they resemble them in being fond of toys, and every kind of hardware. My chief mate in our first voyage, in 1819, about the Bay of Saint Mathias, bought a young guanacoe, from a Patagonian, for an old knife. He described this man to be of middle stature, and good looking: he came up to the boat's crew on horseback, with great confidence; alighted, and showed the officer that he had taken the animal with a sling.

From the necessity of my remaining on board while under sail, on the coast, I had not opportunities of ascertaining any thing in particular of the native habits, which are no doubt materially different from those of the tribes in the neighbourhood of Buenos Ayres, who, by intercourse with the Spaniards, have become somewhat assimilated to European manners.

I am, upon the whole, fully of opinion, that no men, of the prodigious stature described by Commodore Byron, ever appear now on the sea coast, whatever giants there may be in the interior of the country. Port Desire, and the Bay of St. Joseph, are places at which tribes of Patagonians have been seen by gentlemen of my acquaintance, whose description of the natives accords with what I have stated respecting those seen by my officers. The extent of country inhabited by the native Patagonians only, which lies to the south of the river Negro (on which there is a settlement of a few Spaniards), may be estimated at 770 miles in length, and 300 in breadth, or 232,200 square miles.

A knowledge of what this extent of country affords, of inhabitants, and commercial produce, particularly on the eastern part of the Andes, would be very desirable, as an advantageous traffic might possibly be opened with the natives, who may be more numerous than is supposed. Commodore Anson informs us, that King Charles the Second was of opinion that a country contiguous to a region containing such store of gold and silver as Chili, was worthy of being examined for that precious ore, independent of opening a commerce with the natives for other productions.

Induced by these considerations, he sent out Sir John Narborough, to open a communication with the I atagonians, and to ascertain the value of their possessions. However, it appears that he did not effect either. Commodore Anson says, (Voyage, p. 93.) "It is true that Sir John Narborough did not succeed in opening this commerce, which in appearance promised so many advantages to this nation. However, his disappointment was merely accidental, and his transactions upon that coast, besides the many valuable improvements he furnished to geography and navigation, are rather an encouragement for future trials of this kind, than any objection against them; his principal misfortune being the losing company of a small bark, which attended him, and having some of his people trepanned at Baldivia."

However, it appeared by the precautions and the fears of the Spaniards, that they were fully convinced of the practicability of the scheme he was sent to execute, and extremely alarmed at the apprehensions of its consequences.

It is said that his majesty King Charles II. was so prepossessed with hopes of the advantages which would redound from this expedition, and so eager to be informed of the event of it, that hearing intelligence of Sir John Narborough's passing through the Downs, on his return, he had not patience to attend his arrival at court, but went himself in his barge to Gravesend to meet him."

The coasts of South America are of a different description. The western coast is rocky, high, and rugged, containing many islands, with deep water close to the shores.

The eastern falls into many deep and fine bays, with beaches reaching nearly the whole length of the line; and the water deepens so gradually, that at the distance of 100 miles from land, there is not more than a sounding of seventy fathoms.

The shores, which present a pleasing irregularity of height, consist of a soil of brown mould, something resembling fuller's earth, and impregnated with saltpetre.

In many places on the coast where I have walked inland a few miles, I have found the ground richly clothed with grass, and the interior country presenting a beautiful irregularity of surface. No trees are seen near the sea from the river of Plate to the shores of the Straits of Magellan, where, however, they are abundant. Farther inland, however, it is likely that there are trees, as on the western side of the Andes, in the latitude of 45° the woods are almost impervious. To the north of the river Negro, the country becomes level, with rich pasture, on which great numbers of horses and bullocks run wild.

The animal called the pole-cat was seen by my crew on the coast, and one of them indeed emitted the abominable liquid into his eyes, which they are accustomed to do in the way of defence: and judging by the noise he made, it must have caused him great pain.

The American tiger, called by the Spaniards jaguar, is often seen on the coast. They have been known to wander around a boat turned bottom up on shore, with the crew lying underneath, and to depart without showing any voracious inclination after prey.

The rivers in this country are not inconsiderable, and are conveniently spread along the coast, from latitude 39° 50′; six may be enumerated — the river St. Joseph; Colorado, or Red River; River Negro, or Black River; Port Desire; Port St. Julian; and Sta. Cruz. The four last mentioned afford anchorage, two of them for large vessels, which renders this country highly valuable. Having thus given what information I have by my own observations been able to procure regarding these parts and their inhabitants, as also statements made to me by gentlemen of veracity, I shall dismiss the subject, and return to our passage to the Falkland Islands.

We continued within view of land till the 21st, when in the evening, and about to lose sight of the coast, Coy Bay bore S.S.W. distant about five leagues. During our passage to the Falkland Islands, we had fresh gales between S.S.W. and N.N.W. with an irregular sea, and on the 25th, at six o'clock in the morning, with the wind at west, and the weather hazy, we saw Cape Meredith, bearing N.N.E., about three leagues; and at two P.M., we came to an anchor in Robertson's Bay, in seven fathoms water. Having examined the southern shores for the fur-seal, on the 28th the wind being at N.E. and the weather favourable, we weighed, and proceeded to New Island, which we reached on the 2d of March, and at two P.M. anchored in Ship Harbour, in seven fathoms water. Having observed smoke on the north end of the island as we approached, I thought it might probably be intended by some shipwrecked people as a signal of distress; but it turned out to be only the burning of some tussuck, which had been ignited some months before.

On the 6th having completed our sea-store of water, and taken a quantity of peat on board for fuel, we weighed, and the same day anchored in West Point Harbour. On the 12th we proceeded to Port Egmont, and anchored off the ruins in nine fathoms water.

On the 15th, in the morning, I was surprised to see a line of battle ship and a sloop of war coming round the Point. We presently ascertained by their colours that they were Spanish. I hurried on board, and was politely received. I pointed out the most eligible anchorage; but they chose to run a little beyond it, by which they afterwards drove, and caused themselves a great deal of trouble. The ship of the line was the Asia, of 70 guns. The brig was the Achilles, of 20 guns. They reported themselves from Lima, which I afterwards, from a number of concurring circumstances, discovered to be false. My boat's crew soon ascertained from the sailors, some of whom spoke good English, that they were but ten weeks from Cadiz; but the officers still persisted in this story of being from Lima, and I did not contradict it. Their anxiety to obtain information respecting the navigation of Straits Le Maire, and round Cape Horn, was of itself enough to satisfy me, that they were bound that way.

The crew of this ship, I understood, including their gunners or troops, was about 800 men; and the brig was manned with 150. They appeared in all respects effective, and though they were not so expeditious in their movements, as is the practice in our navy, they were indefatigable and secure in their operations. Their crews were sent on shore to ramble for the benefit of their health; and shooting parties soon killed almost every bird in the neighbourhood.

On the 16th, in a hard gale from the N.W. the Asia drove to a distance of about two miles from the landing place. In the morning of the 17th it moderated, and her boats went on shore, but a very hard gale coming on, they were unable to get off.

Being engaged by the officers to dine on board the Asia, and having two of them on board the Jane with me, I took the opportunity of showing them that our boats could go against a gale, and accordingly manned a fine whale-boat with stout men, and rowed on board with apparent ease.

In looking over their charts, I observed the Auroras laid down, and informed them that no such places existed. Of this they would not be convinced, insisting that the Spanish ship of war Atrevida settled their situation in the year 1796, as I have before mentioned. The Commodore supplied us with some naval stores of which we were much in want, and I sent a quantity of oil in return. He appeared to be about the age of fifty, and seemed to possess a thorough knowledge of the executive duties of a ship, even to the minutest operations, as I observed him correct a sailor in the passing a seizing round the fore-stay. He politely invited me to dine with him, and honoured me by particularly noticing the hazardous voyage we had performed, with other marks of respect, which evinced a disposition to favour and promote enterprise.

I took an opportunity of waiting upon the commander of the brig, who, from having been some time a prisoner in England, spoke very good English. He took me through the mess-deck of the ship, and I was surprised to see how orderly every thing appeared; in short, she was little different, as to the internal arrangement, from our own sloops of war. I presume this officer had noticed the system observed in our navy, and had established it in his own vessel.

On the 19th the wind being southerly, and the weather settled, we weighed, and proceeded again towards the coast of Patagonia. During our passage, we had strong gales from the southward, in which we lost two boats from the quarters. We ran under a close-reefed maintop-sail, and though from not steering well some risk was incurred, we continued to scud before the wind. I had an instance of the danger of scudding too long during my passage home in my first voyage, in the year 1822. Being in the Bay of Biscay, in the month of March, at midnight, with the wind at west blowing a heavy gale; we were running under a close-reefed maintop-sail and foretop-mast staysail, and two men were at the wheel, one of whom was considered an excellent helmsman. I was standing on deck, when the wind freshened, and the night became so dark, that only the foam of the sea was visible. The man at the helm, by some mismanagement, put it the wrong way, and the ship flew to the wind with such rapidity as laid her on her broadside. Two sailors, stationed at the maintop-sail sheets, at my desire let them go, and I hastened to the helm, and lashed it a weather, though, from the ship lying on her side, very little of the rudder remained in the water. The foretop-mast staysail fortunately being new, did not give way, and in about three minutes, every moment of which I expected would complete our ruin, the ship veered, and as the wind drew aft she righted, and we presently hove to.

In our passage to Patagonia, however, nothing more serious happened than losing our boats; and on the 23d we made the coast off Point Lobos, in the latitude of 44°, the rendezvous appointed for our meeting with the Beaufoy; but not finding her, I concluded that the strong southerly winds had driven her to the northward, and that she had, in consequence, proceeded home. We ran close along the coast to the northward; and on the 3d of April, having sprung a leak, and being in the mouth of the river of Plate, we put into Monte Video.

My necessities were politely attended to here by the house of Stewart M'Call and Co., of which James Noble, Esq. is executive partner; and I made application to the British Consul, T. S. Hood, Esq., for a survey to be held on the Jane, to ascertain her defects. Sir Murray Maxwell, commodore on that station, and in command of the Briton frigate, having heard of the arrival of the ships of war at the Falkland Islands, requested to see me. I waited on him, and described them to be Spanish, which did away with a conjecture of their being French in the character of Spaniards, as some *finesse* of that kind was possible; and as several French ships of war were in these seas, their movements were narrowly watched.

Mr. Hood, the British Consul, gave the necessary instructions for the survey, which being made, the requisite repairs were entered upon; and by the favour of Sir Murray Maxwell in sending me the assistance of carpenters from His Majesty's ship Briton, our defects were soon made good, and by the 4th of May, we were ready for sea.

Monte Video, a place generally known, is a

walled city, situated on the north shore of the river of Plate, about seventy miles from its entrance. This city was taken in 1823, from the Portuguese royalists, by the Brazilian imperialists, who now possess it. The present military Governor-general, Le Core, seems to be a person well calculated for improving the circumstances of the country; but the experience of frequent invasions and revolutions within the last twenty years prevents the inhabitants from attending to any thing that cannot be quickly turned into money: hence it is, that houses on magnificent plans are left unfinished; and many, for several miles without the walls, are allowed to remain in a state of ruin, caused by the desolation of war. Many of the streets are so broken up as to be almost impassable. The whole together, at this time, presents the accumulated wreck of a series of years, agitated by almost perpetual civil and foreign contests. The rich, as may be expected, live in ease and authority, without, however, being offensively proud, or cruelly severe, as masters. The labouring class of people are not remarkable for industry, being rather addicted to idleness and inebriety; foreign labourers more particularly. Three days' work in the week, on account of the cheapness of provisions, is sufficient to support them during the other four days in riot and dissipation; and there is scarcely any

European, however industrious he may be at his arrival, who does not fall into this course of idleness.

The guachos, or countrymen, who come occasionally into town, are people of tall stature, with ruddy complexions. They are not considered the most honest class of men; and they have, perhaps, committed more assassinations than any other.

The ladies of Monte Video are generally somewhat below the middle stature, and inclined to be lusty. The custom of wearing small shoes, I presume, has made them clumsy about the feet; but the beauty of their faces amply compensates for that deformity. The contour of their countenances is what may be called Grecian, with complexions sallow enough to take off the character of common-place ruddiness; and their expressive black eyes, together with their simple elegance and complacency of manner, does not fail to render them interesting.

The priesthood of this place appear to be dwindling in authority, and poverty is conspicuous in their churches. That grandeur which the internal structure of their sanctuaries used to present in this quarter of the globe, is now diminished almost to the bare walls.

The English merchants are a respectable body, and lately a British consul has been appointed to attend to their interests. These gentlemen never omit celebrating the anniversary of His Britannic Majesty's birth-day with a public dinner. I was so fortunate at this time as to be of the party at this annual feast. The company sat down at six o'clock, about fifty in number. Sir Murray Maxwell, the British Consul, and several Spanish and Portuguese officers of high rank, civil and military, were present. By eight o'clock the cloth was removed, and the health of His Majesty, King George the Fourth, was drunk. To this the Portuguese band, who were placed in the court-yard, struck up the air of God save the King, and at the same moment the Briton frigate discharged a quantity of rockets, and fired a royal salute. The coincidence of these feats, which had been previously well arranged, was so complete that the effect was admirable. The Portuguese band had been taught the music of Rule Britannia, which they played with great spirit; and the bumpers went round to appropriate toasts. The Spanish gentlemen, in order to manifest their total disregard of worldly goods, began to break the plates and glasses, as if they had been of no value. Every toast was accompanied with a sacrifice of these articles; and one old Spaniard was remarkable for rubbing two dessert plates together at every bumper, and throwing them over his shoulder;

on which Sir Murray Maxwell facetiously remarked, that the word Plate (the name of the river) must be derived from the table utensil of that name, from the evident pleasure that was here taken in its destruction. As the evening advanced, the company fell off to their respective homes, and I to mine.

A Spanish public dinner was also given during my stay, to which I was invited by my friend, Mr. Noble. This feast exhibited a very different figure to that I have described. The dinner was given in celebration of the tranquil establishment of the new government.

We were to dine at the house of John Dios de Solis, at the distance of about seven miles from town; and, as few people here walk far without the walls, a conveyance was provided, such as by us is called a noddy, having but two wheels, and being drawn by two horses a-breast, on one of which rode the driver. In this vehicle six of us were seated, and travelled at the risk of being overturned a hundred times by the badness of the roads. The country in this direction to the N.E. appeared to be in a very broken state, barren, and full of deep sand-holes. This, however, being the only road by which a besieging army could approach the town, this part had suffered much by having been many times occupied by the enemy.

About two o'clock, we arrived at the house of our host, and found the company assembled, among whom we presently took our seats at the table, which was continued through two rooms. The party consisted partly of patriot Spaniards, with some Americans, French, and Portuguese, altogether about sixty in number. The dinner was profusely abundant; but no dish appeared very remarkable, except a large roast of beef with the hide on. This mode of cooking has the effect of retaining the juice of the meat, and from the number who partook of it, it appeared to be a favourite viand. The wine, of which there was variety, went merrily round during the entertainment, and by the time the cloth was removed, the organs of articulation had become so volatile, that you could scarcely hear your next neighbour. Some Spaniards, who were less clamorous, amused themselves with shooting little bread balls at one another across the table, and aiming at the face. This amusement was an annoyance to me, but by my remaining neutral, they allowed me to sit in peace. Their national toasts were drunk in quick succession, but on their vice-president proposing the toast of "Long live King Ferdinand the Seventh," nearly the whole company dissented, and loaded him with a torrent of abuse; to which he replied with so much acrimony, that the table of expected friendship and conviviality soon presented a scene of the most inveterate warfare. The vice-president prudently, however, sat in silence for a few minutes, by which means order was restored, and the offended party vented their rage on the wine, which in half an hour was fast becoming conqueror. Glasses and plates flew to destruction, and, to crown the whole, an agile Spaniard mounted the table, making a variety of antics, which so destroyed the economy of it, that no further hint was necessary to advise us to depart, and we rose, got seated in our noddy, and drove homewards. Thus ended the dinner, which in the whole had occupied not more than two hours and a half.

This company, as far as I could understand, were evidently much divided in politics: all probably were patriots, but so variously modified, as to create a great difference of opinion; — nor can it be otherwise. The diversity of interest, with the frequent change of political sentiment, which a change of government induces, renders them fickle and inconsistent. The present code of laws, however, gives the inhabitants more satisfaction than any hitherto enacted: the murderer cannot now, as formerly, escape death by the payment of money, or by suffering a short imprisonment; and in other cases, the present governor is rigidly careful to protect the pecuniary interests and personal safety of the citizens. These amendments, with the firm establishment of the Brazilian government, promise fair to put an end to the ravages of anarchy.

The exports of this place consist, principally, of horses and bullocks, hides and horns. These animals have much diminished in number within the last fifteen years, or since the time that our troops had possession of the place; and they have consequently risen in price. A mound of the bones of horses was shown me, which at the time they were killed, about fifteen years ago, were brought to the slaughter-house for two shillings a head. A good horse now costs two pounds sterling. Bullocks are, no doubt, still numerous in the interior, but in the neighbourhood of the city they are scarce. At this time, a well fed bullock costs about eighteen dollars, such as a dozen years ago was killed only for its hide and tallow. Vegetables are exorbitantly dear; and every thing else that the country produces is increased in price in a similar proportion.

As the late siege of Monte Video has been, however, partly the cause of this diminution of supplies, two or three years with a settled government will do much in restoring the plenty of former times.

Little need be said of the harbour of Monte Video, as it has been well described by former visitors. I may remark, however, that it affords so little shelter from south to west, and is so shallow, having only two fathoms at a mean state, that there is nothing commodious about it.

A vessel drawing twelve or thirteen feet water is seldom afloat in what may be called the harbour, though the bottom is of mud, in which a vessel sits without receiving damage; but sometimes, if lying across the harbour when the pamperos sets in, it is caught by these hurricanes, which is, if not injurious, at least inconvenient.

These winds, blowing from the south-west over a plain nearly reaching the foot of the Andes, acquire such force, that they fall into the river of Plate and harbour of Monte Video with so great violence, that the best anchors and cables are requisite for the securing of ships.

The several dangerous shoals with which this river is bedded, cause the navigation to Buenos Ayres to be attended with danger. Many commanders of ships, entering with a fair wind, are often induced to proceed without a pilot, and by the time they have arrived in the vicinity of danger, the wind becomes contrary, and the weather unsettled, and not being acquainted with the set of the currents, they ground their ships. The lapse of a short time frequently makes great alteration, in the facilities afforded to this pilot-ground. The buoys are often shifted or washed away, and you are left without the guide of land-marks. Banks have moved, and neither the depth of the river, nor the set of the currents are accurately known; all of which uncertainties contribute to embarrass those even of long experience in this passage. During my stay of a month at Monte Video, two vessels were totally lost in the river; and one, a month or six weeks before, was wrecked, with the loss of several lives, in a manner truly distressing, as they died on a raft, drifting with the direction of the wind and current.

On the mount of Monte Video, the lantern, which is nightly lighted, is so faint as scarcely to be seen at the harbour anchorage: it is therefore of little use; but, if placed on the Island of Flores, and properly attended to, it would be a great guidance to ships passing up in dark nights. English and American pilots are to be had at Monte Video, but they get so little encouragement, that they never put to sea to look out for ships.

The harbour of Maldonado would be convenient for a rendezvous for pilots, being near the fair way, and without all the banks.

Could captains be brought under an obligation to take pilots, a system might be pursued similar to that on our own coasts, and in other parts of the world, by establishing two pilot vessels, (schooners or cutters of about 50 tons each,) to cruise off the mouth of the river, with ten or twelve pilots on board.

I have given these hints for the benefit of insurers and others concerned in the trade to the river Plate, to whom such an arrangement would be most advantageous; leaving it to themselves to devise how it could be made obligatory on captains to take the pilots. Were such a system established, the constant employment and encouragement which would be thereby given to the pilots, would enable them to reduce their charges much below what they are at present.

On the 4th of May, with the wind at W. S.W. we weighed anchor, and after waiting upon Sir Murray Maxwell on board his own ship, we made all possible sail to the eastward. We met with the usual winds and weather on our passage home, and in fifty-nine days from our sailing from Monte Video arrived off Falmouth, before the packet that sailed two days before us. We made the Land's End of England, after an absence of nearly two years.

POSTSCRIPT.

I AM aware that many of the details in this volume militate considerably against the prevailing conjectures upon those regions of the earth to which they refer, and interfere, in some measure, with the statements of former navigators; for this, if any apology be necessary, I would rather make it here than to have interrupted the work in its progress by frequent notes. And it seemed more becoming in one who has hitherto had so little leisure for the profound study of geographical literature, to confine himself almost entirely to a simple account of what came practically under his own observation, waiting to be guided, should occasion require it, hereafter, by the judgment of those, whose province it is to mark the deficiencies of authors, and point out what is really worthy of public attention for its novelty or truth.

Recent events in South America have contributed to throw a certain degree of interest over some of the matters mentioned by the author: the present state of Monte Video; the surrender of the Asia man of war, and its consort, to the Government of Mexico, need hardly be particularised.

APPENDIX.

OBSERVATIONS

ON THE

NAVIGATION ROUND CAPE HORN, &c.

MANY commanders of ships, who have been successful in making a passage round Cape Horn to the westward, have treated with unmerited derision the accounts given by Commodore Anson of this navigation.

I am quite satisfied, from my own experience, that the month of March might be productive of all the distresses described by the journalist. Captain Porter, who passed the Cape in the American frigate Essex, in March, 1814, says, "Indeed our sufferings, short as has been our passage, have been so great, that I would advise those, bound into the pacific, never to attempt the passage of Cape Horn, if they can get there by any other route."

The difficulty, however, in making this passage is removed by choosing the proper season, which, when attended to, must at least save much time, and wear and tear of the ship. In the beginning of November the winds begin to draw from the northward, and continue to be frequent till about the middle of February, when they shift into the south-west quarter; during these months the westerly winds are not lasting, hence the passage may be easily effected. From about the 20th of February to the middle of May, the winds are generally between S.W. and N.W., and blow with great violence. During this interval, no ship need expect to make a passage round the Cape, that is not well equipped in every respect. From the middle of May to the end of June, the winds prevail from the eastward with fine weather. During these six weeks, a vessel may round the Cape in sight of the Diego Ramirez. In July, August, September, and October, the winds prevail again between S.W. and N.W.; but August and September are more particularly tempestuous. In regard to the route, which ships should take round the Cape, much depends on the season of the year, as relates to the force of the prevailing westerly winds. I prefer, at all times, passing to the westward of the Falkland islands; and, in the summer season, to pass through Straits Le Maire, as it saves fifty or sixty miles of westing, and can be attended with no risk if you have sufficient daylight to see to run back through the Straits, in the event of being caught with a southerly gale at the southern entrance.

Cape Horn lies from Cape Good Success S. S.W. ½ W. distant thirty-one leagues. In this line lies Barnavelt's island. If intending to touch at an anchorage about Cape Horn, a S. by W. ¼ W. course through the night, will but well avoid the indraught which sometimes sets to the N.W. among the islands, at the entrance of Nassau Straits: if not intending to go into harbour, a south course from Straits Le Maire to the south of Cape Horn, edging to the westward, and passing the Diego Ramirez on the south side, at the distance of a few miles, is the most advisable track. Ships working to the westward, off the Cape, in the summer season, should stand towards the shore of Tierra del Fuego in the evening, when the wind will often be found to draw from the northward off the land, and western again in the morning.

These observations refer to the seasons I have recommended for passing the Cape, but during those months which are attended with the most violent gales, viz. March, August, and September, I have only to recommend the advice given by Commodore Anson, that of standing to the southward, in the latitude of 60°, where the sea is more regular, and the winds more equal. If, however, a ship be making a coasting passage, and should require to anchor, the following instructions may be found useful. The prominent situation of Cape Horn at once points out the neighbouring bay of Saint Francis, in which are two harbours perfectly safe for vessels of any draught of water. Their approach is so easy as to make it necessary only to remark, that Wigwam Cove is the second opening on the west side of the bay, and by steering along the western shore about N. by E. it will be easily found.

On account of the violent gusts that blow out of the cove in westerly gales, a vessel had better anchor at the entrance, where is twenty-one fathoms water, and a bottom of sand and mud, and wait an opportunity of kedging into the cove, till South Head shuts in Cape Horn, when the anchorage will be perfectly safe.

The second harbour in this bay is pointed out on the chart by the name of Maxwell's harbour. The entrance is on the north side, between Saddle Island and Jerdan's Island; but is so narrow, that with a contrary wind a vessel must anchor at the entrance, and kedge to her berth, which may be chosen at pleasure, every part being perfectly secure. Here the water is so smooth that repairs upon a ship can be carried on with great convenience. Wood is abundant on the south side, and water may be obtained in several places.

In proceeding westward New Year's Sound next presents itself. In this sound are several anchorages, but Indian Cove may be considered the most commodious. Indian Island stands at the mouth of the cove, and bears from Sanderson's Island at the entrance of the sound W.N.W. sixteen miles. The anchorage in this cove is at the upper end, in the south corner, in fourteen or fifteen fathoms water, within three cables' lengths of the shore; in most other parts the ground is rocky, and the water deep. The entrance not being more than three fifths of a mile broad, a large vessel in working against a strong S.W. wind, which blows out of the cove, would require to be worked quickly to take advantage of the flaws of wind that play about the entrance. The shoals and spots of foul ground are indicated by kelp about them, and should consequently be avoided. At the entrance of the cove, on the south side of Mid-channel, are two patches; in the inner one is a depth of three fathoms, and in the outer one eight. The tide flows on the full and change of the moon at fifty minutes past three, and rises about seven feet. Wood and water are abundant, and can be conveniently procured.

Clear Bottom Bay is an anchorage which, by being close to the coast, is convenient for a vessel to touch at for wood and water: to sail into it from sea, bring the east Il Defonsos S. ½ E., and steer N. ½ W. for Turn Point. About a mile and a half to the E.N.E. of this point is the anchorage, and at the distance of three cables' lengths from the shore, in twenty-two fathoms water, in a bottom of sand and clay, is the most eligible berth.

A peculiar shaped land, which I called Leading Mountain, on the west side of Duff's Bay, may be seen from a distance of six or seven leagues at sea, and at once points out the entrance of the bay. A view of this mountain with the land adjacent is annexed.

The soundings round the Diego Ramirez are regular, and at the distance of half a mile from the southern island. On the east side is a depth of thirty fathoms, with a bottom of fine green sand. The tides here are regular when the winds are moderate, and by the report of my officers, who were several days on the island, it is high water on the full and change of the moon at two hours fifteen minutes, and rises about five feet. The tide of flood, contrary to former reports, was observed to run to the N.E., and it evidently runs to the eastward between many of the main islands. The currents, or those streams which are propelled by prevailing winds, interfere so much with the natural tendency of the tide, that great doubt is created in regard to the proper direction of it.

Staten Land affords several harbours; that of St. John's, on the north side, and near to the east end, is the one with which I am best acquainted. By the view of the land which I have subjoined, the entrance of the harbour may easily be found. Slack tide is the proper time to sail in, as at the entrance, which is narrow, the winds are so baffling as to cause some risk when the tide is running strong across the passage. The harbour runs up to the W. S.W. about a mile and a quarter, and the anchorage is at the upper end, in twelve fathoms, in a muddy bottom; in most other parts, the depth is twenty fathoms, and rocky. There is a flat extending from the head of the harbour, a full cable's length, in which a small vessel might be laid for repairs.

Wood and water are in great plenty, close to the shore. The wood is much of the same description as that found on Tierra del Fuego: none of it being large enough for ship-building. At the east end of the island is a very heavy tide-rip, and when the wind is strong it should be carefully avoided.

In sailing along the coast of Patagonia to the southward of the river Santa Cruz, vessels should not run within a depth of ten fathoms water, as in many places extensive ledges of rocks lie more than a mile from the shore.

The river of Santa Cruz does not appear from a great distance at sea, but can of course be easily found by the latitude. The meeting of the tides has thrown up a bank about the entrance, on which at low water there is but two fathoms and a quarter.

On the south point of the entrance lies a reef of rocks which appear at low water; and at the north side of the fair way is a shoal, proceeding from the bar, which probably shifts.

The leading mark into the river is a bluff in the middle of the entrance, bearing N.W. by W. ½ W. by compass. After passing the points of the entrance, two indentations will be seen on the south shore, and in the second one is the best anchorage, in five fathoms, in a bottom of gravel and clay. All the north side of the river is shoals, and much of it dries at low water. The tide of flood runs to the northward on the coast, and in strong southerly winds continues to run two hours after it is high water by the shore.

OBSERVATIONS ON THE WINDS AND WEATHER.

The heaviest and most lasting gale that blows in the neighbourhood of Cape Horn is from south, occasionally shifting a point or two each way. This gale I have frequently known to come on in a squall, and continue in the tempestuous months to blow from thirty-five to forty hours together. The southern horizon, filled with rising clouds, heavy and white in a blue sky, is a sure indication of a lasting gale, with snow squalls. A complete calm generally follows this wind, which, however, is not very frequent. The wind at east invariably rises light, and gradually increases to a strong breeze; but when it vears from E. to S.E., a strong gale may generally be expected, with snow or rain squalls.

A north gale also comes on gradually, and towards the end, which is generally about thirty hours, it draws from the N.W. and brings rain, and presently shifts into the S.W. without ceasing to blow, and continues from that point twelve or fifteen hours. All gales are of shorter duration in summer than in winter; and it may be remarked, that a vessel may anchor any where for shelter from a S.W. wind, without the fear of its shifting to the northward; but the contrary must be guarded against, as the wind shifts from N.W. to S.W., continuing to blow with great violence.

In the most windy months N.W. gales blow with great force, when they rise rapidly near that point, and generally last twelve or fourteen hours. To the S.W. of Cape Horn, they blow with less violence, but are more durable. In the summer season, the winds between S.W. and N.W. frequently blow in gusts of six or eight hours' continuance, at the strength of a brisk gale; it then becomes moderate, and the wind inclines to the northward.

In the summer I have observed the coincidence of fine weather with light easterly winds at the time of new moon, when in south declination, and at the time of full moon, to blow strong from the northward. There being many exceptions, however, to the natural action of the wind, produced by localities, I have found it impossible to systematise the indications of the winds and weather satisfactorily. We must, therefore, rest contented with an approximation to certainty in these matters.

OBSERVATIONS for rating CHRONOMETERS at Port St. Elena, 22d *Dec.* 1822.

Time	1h	13′	45″
	0	15	22
	0	16	23
	0	17	24
	0	18	23
	0	19	18
	0	20	24
	0	120	59
	1	17	17
App. time	9	1	45.8
Equa. —	0	1	11.7
	9	0	34.1
	13	17	17.0
N° 403. slow of mean time at Port St. Elena on the 22d	4	16	42.9
Time by 403	1	17	17
403 slow of 820	0	10	42
Time by 820	13	27	59
App. time -	9	0	34.1
N° 820. fast of mean time at Port St. Elena on the 22d	4	27	24.9

Sun's alt.	94°	39′	0″	
	95	13	30	
	5	34	0	
	5	54	0	
	96	15	0	
	6	34	0	
	6	55	30	
	41	5	0	
	95	52	9	
	47	56	4	
	0	16	17	
	48	12	21	
Index error ½	0	1	37	
	48	10	44	
Ref.-Par.	0	0	45	
Altitude	48	9	59	Logs.
Latitude	44	34	16	
P. D.	66	32	7	

Meridian altitude	68°	48′	30″	
Sum of cor.	+0	4	57	
	68	53	27	
	90	0	0	
	21	6	33	
	23	27	43	
Lat. at Port St. Elen.	44	34	16	
Dec. 23d, App. time	8	3	10	
Equation —	0	0	42.5	
Mean time -	8	2	27.5	
Time at Greenwich	12	25	44.0	
Longitude in time	4	23	16.5	= 65 49 15 Long. of Port St. Elena.

OBSERVATIONS for rating CHRONOMETERS — *continued.*

Time	12h	13′	39″
	0	14	26
	0	14	53
	0	15	55
	0	16	29
	0	16	58
	0	17	25
	0	39	45
	12	15	40.7
403slowof820	+0	11	8.0
	12	26	48.7
	7	59	1.2
On the 26th	4	27	47.5
On the 22d	4	27	24.9
	Days 4)		22.6
N° 820. gaining per day			5.6

Sun's alt.	72°	44′	30″	
	73	1	15	
	3	11	0	
	3	33	0	
	3	45	30	
	3	54	30	
	74	5	0	
	24	14	45	
	73	27	49	
	36	43	54	
Index error ½	0	1	37	
	36	42	17	
S. D.	0	16	17	
	36	58	34	
Ref.-Par.	0	1	8	
Sun's alt.	36	57	26	Logs.
Lat.	44	34	16	Logs.
P. D.	66	36	11	Logs.

App. time - - -	7h	58′	14.2″
Equation - - -	0	0	47.0
Mean time - -	7	59	1.2
	12	15	40.7
Fast on the 26th - -	4	16	39.5
Do. 22d - -	4	16	42.9
Lost in four days - - -			3.4
			10.0
Days 4)			34.0
Losing per day - - -			0.8
But having from the 22d to the 23d lost in 24h			2.2
And the former rate being two seconds per day, I shall estimate the present rate *thus :*			3.0
The mean may be assumed, losing per day			1.5

OBSERVATIONS for rating CHRONOMETERS — *continued.*

By the mean of several sets of lunar observations, I make the longitude deduced from chronometers 15 miles too far westward. The Grand Spanish Survey, published by Faden, places Port St. Elena in 65° 33′ 30″.—I shall therefore take a mean: thus,

My chronometer longitude -	65°	49′	15″	
By lunars.—Diff. - -	0	15	0	
	65	34	15	
Spanish Survey - -	65	30	30	
	0	4	45	
Longitude of Port St. Elena -	65	32	22	
Longitude of Port St. Elena in time - -	4h	22′	9″	
Mean time at Port St. Elena - -	7	59	1	
	12	21	10	Time at Greenwich.
Time by chronometer 403. on the 26th — A. M. -	12	15	36	
	0	5	34	N° 403. slow of Greenwich.
Time by chronometer 403. on the 26th - -	12	15	36	
N° 403. slow of N° 820. - - - -	0	11	13	
Time by N° 820. - - - -	12	26	49	
Time at Greenwich - - - -	12	21	15	
	0	5	34	N° 820. fast of Greenwich.

On the 26th at 9 hours A. M., Chronometer N° 3540. was slow of Greenwich 2′ 55″, and losing 13″ per day.

OBSERVATIONS for finding the Longitude by Chronometers with the Ship's Place at Noon.

Date.	Time by No. 403.	Mean Time.	Altitude of the Sun's Centre.	Latitude at Observation.	No. 403. Slow.	No. 820. Fast.	3540. Slow.	Latitude by Observation at Noon.	Latitude by Account.	Longitude by Mean of Chronometers at Noon.	Longitude by Account.
Jan. 1.	1h 25′ 7″	9h 5′ 0″	46° 1′	50° 15′	5′ 43·0″	6′ 7.0″	4′ 13″	50° 30′ 53″	50° 39′	66° 10′ 30″	66° 0′ 0″
2.	2 2 36	9 47 15	—	—	5 44.5	6 12.5	4 26	51 55 0	51 59	65 7 15	65 16 0
										Brought forward.	
3.	—	—	—	—	5 46.0	6 18.0	4 39	—	53 15	63 48 0	63 57 0
4.	12 50 1	8 53 44	42 53	53 19	5 47.5	6 23.5	4 52	53 24 0	53 28	60 24 0	62 0 0
5.	12 42 1	8 54 43	42 42	53 46	5 49.0	6 29.0	5 5	43 49 0	53 48	58 1 50	60 7 0

Time by 403.	12h	42′	1″	
403. slow	0	5	49	
Time at Greenwich	12	47	50	
Mean time	8	54	43	
	3	53	7	Difference of Meridians.

Time by 403.	12h	42′	1″	
No. 403. slow 3540.	0	0	36	
	12	42	37	
3540. slow	0	5	5	
Time at Greenwich	12	47	42	
Mean time	8	54	43	
	3	52	59	Difference of Meridians.

Time by 403.	12h	42′	1″	
No. 403. slow of 820.	0	12	15	
Time by 820.	12	54	16	
Fast	0	6	29	
Time at Greenwich	12	47	47	
Mean time	8	54	43	
	3	53	4	Difference of Meridians.

Longitude by 403.	58h	16′	45″	
Do. 820.	58	16	0	
Do. 3540.	58	14	45	
	0	17	30	
	58	15	50	Mean.
	0	14	0	
Easting	58	1	50	Longitude at noon.

OBSERVATIONS for finding the Longitude by Chronometers with the Ship's Place at Noon.

Date.	Time by No. 403.	Mean Time.	Altitude of the Sun's Centre.	Latitude at Observation.	No. 403. Slow.	No. 820. Fast.	3540. Slow.	Latitude by Observation at Noon.	Latitude by Account.	Longitude by Mean of Chronometers at Noon.	Longitude by Account.
										Bro't. forward.	
Jan. 6.	—	—	—	—	5′ 50.5″	6′ 34.5″	5′ 18″	53° 54′ 0″	53° 54′	56° 24′ 0″	58° 30′
7.	12h 48′ 5″	9h 14′ 59″	44° 42′	54° 39′	5 52.0	6 40.0	5 31	54 59 0	55 28	54 28 0	55 8
										Bro't. forward.	
8.	—	—	—	—	5 53.5	6 45.5	5 44	—	56 9	53 0 0	54 9
9.	12 20 48	9 3 58	41 47	57 18	5 55.0	6 51.0	5 57	57 30 0	57 34	50 41 15	52 24
10.	11 53 56	8 42 44	38 46	58 0	5 56.5	6 56.5	6 10	58 15 0	58 32	48 8 0	51 48
										Bro't. forward.	
11.	—	—	—	—	5 58.0	7 2.0	6 23	—	59 37	46 1 0	49 41
12.	7 46 58	4 57 12	27 34	60 15	5 59.5	7 7.5	6 36	60 25 0	—	44 4 25	48 28

Time by 403.	7h 46′ 58″
403. slow	0 5 59
Time at Greenwich	7 52 57
Mean time	4 57 12
Difference of Meridians by 403.	2 55 45

Time by 403.	7h 46′ 58″
403. slow of 820.	0 13 20
	8 0 18
820. fast	0 7 7
Time at Greenwich	7 33 11
Mean time	4 37 12
Difference of Meridians by 820.	2 55 59

Time by 403.	7h 46′ 58″
3540. fast of 403.	0 0 23
	7 46 35
3540. slow -	0 6 36
Time at Greenwich	7 53 11
Mean time -	4 57 12
Difference of Meridians by 3540.	2 55 59

Longitude by 403.	-	43h 56′ 15″
Do. 820.	-	43 59 45
Do. 3540.	-	43 59 45
		0 25 25
		43 58 28 Mean longitude.

OBSERVATIONS for finding the Longitude by Chronometers with the Ship's Place at Noon.

Date.	Time by No. 403.	Mean Time.	Altitude of the Sun's Centre.	Latitude at Observation.	No. 403. Slow.	No. 820. Fast.	3540 Slow.	Latitude by Observation at Noon.	Latitude by Account.	Longitude by Mean of Chronometers at Noon.	Longitude by Account.
Jan. 14.	1h 1′ 58″	10h 8′ 45″	45° 33′ 30″	60° 3′ 1″	6′ 2.5″	7′ 18.5″	7′ 2″	60h 43′ 1″	—	—	—

Time	1h	1′	35″
	0	1	59
	0	2	31
	0	5	55
	1	1	58
Slow	0	6	2
	1	8	0

Sun's altitude	45h	8′	0″
	0	11	30
	0	14	0
	0	33	30
	45	11	10
	0	12	20
Cor. altitude	45	23	30
Latitude	60	43	1
P. D.	68	36	56

App. time	9h	59′	28″
Equation	0	9	17
	10	8	45
Time at Greenwich	13	8	0
Difference of Meridians	2	59	15
Longitude	44°	48′	45″

Obs. Meridian Altitude	50°	19′	30″
Sum of corr.	+0	12	29
	50	31	59
	90	0	0
	39	28	1
	21	11	49
	60	39	50
Bearing - -	0	2	0
Latitude of Saddle Island	60	37	50

Saddle Island bearing north-west by west three miles, makes the longitude of that island 44° 52′ 45″.

OBSERVATIONS for finding the Longitude by Chronometers, and the Variation of the Compass, with the Ship's Place at Noon.

Date.	Time by No. 403.	Mean Time.	Altitude of the Sun's Centre.	Latitude at Observation.	No. 403. Slow.	No. 820. Fast.	3540. Slow.	Latitude by Observation at Noon.	Latitude by Account.	Longitude by Mean of Chronometers at Noon.	Longitude by Account.
Jan. 19.	12h 30′ 34″	9h 35′ 21″	41h 37′ 40″	60h 21′	6′ ·9.5″	7′ 46″	8′ 7″	60° 17″	—	45° 24′ 40″	—

Time	12h	29′	45″	
	0	30	34	
	0	31	24	
	0	31	43	
	12	30	34	
	0	6	9	
	12	36	43	
Long. by 403. -	45	20	30	
Do. 820. -	45	25	15	
Do. 3540. -	45	28	15	
	0	14	0	
	45	24	40	

Sun's altitude	41°	21′	0″	
	0	26	0	
	0	29	30	
	41	25	30	
	0	12	10	
Sun's corr. altitude	41	37	40	
Latitude -	60	21	0	
P. D. -	60	34	0	
App. time -	9	24	22	
Equa. -	0	10	59	
Mean time -	9	35	21	
Time at Greenwich	12	36	43	
	3	1	22	by 403. d. of merids.

Time by 403. -	12h	30′	34″	
403. slow of 820.	0	14	14	
	12	44	48	
	0	7	46	
Time at Greenwich	12	37	2	
Mean time -	9	35	21	
	3	1	41	by 820. d. of merids.
3540. -	12	30	34	
403. fast of 3540.	0	1	27	
	12	29	7	
3540. slow -	0	8	7	
Time at Greenwich	12	37	14	
Mean time -	9	35	21	
	3	1	53	difference of merids. by 3540.

OBSERVATIONS for finding the Longitude by Chronometers, &c.—*continued.*

Date.	Time by No. 403.	Mean Time.	Altitude of the Sun's Centre.	Latitude at Observation.	No. 403. Slow.	No. 820. Fast.	3540. Slow.	Latitude by Observation at Noon.	Latitude by Account.	Longitude by Mean of Chronometers at Noon.	Longitude by Account.
Jan. 21.	7h 9′ 20″	4h 10′ 32″	31h 58′	60h 43′	6′ 12.5″	7′ 57″	8′ 33″	60° 39′ 50″	46° 19′	46° 24′ 10″	—

Time - -	7h	9′	0″
	0	9	21
	0	9	39
	0	0	60
	7	9	20
403. slow -	0	6	12
Time at Greenwich	7	15	32
Mean time -	4	10	32
	3	5	0
Longitude -	46	15	0
Bearing -	0	5	0
	46	20	0
Westing, &c.	0	4	10
Mean long. by chronometers	46	24	10

Sun's altitude -	31°	48′	0″
	0	46	0
	0	44	0
	8	18	0
	31	46	0
	0	12	5
Sun's corrected altitude	31	58	0
Latitude -	60	43	0
P. D. -	70	3	0

App. time -	3h	58′	53″
Equa. - -	+ 0	11	39
Mean time -	4	10	32

with the bearing makes the longitude of the West Cape - 46° 23′ 52″

OBSERVATIONS for finding the Longitude by Chronometers, &c. — *continued.*

Date.	Time by No. 403.	Mean Time.	Altitude of the Sun's Centre.	Latitude at Observation.	No. 403. Slow.	No. 820. Fast.	3540. Slow.	Latitude by Observation at Noon.	Latitude by Account.	Longitude by Mean of Chronometers at Noon.	Longitude by Account.
Jan. 22.	12h 58′ 56″	10h 6′ 31″	43h 32′ 11″	60h 40′	6h 14′	8′ 2.5′′	8h 56′	—	—	44° 39′ 10″	—

Sun's altitude -	43° 32′ 10″				
Latitude -	60 40 0	Sec. -	0 30990		
P. D. - -	70 13 0	Co-sec. -	0 02642		
	174 25 10				
	87 12 35	Co-sine -	9 68737	Time by 403	12° 58′ 56″
	43 32 10			Slow	0 6 14
	43 40 25	Sine -	9 83982		13 5 10
				Mean time at ship	10 6 31
			18 86289		
Apparent time	9h 54′ 40″			Long. in time	2 58 39
Equa. +	0 11 51		9 43144		
				Long.	44 39 45
	10 6 31 mean time at ship.			Bearing	0 4 0

Cape Dundas south-east by so. 6 miles 44 35 45 long. of Cape Dundas.

OBSERVATIONS for finding the Longitude by Chronometers, &c. — *continued.*

Date.	Time by No. 403.	Mean Time.	Altitude of the Sun's Centre.	Latitude at Observation.	No. 403. Slow.	No. 820. Fast.	3540. Slow.	Latitude by Observation at Noon.	Latitude by Account.	Longitude by Mean of Chronometers at Noon.	Longitude by Account.
Jan. 23.	—	—	—	—	6′ 15.5″	8′ 8″	9ʰ 9′	—	61° 59′	43° 0′ 0″	43° 0′
24.	—	—	—	—	6 17.0	8 13	9 22	—	62 35	42 2 0	42 2
25.	—	—	—	—	6 18.5	8 19	9 35	—	63 2	40 51 0	40 51
									By double Altitudes.		
26.	6ʰ 51′ 4″	4ʰ 17′ 25″	29ʰ 3′ 0″	64° 52′	6 20.0	8 24	9 48	64° 33′ 0″	64 24	40 13 30	40 19
27.	11 31 10	8 59 1	33 45 0	64 51	6 21.5	8 29.5	10 1	64 58 0	65 22	39 40 30	40 18

Time by 403.	11°	31′	10″
Slow	0	6	21
	11	37	31
	8	59	0
	2	58	30 = 39° 37′ 30″
			+ 3 -
			39 40 30 long. at noon.

About 10 A. M. with the ship's head S. by W. the mean of 10 sights gave azimuth 24° 33′ sun's altitude, 40° 9′ corrected.

P. D. - -	71° 25′	Sec. -	0° 37243′
Latitude -	64 54	Sec. -	0 11670
Sun's altitude -	40 9		
	176 28	Co-sine -	8 48896
	88 14		
	71 25	Co-sine -	9 98102
			18 95911
	16 49	72° 26′ ½ Co-sine	9 47955
	24 33	× 2	
	180 0		
From south -	155 27	144 52	
From do. -	144 52		
Variation easterly	10 35		

OBSERVATIONS for finding the Longitude by Chronometers, &c.—*continued.*

Date.	Time by No. 403.	Mean Time.	Altitude of the Sun's Centre.	Latitude at Observation.	No. 403. Slow.	No. 820. Fast.	3540. Slow.	Latitude by Observation at Noon.	Latitude by Account.	Longitude by Mean of Chronometers at Noon.	Longitude by Account.
										Brot. forward.	
Jan. 28.	—	—	—	—	6′ 23.0″	8′ 35.0″	10° 14″	63° 25″	63° 35′	39° 54′ 30″	40° 32′ 0″
29.	5^h 1′ 31″	2^h 25′ 20″	41° 1′	61° 5′	6 24.5	8 40.5	10 27	61 18	61 20	40 32 15	42 9 0
										Brot. forward.	
30.	—	—	—	—	6 26.0	8 46.0	10 40	60 31	60 23	42 48 0	44 25 0
31.	5 43 15	3 4 34	37 52	59 33	6 27.5	8 51.5	10 53	59 50	59 51	40 52 0	43 59 0
										Brot. forward.	
Feb. 1.	—	—	—	—	6 29.0	8 57.0	11 6	58 50	58 46	38 51 0	41 58 0
2.	9 24 4	6 58 50	9 4	60 34	6 33.5	9 2.5	11 19	60 16	60 14	38 22 25	40 54 0

Time by 403.	9^h 24′ 4″
403. slow	0 6 33
Time at Greenwich	9 30 37
Mean time	6 58 50
Difference of merids. by 403.	2 31 47

Time by 403.	1^h 6′ 19″
820.	1 22 20
No. 403. slow of 820.	0 16 1
	9 24 4
	9 40 5
Fast	0 9 2
	9 31 3
	6 58 50
Diff. of Mer. by 820.	2 32 13
Time by 403.	1 9 25
3540.	1 4 45
No. 3540. slow of 403.	0 4 40
	9 24 4
	9 19 24
Slow	0 11 19
	9 30 43
	6 58 50
Diff. of Meridians by 3540.	2 31 53

Longitude by 403.	-	37° 56′ 45″
Do. 820.	-	38 3 15
Do. 3540.	-	37 58 15
	3)	113 53 15
		37 59 25
	Easting	0 23 00
		38 22 25 Longitude at noon.

OBSERVATIONS for finding the Longitude by Chronometers, &c.—*continued.*

Date.	Time by No. 403.	Mean Time.	Altitude of the Sun's Centre.	Latitude at Observation.	No. 403. Slow.	No. 820. Fast.	3540. Slow.	Latitude by Observation at Noon.	Latitude by Account.	Longitude by Mean of Chronometers at Noon.	Longitude by Account.
Feb. 3.	—	—	—	—	6′ 35.0″	9′ 8.0″	11° 32′	60° 59′	—	36° 58′ 0″	38° 31′ 0″
4.	9h 21′ 21″	7h 11′ 50″	21° 15″	60° 56′	6 33.5	9 13.5	11 45	60 44	61° 5′	33 27 0	35 58 0
5.	10 36 34	8 37 32	30 53	61 17	6 35.0	9 19.0	11 58	61 44	61 43	31 16 15	34 35 0
6.	10 55 1	8 58 32	32 18	62 19	6 36.5	9 24.5	12 11	—	62 52	30 42 15	34 24 0
7.	10 56 46	9 1 4	31 22	63 59	6 38.0	9 30.0	12 24	64 ·15	64 20	30 46 0	34 50 0
8.	12 34 48	10 37 47	37 18	65 16	6 39.5	9 35.5	12 37	65 24	65 33	30 58 30	35 3 0
9.	—	—	—	—	6 41.0	9 41.0	12 50	—	66 10	31 25 30	35 25 0
10.	—	—	—	—	6 46.5	9 46.5	13 3	—	66 24	32 32 30	36 37 0
11.	10 54 44	8 45 35	28 0	65 27	6 44.0	9 52.0	13 16	65 34	65 45	34 7 15	37 24 0

P. M. the Ship's head S. E. by S. and the compass at the binnacle, the mean of 7 azimuths gave N. 83 W. and sun's apparent altitude at the same time was 23° 43′.

Time by 403.	10° 55′ 44″	
Slow	0 6 44	
	11 1 88	
	8 45 35	
	3 16 53	=34° 13′ 15″
	Easting	0 9 0
		34 4 15 Longitude at noon.

P.D.	75° 54′		
Lat.	65 44	Sec.	38618
Alt.	23 43	Sec.	3832
	165 21		
	82 40	Co-sine	9 10599
	75 54		
	6 46	Co-sine	9 99696
			19 52745
			9 76372

Half co-sine	54 31
	2
From south	109° 2′
	97 0
	12 2 Variation Easterly.

OBSERVATIONS for finding the Longitude by Chronometers, &c.—*continued.*

Date.	Time by No. 403.	Mean Time.	Altitude of the Sun's Centre.	Latitude at Observation.	No. 403. Slow.	No. 820. Fast.	3540. Slow.	Latitude by Observation at Noon.	Latitude by Account.	Longitude by Mean of Chronometers at Noon.	Longitude by Account.
Feb. 12.	—	—	—	—	6′. 45.5″	9′ 57.5″	13′ 42″	—	66° 45′	32° 32′ 00″	35° 49′
13.	—	—	—	—	6 47.0	10 3.0	13 55	67° 5′	67 33	31 17 00	34 34
14.	10h 57′ 17″	9h 11′ 28″	27° 43′	68° 8′	6 48.5	10 8.5	14 8	—	68 22	28 19 15	33 00

P.M. the Ship's head S. by W. and the compass at the binnacle, the mean of 9 azimuths gave N. 78° 23′ W. and sun's apparent altitude at the same time was 21° 38′.

Time by 403	10h 57′ 17″	
Slow	× 6 48	
	11 4 5	
	9 11 28	
	1 52 37 = 28° 9′ 15″	
	Westing, &c. + 10 0	
	28 19 15	Longitude at noon.

P.D.	76° 53′		
Lat.	68 22	Sec.	43337
Alt.	21 38	Sec.	3172
	166 53		
	83 26	Co-sine	9 05827
	76 53		
	6 33	Co-sine	9 99716
			19 52052
			9 76026

Half co-sine	54° 51′	
	× 2	
From south	109 42	
Mag. from south	101 37	
	8 5	Variatio Easterly.

OBSERVATIONS for finding the Longitude by Chronometers, &c.—*continued.*

Date.	Time by No. 403.	Mean Time.	Altitude of the Sun's Centre.	Latitude at Observation.	No. 403. Slow.	No. 820. Fast.	3540. Slow.	Latitude by Observation at Noon.	Latitude by Account.	Longitude by Mean of Chronometers at Noon.	Longitude by Account.
Feb. 15.	10^h 56′ 36″	9^h 5′ 32″	26° 41′	68° 36′	6′ 50″	10′ 14″ 0‴	14′ 21.5″	68′ 44″	69° 0′	29° 37′ 0″	33° 55′ 0″

A. M. The Ship's head S. by W. and the compass at the binnacle, the mean of 15 magnetic azimuths gave N. 30°, 18 E., and the sun's apparent altitude at the same time was 31° 31′.

10°	56′	36″				
0	6	50				
11	3	26				
9	5	32				
1	57	54	= 29°	28′	30″	
			0	6	0	Westing.
			29	34	30	Longitude at noon by 403.

P.M. The Ship's head S. by W. and the compass at the binnacle, the mean of 11 magnetic azimuths gave N.88° 18′ W., and the sun's altitude at the same time was 16° 16′.

P.D.	77°	14′			
Latitude	68	52	Sec.	0°	44305′
Altitude	16	16	Sec.	0	1774
	162	22			
	81	11	Co-sine	9	18547
	77	14			
	3	57	Co-sine	9	99897
				19	64523
			Co-sine	9	82261

OBSERVATIONS for finding the Longitude by Chronometers, &c.—*continued.*

P.D.	77°	10′			
Latitude	68	38	Sec.	0°	43850′
Altitude	31	31	Sec.	0	6931
	177	19			
	88	39	Co-sine	8	37217
	77	10			
	11	29	Co-sine	9	99122
				18	87120
	74	11	Half co-sine	9	43560
	×	2			
	148	22	from south.		
	149	42	from south.		
	1	20	variation easterly in the morning.		

	48	20	½ Co-sine.
	×	2	
time	96	40	from south.
	91	42	from south.
	4	58	variation easterly in the evening.

OBSERVATIONS for finding the Longitude by Chronometers, &c.—*continued.*

Date.	Time by No. 403.	Mean Time.	Altitude of the Sun's Centre.	Latitude at Observation.	No. 403. Slow.	No. 820. Fast.	3540. Slow.	Latitude by Observation at Noon.	Latitude by Account.	Longitude by Mean of Chronometers at Noon.	Longitude by Account.
										Brot. forw.	
Feb. 16.	—	—	—	—	6′ 51.5″	10′ 19.5″	14′ 34″	—	70° 26′	29° 58′ 0″	34° 16′ 0″
17.	—	—	—	—	6 53.0	10 25.0	14 47	—	71 34	30 12 0	34 30 0
18.	10h 24′ 48″	8h 13′ 28″	20° 1′	72° 28′	6 54.5	10 30.5	15 00	72 38	74 24	34 54 30	37 45 0

A.M. With the Ship's head S.W. by S., and the compass at the binnacle, the mean of 18 magnetic azimuths gave 47° 13′; and the sun's apparent altitude at the same time was 21° 3′.

10° 24′ 48″						
0 6 54						
10 31 42						
8 13 28						
2 18 14	=	34° 33′ 30″	
		0 18 00	Westing
		34 51 30	Longitude at noon.

P.M. With the Ship's head S. by E. and the compass at the binnacle, the mean of 15 magnetic azimuths gave N. 82° 52′ W.; and the sun's apparent altitude at the same time was 20° 16′

P.D.	78° 17′		
Latitude	72 40	Sec. -	0° 52589′
Altitude	20 16	Sec. -	0 2776
	171 13		
	85 36	Co-sine	8 88490
	78 17		
	7 19	Co-sine	9 99645
			19 45300
			9 71750

N. 48°	E. Sun's obs. alt.	
51	20° 26′	
49		
3) 148° 0′		
49 20		
47 30		
48 0	20° 31′	
48 0		
3) 23 30		
74 50		
47 0		
46 30	20 37	
48 0		
3) 21 30		
47 10		
47 30		
47 30	20 42	
48 0		
3) 23 0		
47 40		
45 0		
45 30	20 54	
46 0		
3) 17 30		
45 50		
45 30		
45 0	21 7	
46 0	4 17	
16 30	20 51	
45 30	0 12	
	21 3	Sun's app. alt.

P.D.	78°	12′			
Latitude	72	30	Sec. -	0°	52186′
Altitude	21	3	Sec. -	0	2999
	171	45			
	85	52	Co-sine	8	85780
	78	12			
	7	40	Co-sine	9	99610
				19	40575
				9	70287

	47°	13′
	180	0
Magnetic azimuth	132	47

59°	42′ ½	Co-sine.
× 0	2	
119	24	from South.
132	47	from South.
13	23	variation easterly.

Means	49°	20′	
	47	50	
	47	10	
	47	40	
	45	50	
	45	30	
	43	20	
	47	13	mag. azimuth.

N. 84° 0′	W. Sun's obs. alt.		
83 30	20° 9′		
83 30			
11 0			
83 40			
82 0			
82 0	20 7		
84 0			
8 30			
82 50			
83 30			
83 0	20 6		
84 0			
10 30			
83 30			
82 0			
82 0	20 4		
82 0			
82 0			
82 0			
82 0	-	20 2	
83 0		5) 0 28	
82 20		20 6	
		0 10	
		20 16	Sun's apparent altitude.

58°	33′ ½	Co-sine.
× 0	2	
117	6	from South.
97	8	from South.
19	58	variation easterly.

82°	20′	
82	0	
83	30	
82	50	
83	40	
5) 14	20	
N. 82	52	W. Mag. azim.

N. B. I had all the compasses upon deck, and found them to agree, but slow in their movements.

OBSERVATIONS for finding the Longitude by Chronometers, &c.—*continued.*

Date.	Time by No. 403.	Mean Time.	Altitude of the Sun's Centre.	Latitude at Observation.	No. 403. Slow.	No. 820. Fast.	3540. Slow.	Latitude by Observation at Noon.	Latitude by Account.	Longitude by Mean of Chronometers at Noon.	Longitude by Account.
Feb. 19.	11h 57′ 11″	9h 33′ 32″	23° 56′	73° 15′	6′ 56″	10′ 36″ 0‴	15′ 13.5″	73° 17′ 0″	73° 26′	35° 54′ 35″	38° 15′

A.M. With the Ship's head S. by E., and the compass at the binnacle; the mean of seven sights gave magnetic amplitude E. 28°, 30° S.

Latitude	-	73 7	Sec.	-	0° 53697′
Sun's declination	-	11 34	Sine	-	9 30213
				Sine	9 83910

True from East	-	43° 40′
Magnetic from East		28 30
		15 10 variation easterly.

P. M. With the Ship's head S. E. by E., and the compass in midships; the magnetic amplitudes were observed when the ship's latitude was 73° 34′.

Amplitude -	S. 40	°0′	W.
	40	0	
	39	0	
	40	0	
	40	0	
	39	0	
	40	0	
	41	30	
	40	0	
	39	0	
	398	30	
	39	51	
	90	0	
From West -	50	9	
True from West -	43	41	
Variation - -	6	28	
Do. - -	3	49	
Do. - -	5	58	
Sum	16	15	
Mean variation easterly	5	25	

Amplitude S.	40°	0′	W.
	40	0	
	40	0	
	39	0	
	40	0	
	40	0	
	40	0	
	40	0	
	39	0	
	39	0	
	39	0	
	40	0	
	41	0	
	40	0	
	40	30	
	41	0	
	40	30	
	40	0	
	39	0	
	40	0	
	41	0	
	40	40	
	40	0	
Mean	40	21	

Lat. 73 34 sec.	10.54836	90°	0′	
Dec. 11. 16 sine.	9.29087	40	21	
43 41 sine.	9.83923	49	39	from W.
		43	41	from W.
	Variation	5	58	

Compass shook and extremes taken thus -	50°	0′
	35	0
2)	85	0
	42	30
	90	0
	47	30
	43	41
Variation	3	49

OBSERVATIONS for finding the Longitude by Chronometers, &c.—*continued.*

Date.	Time by No. 403.	Mean Time.	Altitude of the Sun's Centre.	Latitude at Observation.	No. 403. Slow.	No. 820. Fast.	3540. Slow.	Latitude by Observation at Noon.	Latitude by Account.	Longitude by Mean of Chronometers at Noon.	Longitude by Account.
Feb. 20.	—	—	—	—	6′ 57.5″	10′ 41.5″	15′ 26″	74° 6′ 26″	74° 8′	34° 16′ 45″	36° 36′ 0″

A. M. With the Ship's head E. S. E. and the compass at the binnacle, the mean of 12 magnetic azimuths gave N. 20° 32′ E. and the sun's apparent altitude at the same time was 24° 43′.

Sun's Meridian Altitude - -		26 46 0
Sum - - -	+	0 11 4
		26 57 4
		90 0 0
		63 2 56
		11 33 0
Latitude at noon - - -		74 6 56

A. M. With the Ship's head E. S. E. and the compass in midships, the mean of 12 magnetic azimuths gave N. 22° 17′ 30″ E. and the sun's apparent altitude at the same time was 25°.

P. D.	78° 55′		
Lat.	74 12	Sec. -	56498
Alt.	25 0	Sec. -	4272
	178 7		
	89 3	Co-sine	8 21958
	78 55		
	10 8	Co-sine	9 99317
			18 82045
			9 41022

N. 21 0 } E. Sun's obs. alt.
21 0 } 24° 26′
20 30 }

2 30
20 50

18 30 }
19 30 } 24 31
21 30 }

59 30
19 50

21 30 }
20 30 } 24 35
20 30 }

2 30
20 50

20 30 }
20 30 } 24 37 0
21 0 } 0 129 0
24 32 15
2 0 0 11 0
20 40 24 43 15

P. D.	78°	55′			
Latitude	74	12	Sec.	-	56498
Altitude	24	43	Sec.	-	4173
	177	50			
	88	55	Co-sine	8	27661
	78	55			
	10	0	Co-sine	9	99335
				18	87667
				9	43833

74° 4′ ½ Co-sine.
× 2
148 8 from south.
159 28 from south.
11 20 var. easterly.

Means	N. 20°	50′	E.
	19	50	
	20	50	
	20	40	
	82	10	
Magnetic N.	20	32	
	180	0	
	159	28	

N. 19 30 } E. Sun's observed altitude.
22 30 } 24° 44′
22 30 }

64 30
21 30

23 0 }
23 0 } 24 48
23 0 }

23 0

21 0 }
22 0 } 24 50
23 0 }

6 0
22 0

22 0 }
23 0 } 24 53
23 0 }
0 195
8 0 24 49
22 40 0 11
25 0

75 6 0 ½ Co-sine.
× 0 2 0
150 12 0 from south.
157 42 30 from south.
7° 30′ 30″ variation easterly.

Means N.	21	30	0	E.
	23	0	0	
	22	0	0	
	22	40	0	
	9	10	0	
Mag.	22	17	30	

OBSERVATIONS for finding the Longitude by Chronometers, &c.—*continued.*

Date.	Time by No. 403.	Mean Time.	Altitude of the Sun's Centre.	Latitude at Observation.	No. 403. Slow.	No. 820. Fast.	3540. Slow.	Latitude by Observation at Noon.	Latitude by Account.	Longitude by Mean of Chronometers at Noon.	Longitude by Account.
Feb. 21.	—	—	—	—	6′ 59.0″	10′ 47.0″	15′ 39″	—	73° 18′	35° 7′ 45″	37° 27′ 0″
22.	11h 44′ 4″	9h 37′ 29″	94° 21′	71° 33′	7 0.5	10 52.5	15 52	71° 25′	71 35	33 24 45	37 47 0
23.	10 58 53	8 47 24	21 47	70 9	7 2.0	10 58.0	16 5	70 12	70 25	34 40 45	39 50 0

Time by 403. -	10h 58′ 53″
403. slow -	0 7 2
Time at Greenwich -	11 5 55
Mean time -	8 47 24
Difference of Meridians	2 18 31

Time by 403. -	10° 58′ 53″
403. slow of 820.	0 18 48
	11 17 41
820 fast of Greenwich -	0 10 58
Time at Greenwich -	11 6 43
Mean time -	8 47 24
Difference of Meridians	2 19 19

Time by 403. -	10° 58′ 53″
403. fast of 3540.	0 8 47
	10 50 6
3540. slow -	0 16 5
Time at Greenwich -	11 6 11
Mean time - -	8 47 24
Difference of Meridians	2 18 47

No. 403.	34° 37′ 45″
No. 820.	34 49 45
No. 3540.	34 41 45
	119 15
Mean Longitude	34 39 45

OBSERVATIONS for finding the Longitude by Chronometers, &c.—*continued.*

Date.	Time by No. 403.	Mean Time.	Altitude of the Sun's Centre.	Latitude at Observation.	No 403. Slow.	No. 820. Fast.	3540. Slow.	Latitude by Observation at Noon.	Latitude by Account.	Longitude by Mean of Chronometers at Noon.	Longitude by Account.
Feb. 24.	—	—	—	—	7′ 3.5″	11′ 3″	16′ 18″	69° 7′	69° 9′	37° 32′ 45″	42° 44′ 0″
25.	11h 22′ 26″	8h 54′ 23″	22° 26′	68° 42′	7 5.0	11 9	16 31	68 21	68 35	38 48 0	44 6 0

OBSERVATIONS for finding the Longitude by Chronometers, &c. — *continued.*

Date.	Time by No. 403.	Mean Time.	Altitude of the Sun's Centre.	Latitude at Observ-ation.	No. 403. Slow.	No. 820. Fast.	3540. Slow.	Latitude by Obser-vation at Noon.	Latitude by Ac-count.	Longitude by Mean of Chro-nometers at Noon.	Longitude by Account.
Feb. 26.	11h 36′ 33″	9h 2′ 15″	23° 23	67° 39′	7′ 6.5″	11′ 14.5′	16′ 44″	67° 33′	67° 21′	40° 2′ 45″	45° 13′ 00″

P. M. with the Ship's head west, and the compass at the binnacle, the mean of 15 magnetic azimuths gave 72° 54′, and the sun's apparent altitude at the same time was 22° 4′.

Time by 403.	11h	36′	32″				
	0	7	6				
	11	43	38				
	9	3	15				
	2	40	23	=	40°	5′	45″
				Easting —		5	0
					40	0	45 Longitude by 403. at noon.

P. D.	81° 12′			
Latitude	67 29	Sec.	- -	0° 41686
Altitude	22 4	Sec.	-	0 03304
	170 45			
	85 22	Co-sine	-	8 90730
	81 12			
	4 10	Co-sine	-	9 99885
				19 35605
				9 67802

N. 70°		W.		Sun's observed altitude.
74		22°	26′	
71				
5				
71	40			
72	30			
72	30	21°	59′	
71	0			
6	0			
72	0			
72	30			
72	0	21	55	
72	30			
72	0			
74	30			
74	0	21	49	
72	30			
11	0			
73	40			
74	30			
75	0	21	43	
76	0			
		9	32	
15	30	21	54	
5	10	—	10	
		22	4	Sun's apparent altitude.

Co-sine	61°	32′	
	×	2	
From South	123	4	
	107	6	
	15	58	variation easterly.

Means		71°	40′	
		72	0	
		72	0	
		73	40	
		75	10	
		14	30	
	N.	72	54	W. mag.
		180	0	
		107	6	

OBSERVATIONS for finding the Longitude by Chronometers, &c.—*continued.*

Date.	Time by No. 403.	Mean Time.	Altitude of the Sun's Centre.	Latitude at Observation.	No. 403. Slow.	No. 820. Fast.	3540. Slow.	Latitude by Observation at Noon.	Latitude by Account.	Longitude by Mean of Chronometers at Noon.	Longitude by Account.
Feb. 27.	11° 44′ 34″	9° 10′ 38″	24° 15′	66° 37′	7′ 8″	11′ 20″	16′ 57″	66° 36′	66° 33′	40° 22′ 00″	45° 52′ 00″

A. M. with the Ship's head N. W. and the compass in midships, the mean of 15 magnetic azimuths gave N. 25° 42′, E. and the apparent altitude at the same time was 25° 7′.

11°	44′	34″					
—	7	8					
11	51	42		30°	0′	0″	
9	10	38		10	0	0	
2	41	4		40	16	0	
			Westing		4	0	
				40	20	0	Longitude by 403.

P. M. with the Ship's head N. W. and the compass in midships, the mean of 15 magnetic azimuths gave 63° 2′, and the apparent altitude at the same time was 23° 51′.

P. D.	81°	34′			
Latitude	66	31	Sec. - -	0°	39959′
Altitude	23	51	Sec. - -	0	03877
	171	56			
	85	58	Co-sine - -	8	84718
	81	34			
	4	24	Co-sine - -	9	99872
				19	28426
				9	64213

N.	26° 30	E.	E. Sun's obs. alt. 24° 48′	
	26 30			
	27 0			
	27 0			
	27 0			
	26 45			
	26 0			
	26 0	24° 53′		
	25 0			
	25 0			
	22 0			
	25 30			
	25 0			
	26 0	24 56		
	27 0			
	25 0			
	23 0			
	25 45			
	26 0			
	26 0	25 1		
	26 0			
	26 0			
	26 0			
	23 30			
	24 30	25 6		
	25 0	24 44		
	25 0	24 57		
	18 0	10		
	24 30	25 7	Sun's app. alt.	
	26 0			
	25 45			
	25 30			
	26 45			
	28 30			
	25 42			
	180 0			
	154 18			

P.D.	81° 29′		
Latitude	66 37	Sec.	0 40134
Altitude	25 7	Sec.	0 04314
	173 13		
	86 36	Co-sine	8 77310
	81 29		
	5 7	Co-sine	9 99827
			19 21585
			9 60792

66° 5′	Co-sine.
× 2	
132 10	from south.
154 18	from south.
22 8	variation easterly.

Means	26° 45′	
	25 30	
	25 45	
	26 0	
	24 30	
	25 42	
	34 12	
	25 42	mag. azimuth.

N.	61° 30′	W. 23° 51′	
	62 0		
	62 30		
	6 0		
	62 0		
	61 30		
	62 30	23 47	
	63 30		
	7 30		
	62 30		
	61 30		
	62 30	23 39	
	63 0		
	7 0		
	62 20		
	63 30		
	63 30	23 34	
	64 30		
	11 0		
	63 40		
	64 30		
	64 30	23 31	
	65 0	22	
Means	14 0	23 40 24	
	64 40	10 36	
	63 40	23 51 00	Sun's app. alt.
	62 20		
	62 30		
	62 0		
	15 10		
	63 2		
	180 0		
	116 58		

63° 59′	½ Co-sine.
× 2	
127 58	from south.
116 58	from south.
11 0	variation easterly.

OBSERVATIONS for finding the Longitude by Chronometers, &c. — *continued.*

Date.	Time by No. 403.	Mean Time.	Altitude of the Sun's Centre.	Latitude at Observation.	No. 403. Slow.	No. 820. Fast.	3540. Slow.	Latitude by Observation at Noon.	Latitude by Account.	Longitude by Mean of Chronometers at Noon.	Longitude by Account.
Feb. 28.	—	—	—	—	7′ 9.5″	11′ 25.5″	17′ 10″	—	64° 57′	41° 6′	46° 39′
March 1.	11h 19′ 51″	8h 36′ 22″	22° 20′	63° 32′	7 11.0	11 31.0	17 23	63° 29′	63 28	42 47	49 1

A.M. With the Ship's head N.W. and the compass at the binnacle, the mean of 18 magnetic azimuths gave N. 15° 13′ E.; and the sun's apparent altitude at the same time was 31° 16′.

11°	19′	51″				
0	7	11				
11	27	2				
8	36	22				
2	50	40	=	42°	40′	Longitude by 408.
	Westing		—	0	5	
				42	45	

P.M. With the Ship's head W. by S., and the compass in midships, the mean of 15 magnetic azimuths gave N. 62° 46′ W.; and the sun's apparent altitude at the same time was 27° 40′.

P.D.	82°	20′				
Latitude	63	28	Sec.	-	0°	34997′
Altitude	27	40	Sec.	-	0	05273
	173	28				
	86	44	Co-sine	-	8	75575
	82	20				
	4	24	Co-sine	-	9	99872
					19	15717
					9	57858

N.	E. Sun's obs. alt.		
15° 30′	30° 50′		
15 30			
18 0			
19 0			
16 20			
14 30			
16 0	30 56		
16 0			
16 30			
15 30			
15 30			
16 30	30 1		
16 30			
18 30			
16 10			
14 30			
14 30	31 3		
15 30			
14 0			
14 40			
14 30			
14 30	31 7		
13 30			
12 30			
14 10			
14 30			
14 30	31°	9′	0″
14 30	0	26	0
14 30	31	5	12
	0	10	48
	31	16	0 Sun's app. alt.

P. D.	82° 14′			
Latitude	63 32	Sec.	0°	35098′
Altitude	31 16	Sec.	0	06777
	176 57			
	88 28	Co-sine	8	42746
	82 14			
	6 14	Co-sine	9	99742
			18	84363
			9	42181

74°	41′	½ Co-sine.
×	2	
149	22	from south.
164	47	from south.
15	25	variation easterly.

Means	14°	30′	
	14	10	
	14	40	
	16	10	
	15	30	
	16	20	
	31	20	
	15	13	mag. azimuth.

N.	W.		
64° 0′	27° 37′		
62 30			
62 30			
9 0			
63 0			
61 30			
61 30	27 32		
63 0			
6 0			
62 0			
62 30			
62 30	27 29		
63 0			
8 0			
62 40			
62 30	27 25		
62 30	27 21		
63 0	0 144		
8 0	27 29		
62 40	0 11		
63 30			
63 30	27 40	Sun's app. alt.	
63 30			

67°	44′	½ Cosine.
× 0	2	
135	28	from south.
117	14	from south.
18	14	variation easterly.

Means	63°	30′	
	62	40	
	62	40	
	62	0	
	63	0	
	13	50	
	62	46	mag. azimuth.
	180	0	
	117	14	

OBSERVATIONS for finding the Longitude by Chronometers, &c. — *continued.*

P. M. With the Ship's head N. W. and the compass at the binnacle, the mean of 15 magnetic azimuths gave N. 59° 6′ W. and the sun's apparent altitude at the same time was 28° 12′.

Azimuths		Sun's alt.
N. 55° 30′	W.	
58 0	}	28° 15′
57 30		
21 0		
57 0		
59 0		
59 30	}	28 7
59 0		
59 10		
60 0		
58 30	}	27 58
59 0		
117 30		
59 10		
61 0		
59 0	}	27 53
59 0		
179 0		
59 40		

Means	57° 0′	
	59 10	
	59 10	
	59 40	
	60 30	
	295 30	
	59 6	
	180 0	
	120 54	from south.

P. D.	82° 20′		
Lat.	63 29	Sec.	0° 35022′
Alt.	28 12	Sec.	0 05487
	174 1		
	87 0	Co-sine	8 71880
	82 20		
	4 40	Co-sine	9 99856
			19 12245
			56122

Variation by 1st.	-	15° 25′
Do. 2d.	-	16 24
Do. 3d.	-	18 14
		20 3
		16 41 mean variation easterly.

61 0
61 0 } 27 51
59 30
181 30 — 40 4
60 30 — 28 1
0 11
28 12 Sun's apparent altitude.

68° 39′ ½ Co-sine.
×0 2
137 18 from south.
120 54 from south.
16 24 variation easterly.

Date.	Time by No. 403.	Mean Time.	Altitude of the Sun's Centre.	Latitude at Observation.	No. 403. Slow.	No. 820. Fast.	3540. Slow.	Latitude by Observation at Noon.	Latitude by Account.	Longitude by Mean of Chronometers at Noon.	Longitude by Account.
March 2.	—	—	—	—	7′ 12.5″	11′ 36.5″	17′ 36″	63° 7′	63° 9′	43° 55′ 0″	50° 10′
3.	—	—	—	—	7 14.0	11 42.0	17 49	—	63 1	46 9 0	52 24
4.	11ʰ 46′ 4″	8ʰ 53′ 41″	23° 6′	63° 17′	7 15.5	11 47.5	18 2	63 22	63 17	45 22 30	53 51
5.	—	—	—	—	7 17.0	11 53.0	18 15	63 4	63 4	44 31 30	53 0
6.	6 8 16	3 21 31	24 4	61 37	7 18.5	11 58.5	18 28	61 55	61 45	43 52 45	53 9
7.	—	—	—	—	7 20.0	12 4.0	18 41	—	59 36	42 30 45	51 47
8.	7 10 59	4 43 46	16 0	56 47	7 21.5	12 9.5	18 54	57 14	56 49	38 38 0	48 55
9.	—	—	—	—	7 23.0	12 15.0	19 7	51 21	55 25	38 21 0	48 38
10.	—	—	—	—	7 24.5	12 20.5	19 20	—	55 23	38 11 0	48 27
11.	—	—	—	—	7 26.0	12 26.0	19 33	—	54 41	39 24 0	49 40
12.	11 51 1	9 26 28	29 17	54 27	7 27.5	12 31.5	19 46	54 17	54 11	37 52 10	49 32

DIFFERENCES of CHRONOMETERS between the 26th of *December* 1822, and the 12th *March* 1823.

Time by 403.		11h	51′	1″	
403. fast of 3540.	—		12	40	
		11	38	21	
3540.slow of Greenwich	+		19	46	
Time at Greenwich		11	58	7	
Mean time at ship		9	26	28	
		2	31	39	Difference of Meridians by 3540.
Time by 403.		11	51	1	
403. slow of 820.	+		21	4	
Time by 820.		12	12	5	
820. fast of Greenwich	—		12	31	
Time at Greenwich		11	59	34	
Mean time at ship		9	26	28	
		2	33	6	Difference of Meridians by 820.

Time by 403.		11h	51′	1″	
403. slow of Greenwich	+		7	27	
Time at Greenwich		11	58	28	
Mean time at ship		9	26	28	
		2	32	0	Difference of Meridians by 403.
Longitude by 3540.		37°	54′	45″	
do. 820.		38	16	30	
do. 403.		38	0	0	
	3)	24	11	15	
		38	3	45	Mean Longitude of Chronometers, 12th March, 1823.

LATITUDE and LONGITUDE of Places, deduced from Observations.

Islands, &c.	Harbours, Headlands, &c. &c.	Latitude.	Longitude.	Variation.
Madeira	Funchall	32° 37′ 45″	16° 52′ 28″	
Bonavista	Cape de Verds	16 5 0	22 59 0	15° 20′ West
Trinidad	North End	20 26 55	29 12 30	
Patagonia	River Santa Cruz	50 12 16	68 14 30	
———	Saint Elena	44 34 16	65 32 22	
Falkland Islands	Ship Harbour, New Island	51 42 36	61 9 0	
———	West Point Harbour	51 24 15	60 36 30	
———	Port Louis	51 32 0	58 3 30	
Tierra del Fuego	Cape Horn	55 59 21	67 13 45	23 29 East
———	Barnavelt's Island	55 48 16	66 39 0	
———	St. Martin's Cove	55 53 37	67 29 45	
———	Clear Bottom Bay	55 32 50	69 1 15	
———	Ildefonsos, North Island	55 48 38	69 20 50	26 42 Easterly
———	South Island	55 50 38	69 16 50	
———	Diego Ramirez, North Island	56 28 0	68 27 45	
———	South Island	56 32 15	68 24 15	
South Georgia	Adventure Bay, West End	54 2 48	38 8 4	11 15 Easterly
South Orkneys	Cape Dundas	60 46 30	44 35 45	
———	Saddle Island	60 37 50	44 52 45	16 1 Easterly
———	West Cape	60 42 0	46 23 52	

LATITUDE, &c.—*continued.*

Islands, &c.	Harbours, Headlands, &c. &c.	Latitude.	Longitude.	Variation.
New S. Shetland	O' Brien's Islands	62° 32′ 0″	56° 20′ 0″	
———	Cape Melville	62 1 0	57 45 45	
———	Seal Rocks	61 1 0	55 32 0	
———	James Island, East End	62 52 45	62 26 30	27° 30′
———	Start Point	62 41 30	61 16 30	
———	Cape Sheriff	62 26 0	60 40 0	28 0
———	Deception Island, East End	63 2 0	60 45 0	
———	Bridgeman's Island	62 4 0	56 57 30	
———	Cape Bowles	61 18 0	54 25 0	
———	Hope Island	63 5 30	56 44 0	
———	Jameson's Island, Centre	63 4 0	62 17 30	28 0
———	James's Island, West End	62 49 30	62 55 0	
———	Cornwallis Island	61 2 0	54 41 0	
———	Basil Hall's Island, Centre	62 47 30	61 40 0	
———	St. George's Bay	62 6 0	58 6 0	

TABLE exhibiting the Temperature of AIR and WATER.

Date.	Latitude.		Longitude.		Thermometer. Mean Temperature of Air and Water.				Winds.	Weather.
					Air.		Water.			
Jan. 3.	53°	15′	63°	48′	39°	30′	49°	30′	S. by E.	Strong gales.
4.	53	24	60	24	40	0	47	0	S.S.W.	Strong gales.
5.	53	49	58	1	50	0	49	0	South.	Moderate breezes.
6.	53	54	56	24	40	0	46	0	South.	Strong gales.
7.	54	59	54	28	43	0	44	0	S.S.W.	Moderate breezes.
8.	56	9	53	0	40	30	43	0	W.S.W.	Fresh breezes.
9.	57	30	50	41	41	0	42	0	S. S.W.	Moderate breezes.
10.	58	15	48	8	39	0	40	0	S.S.W.	Squally with snow.
11.	59	37	46	1	38	0	33	0	S.S.W.	Fresh breezes.
13.	60	40	45	0	34	0	33	0	S. by W.	Under the land of South Orkneys, light breezes.
19.	60	40	45	0	33	30	33	30	S. by W.	Light breezes.
24.	62	35	42	2	36	0	34	0	S.S.E.	Moderate breezes and foggy.
25.	63	2	40	51	36	0	34	0	N.W.	Moderate breezes and foggy.

TABLE, &c.—*continued.*

Date.	Latitude.		Longitude.		Thermometer. Mean Temperature of Air and Water. Air.		Water.		Winds.	Weather.
Jan. 26.	64°	33′	40°	13′	36°	0′	34°	0′	N. by W.	Fresh gales and clear.
27.	64	58	39	40	37	0	34	0	E.S.E.	Light winds and clear.
29.	61	18	40	32	34	0	34	0	S.W.	Fresh breezes.
30.	60	31	42	48	37	30	35	0	N. by E.	Fresh breezes.
31.	59	50	40	52	36	0	35	0	N. by N.	Fresh breezes.
Feb. 2.	60	19	38	21	35	0	34	0	West.	Fresh gales and cloudy.
3.	60	59	36	58	37	0	35	0	W.S.W.	Fresh breezes and clear.
4.	60	44	33	27	34	0	34	0	S.W. by W.	Strong breezes and clear.
5.	61	44	31	16	37	0	36	0	W. by S.	Fresh breezes and cloudy.
6.	62	51	30	42	40	0	36	0	W. by S.	Strong breezes and foggy.
7.	64	15	30	46	39	0	37	0	W. by N.	Moderate breezes with rain.
8.	65	24	35	28	34	0	36	0	West.	Light breezes and cloudy.
10.	66	24	32	32	35	0	34	0	South.	Squally with showers of snow. (Broke the thermometer.)

OBSERVATIONS of the MOON used with Chronometers for settling the Longitude of Places at New South Shetland.

Date.	Time by Chronometer.	Sun's Altitude.	Moon's observed Altitude U.L.	Observed angular Distance between the Sun and Moon's nearest Limbs.	Difference of Meridians.	Longitude of the Ship.
Nov. 10. 1823.	5h 37′ 27″	39° 1′	26° 14′	87° 59′ 40″		
	5 39 7	38 55	26 28	88 1 0		
	5 40 29	38 50	26 34	88 1 15		
	5 43 57	38 29	26 56	88 2 15		
	5 45 44	38 21	27 8	88 2 30		
	5 47 8	38 13	27 15	88 3 15	4h 7′ 31″	61° 52′ 45″ W. from Greenw.
	5 48 7	38 6	27 23	88 3 30		
	5 49 41	38 0	27 31	88 4 15		
	5 51 27	37 51	27 43	88 5 40		
	5 52 42	37 46	27 50	88 6 0		
	5 54 3	37 38	28 0	88 7 0		

REMARKS:

James' Island S. 6° E. distant about 40 miles. Index error of sextant 2′ 10″. sub. Apparent time at ship 2h 21′ 56″. Index error in the moon's altitude 1′. sub.

OBSERVATIONS of the MOON, used with Chronometers, for settling the Longitude of Cape Horn, and Places in its Vicinity.

Date.	Time by Chronometer.	Sun's observed Altitude.	Moon's observed Altitude U.L.	Observed angular Distance between Sun and Moon's nearest Limbs.	Difference of Meridians.	Longitude of the Ship.
Dec. 24. 1823.	2h 33′ 42″	53° 46′	15° 32′	89° 16′ 0″	4h 36′ 17″	69° 4′ 15″ W. from Greenw.
	2 35 32	53 53	15 9	89 14 15		
	2 37 2	54 1	15 0	89 13 40		
	2 38 21	54 6	14 49	89 13 0		
	2 39 52	54 13	14 40	89 12 40		
	2 41 29	54 20	14 26	89 11 30		
	2 43 32	54 28	14 10	89 11 0		
	2 44 43	54 34	14 2	89 10 0		
	2 46 27	54 41	13 46	89 9 0		

REMARKS:

The eastern Island of the Ildefonsos (off Cape Horn), W. ½ S. by compass distant three miles. Index error of sextant 2′ 10″. sub. Apparent time at ship 10° 39′ 34″.

OBSERVATIONS

ON

THE PROBABILITY OF REACHING

THE SOUTH POLE.

ADVERTISEMENT.

The late meritorious expeditions, sent out by our Government to explore the northern parts of the globe, having excited much public interest; and the late voyage performed by me towards the South Pole, having attracted considerable attention; are the circumstances which have induced me to publish the following sheets, containing my opinions on the probable state of the Polar Regions.

JAMES WEDDELL, R. N.

OBSERVATIONS

ON THE

STATE OF THE POLES.

In presenting to the public the following considerations, relating to the probability of the Polar Regions being open, I must necessarily use the data upon which both the early and late expeditions towards the North Pole have been projected, as these must continue to be the principal grounds of reasoning till the matter shall be set at rest by actual observation.

Many arguments have been employed to prove the open state of the Polar Regions, since experimental investigations have been effected, not only by Great Britain, but by several other nations, during more than two centuries.

The numerous unsuccessful attempts which have been made to penetrate the Northern Polar Region, do not by any means destroy the assumption of the Poles being accessible, but rather furnish new matter for further enquiry into that part of geography. And the open state of the Antarctic Sea, as described in my Journal, naturally gives rise to new conjecture, in regard to the southern extremity of the globe.

The natural action of the sun, arising from his particular situation in the heavens, and his continuance above the horizon, as relates to the Poles, I am aware is understood by those whose attention has been directed to the temperature of the extremities of the globe; but by persons generally, the subject is, perhaps, not clearly comprehended. To them an illustration of the movements of the sun, as regards the Polar Regions, may be acceptable; and the subject follows in connection with the supposition I have set forth in my Journal; namely, the prospect of reaching the *South Pole*.

The probability of a temperate Polar Region depends not wholly upon the presence of the sun, but greatly on the properties of matter at and about the Poles. The questions which arise from this latter consideration are, do the Polar Regions contain water only, or land only, or both; and if the latter, what is the quality of the land, and what is its proximity to the Poles? Any one of these peculiar states will, notwithstanding the constant and uniform action of the sun during summer, produce a corresponding change of atmospheric temperature.

There are only two states of the Polar Regions which seem to afford a hope of their being accessible. The first, and most flattering supposition, is that of the extremities of the globe being clear of land, and having a clear expanse of ocean, reaching from about the 83° of latitude, some degrees towards the Equator; and the other state is that of having land immediately about the Poles, consisting of matter, capable of retaining through the winter part of the caloric absorbed during summer.

As we know of no land nearer to the South Pole than 20½ degrees of latitude, or 1230 miles, and as I have ascertained that within 855 miles there is neither field ice, nor land, the supposition that the South Pole may be covered with an expanse of water is at least probable.

The great obliquity of the sun's rays in those regions may be brought forward as an argument for their insufficiency to produce a temperate atmosphere; but their effects at and immediately about the Poles have never, to our knowledge, been witnessed. The point of 81° 50′ appears to have been the highest northern latitude attained, of which we have an undoubted account. Consequently, a nearly stationary altitude, such as would be experienced at the Poles, has never been observed; and hence the analogy afforded by the sun's motion round the horizon in this latitude is weak and unsatisfactory.

Professor Mayer of Gottingen gives a *formula* *, by which the temperature of any latitude may be readily computed; and were the extremities of the globe unaccompanied with local peculiarities, the calculation would be uniformly true. But the rocky and mountainous lands, lying in high latitudes, produce a temperature much below that indicated by the formula. This seems to be the case in each hemisphere respectively; and about the latitude of 60° the two hemispheres themselves differ from each other very materially. The sun being about seven days longer on the *north* side of the

* Let t denote the mean temperature of any parallel of which the latitude is L, m the mean temperature in the latitude of 45°, $m + e$ the mean temperature at the Equator; then is $t = m + e$ cosine 2 L; whence the mean temperature is readily ascertained. The mean temperature in latitude 45° is $58 = m$. At the Equator it is 85°, whence $85 - 58 = 27 = e$; therefore, $t = 58 + 27$ cosine 2 L, which, when 2 L is greater than 90°, the cosine being negative, is less than 58.

Equator than on the *south*, may be assigned as one reason for this difference of temperature; but, as he is about $\frac{1}{32}$ part of his mean distance nearer the earth on the 1st of *January* than on the 1st of *July*, it is evident that he must be nearer the earth from the 23d of *September* to the 20th of *March*, than from the 20th of *March* to the 23d of *September;* and, therefore, upon calculation, it will be found, that this latter circumstance will more than counterbalance the effect produced by his longer continuance on the north side of the Equator.

Captain Scoresby found the mean annual temperature of the latitude of 78° to be 16° below the estimate by calculation; and in the latitude of 61° south, 17° nearer to the Equator, I found by observation the mean temperature of the month of *January* to be nearly 35° of Fahrenheit. The mean temperature of the year in that latitude, by the formula of Professor Mayer, is 44° 5′.* We have not observations sufficient to obtain the real annual temperature of the latitude of 61°; but it must of course be much lower than that of *January*, and must consequently exhibit a great deviation from the result by calculation.

* Professor Leslie, in his notes to his Elements of Geometry, (p. 461. 4th edit.) calculates the mean temperature of latitude 61° to be 44° 3′.

This circumstance of remarkable frigidity in a latitude, which in the northern hemisphere is so temperate, strikingly exhibits the great effects caused by the barren land of the Archipelago of New South Shetland. In proceeding southwards, this deviation of observed temperature from the result by calculation greatly diminishes; so that in the latitude of 74° the formula approaches much nearer the truth. At the summer solstice this parallel will probably be much warmer than that of 61°; and we may suppose, that in winter the cold of these respective latitudes will not materially differ. The little change which I found in the temperature, through a southern route of 13 degrees, as mentioned in the Journal of my voyage, is remarkable, and accords with the observation made by Professor Leslie*, in his calculations of the temperature of the earth at different latitudes.

On the 8th of *February* the influence of the sun's rays must be very different at the Poles from what it is in the latitude of 80°; for on that day the sun passes round the South Pole,

* "Very little increase of heat is therefore observed in advancing through the torrid zone to the Equator; and the intensity of the cold would not be sensibly augmented in penetrating from the Arctic Circle to the Pole. The existence of an open sea towards the extreme north is hence not improbable."— Supplement, 3d vol. to the Encyclopædia Britannica.

at the altitude of 15°, whilst in the latitude of 80° his altitude is diminished to 5°; at which height it can produce but little effect on the surface of the earth. The meridian altitude on the above day (at 80°) is 25° 13′; but the time of his being above the altitude of 15° is only about half what it is at the Pole on that day. In short, it is only from the constant and uniform action of the sun at those low altitudes that an extraordinary degree of heat can be expected.

In bringing this subject as clearly to view as possible, some observations on the movements of the sun in our own latitude, compared with those about the Poles, may be necessary by way of illustration. When the sun is in the first degree of the sign Cancer, on our longest day, (the 21st of *June*,) the meridian altitude at Greenwich is 61° 59′. When in the sign Capricorn, (the 21st of *December*,) on our shortest day, the meridian altitude is 15° 3′; the mean meridian altitude is, therefore, 38° 30′. The longest space of time during which the sun is above the horizon in this latitude, (namely, on the 21st of *June*,) is 16^h 34′. The shortest space, (namely, on the 21st of *December*,) is 7^h 44′; hence the mean day or time that the sun is above the horizon in the latitude of Greenwich is 12° 9′. The temperature of this climate is, therefore, the result of a meridian altitude of 38° 31′, with the sun visible nearly twelve hours out of twenty-four. At the Poles the presence of the sun is of the same duration in the course of a year as at all other points of the globe, but at different periods, and at different altitudes above the horizon, according to the latitude.

At the South Pole (the north being subject to the same law at the opposite season), from the 3d of *November* till the 8th of *February* (more than three months), the sun never descends below 15 degrees; which is the meridian altitude of that body for several days of our winter, when it is only for the space of 7^{h} 44′ above the horizon. This continuance of the sun's presence for more than three months at the Pole is a most important circumstance; and when we consider the warmth of an unclouded winter sun, when on the meridian, or at noon, our curiosity is excited as to what his effects must be where the action of the rays is constant for so long a time as above mentioned.

The little warmth which we receive from the sun, when under 5 degrees, is evident to every one who has paid the least attention to the subject.

The extent of atmosphere through which the rays have to pass, on account of their obliquity, so refract and resist them, that they fall but faintly on the surface of the globe; but, at the altitude of 15°, the rays of the sun pass through so diminished an extent of atmosphere, that at its mean density the refraction is reduced from 9′ 54″ to 3′ 34″, and the calorific effect at 5° is computed by Professor Leslie to be only ·004; but, at the altitude of 15°, it is increased to ·084. The caloric transmitted from the sun to the earth must, therefore, increase above the altitude of 5° to 15° in a very compounded ratio.

The action of the sun on the Polar Regions must be even more powerful than is here mentioned, for during three months (from the 3d of *November* to the 8th of *February*) the sun is considerably above the altitude of 15° at the South Pole. From the 22d of *November* till the 20th of *January* (two months) of that time, the sun is never below 20°; and from the 11th of *December* to the 1st of *January*, never below 23°; being on the 21st of *December* 23°, 28′ and for several days before and after that time about the same altitude.

The continuance of the sun above the horizon of the Poles for these periods, and at so considerable altitudes, cannot fail to persuade us, that the ices there must be annually dissolved, and the Polar Regions assume an appearance as in the annexed sketch.

In this figure I have placed the ices promiscuously in the situations of the latitude they may be supposed to occupy, on being disjoined from South Shetland, and possibly other lands in high southern latitudes which have not yet been discovered.

St. Pierre, whose writings in general do honour to his head and heart, has treated the subject of Polar temperature in a course of reasoning truly inventive; but he establishes his theory by referring to tides and currents, of which, although the latter do exist in a trifling degree, yet experience demonstrates them to bear no adequate proportion to the cause he assigns, namely, large floods proceeding from the Polar regions, by the fusion of their ices.

I am not aware that his philosophical observations on the state of the Poles have ever been replied to: perhaps they have been thought too chimerical to merit an answer; but the many unsuccessful attempts which have been made to penetrate the Northern Polar Sea seem, at first sight, to favour his hypothesis; and it is only by a close examination of his arguments, compared with modern discovery, that the errors of his system can be detected. Actual observation has afforded me proof of the fallacy of his conjectured Polar currents. (See his Studies of Nature, p. 35.) "In our winter, the fluid ocean

Fig. 1.

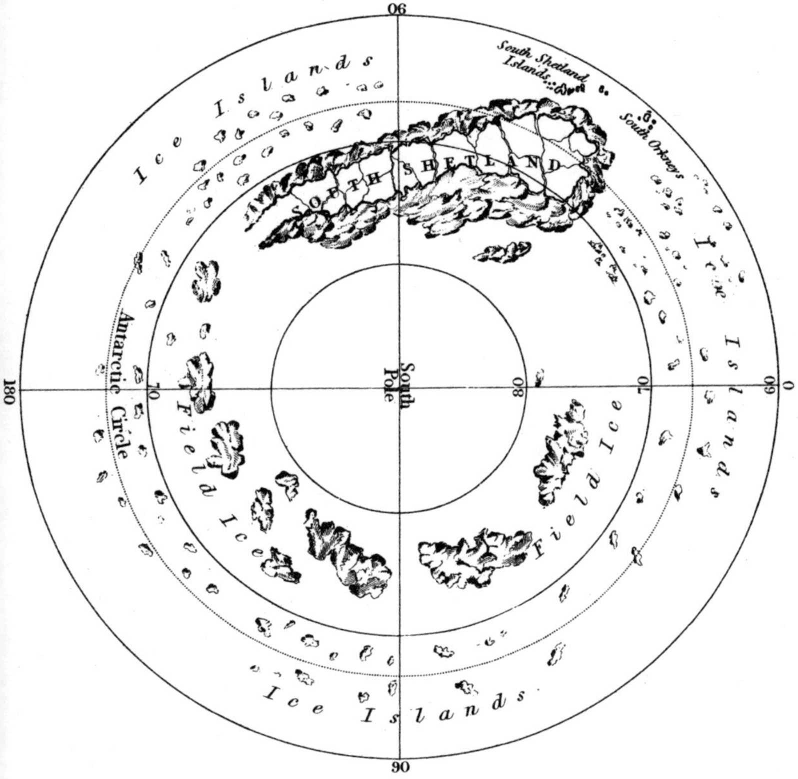

Sidy. Hall Sculpt.

descends from the frozen ocean of the South Pole, at that time four or five thousand leagues in circumference, by the action of the sun, which melts the ice from the equinox of *September* to that of *March*."

On reference to the Journal of my voyage, p. 46. it will be found, that the current which set to the northward was in general scarcely perceptible; and on the 18th of *February* (see p. 35.), it actually ran to the southward.

This proves, certainly, that the current he describes does not constantly prevail; but the cupola he has fancied may exist without producing a northerly flood. If the Poles of the world be pyramids of ice, as he asserts *, I am of opinion that no such flood of ice waters as he mentions could take place; for these supposed cupolas must be the accumulation of, perhaps, the age of the world, subject to a small change in their formation by the change of the obliquity of the ecliptic, and ages since they must have reached that point of the atmosphere, above which there is no condensation of vapour, and consequently no addition to the mass, by means of snow, could be produced. The height of these cupolas will of course depend on the quality of the Polar atmosphere; but we cannot doubt that they

* This assertion I find quoted by respectable authors.

are much above the point of congelation at the summer solstice*, and therefore not subject to fusion by the sun's rays. Around the water line of the base of this imaginary pyramid some fusion of ice would certainly be effected; but, the space occupied by the ice immersed in water being greater than that which it would fall into when dissolved, the waters by this partial fusion could scarcely be impelled enough to produce a current. Snow and ice waters falling from land must unquestionably produce currents. This appears during summer, in the innumerable straits and channels situated in high northern latitudes. When I further call in question the statements made by St. Pierre, I feel sensible that it is only by means of actual observation, such as he had not the advantage of, that I am able to refute his opinions. In accounting for the universal deluge, by the fusion of the Polar ices, he says, "Who then can doubt, that the total effusion of the ices of the two Poles is sufficient to overflow the bed of the ocean, and entirely to inundate the two continents? Must not the elevation of those two cupolas of Polar ice, vast as oceans, far surpass the height of the most lofty lands, since the fragments of their

* The mean temperature here being supposed to be 32°; the point of perpetual congelation is, therefore, in the horizon.

extremities, when half dissolved, are as high as the turrets of Notre Dame, and even rise to the height of fifteen or eighteen hundred feet above the level of the sea?"

This is certainly a mistake; and St. Pierre, we may suppose, was led into this error by the exaggerated accounts of voyagers who had navigated in high latitudes; for I know of no icebergs, afloat, at least in the south, of such a height. And those which are seen floating about do not separate from the supposed Polar glacier, but are formed in straits and indentations of land; and they vary in size not so much according to the latitude, above 60 degrees, in the southern hemisphere, as by peculiarities of the coasts where they are formed. This evidently appeared during my experience in the south. The ice-islands seen in the latitude of 74° were much less than others we know to have been formed in the latitude of from 60 to 65 degrees. If we may draw an analogy for the south from the observations made by Captain Phipps on the northern glacier or ice barrier (the southern not having been seen by me), it appears evident, that there is no coincidence between the northern glacier, which Captain Phipps (see his voyage, p. 60.) found to be twenty-three feet deep, and those fragments mentioned by St. Pierre, of 1500 and 1800 feet high; they cannot, therefore, have separated from the base of the supposed pyramid. I am aware that St. Pierre supposes this mass of ice to reach over land as well as water; but into what latitude, it may be asked, does the base of this cupola extend? If the point of the South Pole be reared to the top of the atmosphere, which must be the case if such a cupola exist, how are we to reconcile the circumstance of higher ice-bergs being formed at the extremity, or base (as at South Georgia), than 1200 miles nearer the supposed point of greatest frigidity? Those ice-islands seen by me in latitude 74° had unquestionably been formed contiguous to land; and should, according to the idea of increasing cold, and the figure of a cupola, have been considerably higher than those formed in latitude 54° (in South Georgia). In this island they are some miles in extent, and are fully 250 feet high. If, then, the influence of the frigidity of the Pole extends so far northward as to be capable of producing such masses of ice, 2160 miles distant from the Pole, it is a very remarkable circumstance, that 1200 miles nearer to that point the sea should be found unfrozen.

I am inclined to hazard an opinion, that the effects of the sun, as caused by his alternate presence and absence on the two simple elements of earth and water, will be periodically the same.

Water unconnected with land will undergo no greater conversion into ice, during the absence of the sun, than can be again destroyed by his presence. No part of visible matter exhibits a tendency to progress in any one state indefinitely. All is alternate; and thus, by the change of seasons in the frigid parts of the globe, nature, whose energy is suspended during the absence of the sun, is, by his presence, again restored to activity; so that we find, for instance, the deer of Spitzbergen, in the latitude of 80° N.*, obtain their herbage annually, where the land is so formed as to supply the demands of animal life. We may receive with tolerable confidence the opinion common to all who have written theories of the earth, that the present distorted form of the terrestrial part of the globe is probably very different from that which it assumed at the creation of the world. The primitive state, philosophically considered, we may suppose exhibited the earthy or lighter strata on the surface of the globe, with a height not exceeding the present low lands; and in such a state, I am of opinion, that every portion of the surface of the globe, at its respective summer sol-

* Deer live and thrive in 80° of latitude on Spitzbergen, but cannot live in 75° in Nova Zembla. — Barrow's Voyages into the Arctic Regions, p. 372.

stice, would be at least free from ice, if not habitable.

The irregular strata, which compose nearly all the lands in high latitudes, interfere materially with the uniform operation of the sun, with regard to the heating of those regions in which they are placed.

The character which those parts of the earth assume, by the accumulations of ice and snow, does not, however, exist entirely uncontrolled. The rocky masses of land in the north have exhibited many changes in their temperature, according to their peculiar form, situation, and quality, and the collections of ice on their shores. But it may be remarked, that whatever accumulation of ice has been at various times formed upon them, after the lapse of a number of years has been removed, and the countries have returned to their original state. East Greenland, for example, is supposed to have been once inhabited. The country was afterwards shut up by ice, and the inhabitants consequently perished by cold and hunger. The country remained enveloped in ice for nearly three centuries, but is now again accessible.

The aqueous part of the globe does not exhibit the same difference. In short, it can be little changed from the original quality it possessed at the formation of the world. The waters of the Equator, and those of the highest latitudes which have yet been attained, differ not materially from one another in saltness and density; and, never having been affected in the same manner as the earthy parts of the globe, they may be supposed to become solid and fluid alternately, in conformity to the presence or absence of the sun. Were the terrestrial parts of the globe formed regularly, that is, by the natural tendency of matter subsiding according to its specific gravity, the lighter and earthy part would occupy the upper stratum; which formation, it may be observed, is most natural, being indispensably necessary for the production of vegetable matter, on which animal life depends for support. If such were the universal construction of the solid part of the globe, I will venture to say, that no ice-islands would be found floating in the ocean, nor bergs fixed upon the land, because the ices would be annually dissolved.

Within the tropics, when the sun, in his course over the meridian, passes through the zenith, the excessive heat which is received during the day is modified by a night of twelve hours, and the whole of the torrid zone is tempered by the sun's change of declination, which is equal to an arc of 47 degrees every six months. If this were not the case, animal life could not be supported in the Equatorial Regions, and every thing inflammable would probably become ignited.*

No material change could take place in the present form and motion of the earth, without destroying entirely the general harmony which exists in the economy of nature.

It is pleasing to observe, that from the Equator to the Poles, as the continuance of the sun above the horizon increases, so the meridian altitude decreases; thus, by the obliquity of his rays, too great an accumulation of heat is prevented.

This harmony, arising from the regularity of the sun's motion in the ecliptic, Dr. Burnet, in his Theory of the Earth, (vol. i. p. 188.) considers not to have been the original order of the solar influence; but he supposes that, previous to the time of the deluge, the sun moved

* "The sun changes his declination every day in Venus, about 14° more at a mean rate than he does in a quarter of a year on our earth. This appears to be providentially ordered, for preventing the too great effects of the sun's heat (which is twice as great on Venus as on the earth, so that he cannot shine perpendicularly on the same places for two days together); and on that account the heated places have time to cool."—Brewster's edition of Ferguson's Astronomy, vol. i. p. 17.

constantly in the Equator, producing a temperature which, he says, caused perpetual spring.

My comments on this opinion shall not take me beyond the consideration of the state of the Poles, that being the sole object of my present research.

In the case supposed by Dr. Burnet, the sun would be constantly in the horizon of the Poles; and round these points, for ten degrees at least, would consequently have perpetual winter, whilst the Equatorial Regions would experience insufferable heat. It is evident that the whole space contained within the Polar Circles would be covered with ice, formed by the condensations of the atmosphere, and which would remain fixed, extending frigid influence some degrees farther.

Following up the Doctor's theory: — The eruption of the earth, which he supposes destroyed the primitive, and produced the present state of the globe, and which changed the position of the Poles $23\frac{1}{2}$ degrees, we may suppose would destroy the Polar ices, and leave the extremities of the globe unencumbered; but if, from the creation of the world, the sun has travelled the same course in the heavens, or, in other words, the axis of the earth has always had the same inclination to its orbit, which is the most probable conjecture, then the conclusion, as relates to the Poles, will be very different.*

The various ices of the Poles we cannot suppose were produced immediately at the creation, they must have been produced by successive winters; and, since the temperature at the Poles, at the summer solstice, is one-fourth greater than at the Equator, may we not reasonably imagine that the heat of the sun during the summer which succeeded the first winter, would be sufficient to reduce to fluidity the ices which had been produced? In this consideration, I am supposing the Poles, as to their quality of matter, to be in one or other of the two states mentioned at page 281.

Many parts of Russia experience the extraordinary degree of summer heat, arising from the long space of time that the sun is above the horizon. At St. Petersburg, in the latitude of 60°, the heat during the month of *July* I have myself experienced to be greater than that of the West Indies; and were the sun's rays to fall less obliquely on that part of Russia, ve-

* Professor Leslie, in the Supplement, vol. iii. of the Encyclopædia Britannica, observes: "At the Pole itself, during the complete circuit of the sun in midsummer's day, the measure of heat would be greater than at the Equator, by about $\frac{1}{4}$th, or 797 thousand parts. The continued endurance of the sun above the horizon more than compensates for the feebleness of his oblique rays."

getation would be destroyed by the violent and almost continual action of his rays. An extract from Captain Scoresby's Voyage to the North is descriptive of the powerful effects of the sun, where he continues for a great length of time above the horizon. (See p. 343.) "The total freeness from clouds of the atmosphere near shore is often remarkable. The sun sometimes sweeps for days together round and round the heavens without for a moment being concealed by a cloud. The heat on shore, I have had occasion to remark, is in such cases very intense. The constant action of the sun, without the suspension of night, produces an influence on the vegetation, which exceeds, perhaps, any thing that elsewhere occurs even in the finest regions of the globe."

In the calculations made for the comparative temperature between that of the Pole and other latitudes, the accumulation of heat produced by the continued action of the sun is not taken into account; though such accumulation is great and quite apparent in many common experiments. I should, in another part of these sheets, perhaps, have introduced the following considerations regarding the probable deposit of congealed matter about the Poles; but, as I have not immediately digressed from the subject of the peculiarities of the Polar Regions, the apparently detached mode of treating it may not be materially objectionable.

I suppose that during the depth of winter the Polar atmosphere becomes so divested of humidity, by intense frost, as to afford little matter for condensation in the form of snow; for when the Polar Regions have received their winter covering of snow and ice, the caloric of the land or water is thereby prevented from escaping, and little or no evaporation can go on.

"In the month of July, for example, when the mean point of deposition may be taken in this latitude (56°) at 45°, the quantity of moisture in the air is 0·2099 grains in 100 cubic inches; whereas, in the month of December, when the mean point of deposition is 15° lower, the quantity of moisture in the same volume of air is only 0·1278 grains."—Edinburgh Philosophical Journal, No. 21. p. 165.

The estimate made by Captain Parry, (Second Voyage, p. 200.) in regard to the quantity of snow which fell during five winter months, about the latitude of 66 degrees, was 4½ inches; but allowing, as he supposes, that as much had been carried off by wind, the accumulation of snow, during the whole five months of winter, would still not exceed the depth of 9 inches. It is impossible to infer exactly, from what fell in this latitude, what quantity would fall during the same period at the Poles; but, for the above reason, of the Polar atmosphere probably possessing less humidity, the falls of snow would be proportionably less. If the Polar Region be an expanse of water, the next object of enquiry is, what is the probable annual production of ice?

Captain Parry's estimate of the depth of ice formed during five winter months, in the latitude of 66°, is the best analogy afforded for calculating that at the Poles; the thermometer having frequently, during that time, indicated a temperature of 31° below zero of Fahrenheit. He says, (Second Voyage, p. 186.) "The thickness of the floe was here 4 feet 7 inches, being the produce of exactly five calendar months. The ice was hard, brittle, and transparent, till within six or eight inches of the lower surface, where it became soft and porous, allowing the water to filter through it. In the offing, or in deep water, the production of ice was very slight when the thermometer stood at 31°." By analogy, according to this estimate, we may suppose that the winter production of ice at the Poles is not so enormous but that the more than equatorial heat of summer, which is presumed to exist there, will dissolve it.

The temperature of the sea-water in high northern latitudes is much above what might be expected if the Pole were a cupola of ice.

Captain Ross found the temperature of the sea to the northward of Davis's Straits, about the latitude of 72°, at the depth of six, seven, and eight hundred fathoms, to be $28\frac{1}{4}°$; and Captain Parry, at similar depths, found it 28°; whereas Captain Phipps, in the latitude of 75°, in the Spitzbergen Sea, at the depth of 600 fathoms, found the temperature of the water to be 40°; and on the 4th of *August*, in the latitude of 80 degrees, 60 fathoms under the ice, he found the temperature to be 39°. From what source can we suppose that these eleven degrees of heat above the freezing point of salt water were derived? It could not proceed from the southward; for, as mentioned by Captains Ross and Parry, at great depths the temperature has been found to be about 28°. The increase of heat was not generated at the surface, for that was at 36°; and the air was at 32°. It most probably came from the Polar Region, where the water, by being heated to a temperature of 70 or 80 degrees, would be so expanded as to force its way southwards to obtain a level.* The incapacity of water to conduct caloric downwards,

* According to the experiments of Mr. Dalton, on the gravity and expansion of water under different temperatures, the bulk of water at 5° is equal to the same bulk of water at 80°. — Manchester Memoirs, vol. v. p. 374.

and the rays of the sun exhausting their calorific effects in passing through a depth of not more than three or four fathoms, makes it difficult to conceive how the heated waters of the Pole could find their way to the depth of sixty fathoms. Supposing them to be heated to the temperature of 70° or 80°, they would become specifically lighter than the waters of the sea in the latitude of 80°; but those of the Pole coming in contact with ice, or a colder stratum of water, might be cooled to what Captain Phipps found it, 39°; and this being nearly the maximum density of water, it would sink beneath that at the surface, which was at a temperature of 36°.*

Captain Scoresby reached the latitude of 80° 33′, so early as the month of *April*, and on the 30th of that month, about the latitude of 80°, he observed a striking instance of the calorific effects of the sun. (See his Voyage to the North in the year 1822, p. 33.) The sun broke through the clouds at the same time, and produced a powerful effect on the temperature. At 2 A.M. the thermometer was 3° or 4° below zero, and at 8 A.M. it was + 6°; and, at 10, about 14° in the shade. But the genial influence of the sun was still more striking; in a sheltered air it produced the

* The density of water at 32°, and at 53°, is precisely the same; hence the maximum density of water is 42·5. — Manchester Memoirs.

feeling of warmth ; the black paint of the side of the ship on which the sun shone was heated to the temperature of 90° or 100°, and the pitch about the bends became fluid. Thus, while on one side there was uncommon warmth, on the opposite was intense freezing.

Although I have, in another place, mentioned the calorific effects experienced in the latitude of 80°, to afford but a weak analogy for deductions respecting the state of the Pole, that observation applies to the motion of the sun round the horizon ; but from this phenomenon, witnessed by Captain Scoresby, an inference may be drawn for the strength of the sun's action at the Pole at the summer solstice, when the altitude is 23° 28′.

Supposing the ship in the latitude of 80° 19′ at noon, and to continue at rest in the position described by Captain Scoresby, the sun, when under the Pole, would have declined in his revolution, to the altitude of 5° 8′ on the frozen side of the ship, at which altitude, from the extreme obliquity of his rays, he would produce scarcely any warmth, whilst the already heated side would have time to cool. But, again, suppose the ship revolved slowly round once in twenty-four hours, and that the sun remained at the altitude of 24° 21′, which would be nearly the meridian altitude at that place ; or, that the sun revolved round the ship, which would be the same thing, it cannot be doubted, that every part of the ship, in a few revolutions, would become temperately heated, and, after a considerable succession of revolutions, would suffer by too great an accumulation of caloric. The result of the sun's action at the Poles would therefore not be materially different from that mentioned by Captain Scoresby, as having been the effect of the meridian sun in the latitude of 80°.

The meridian altitude at the Pole, at the summer solstice, would be only 53′ lower than that in the case above mentioned; and, though the heat absorbed by a sheet of water, supposing the region of the Pole to be such, would not be equal to that taken up by the black side of a ship, yet it would be considerable. I have supposed the ices of the Poles to be dissolved by the 21st of *June;* for, although the process of the fusion of ice is slow, it having no less than 140 degrees of caloric to absorb, before it can become fluid, yet, the sun having swept the horizon for nearly two months, advancing from the altitude of 15° to 23° 28′, we may conclude his effects to have been sufficient to accomplish the dissolution of those ices.

The intervention of the rays by fogs and clouds, both of which are prevalent in high northern latitudes, would, of course, lessen the effects of the sun; but in regard to the Antarctic Region, I remarked, during my navigation in those seas, that the atmosphere became less loaded with vapour as we proceeded southwards, till, in the latitude of 74° 15′, the sky was almost without a cloud.

By referring to the annexed figure, it will be seen in how rapid a proportion the length of day, or the sun's continuance above the horizon, increases from the Arctic and Antarctic Circles to the Poles, thereby affording at those points more than an equivalent of heat for the obliquity of his rays.

Were the globe elongated at the Poles, so that each extremity resembled the small end of an egg, the intervention of night, which in such case would take place during summer, as well as winter, in the latitude of 80°, would probably be sufficient to fill that region with ice; but, the earth being globular, or rather flatted at the Poles, as the sun approaches the regions within the Arctic and Antarctic Circles, they enjoy his presence for a longer time, in proportion to the rapid contraction that takes place in the circles of latitude, as may be understood by the annexed diagram. In the figure, the strait lines represent diameters of circles of latitude, all of which, by the diurnal motion of the earth, revolve in equal spaces of time; but, from the

Fig. 2.

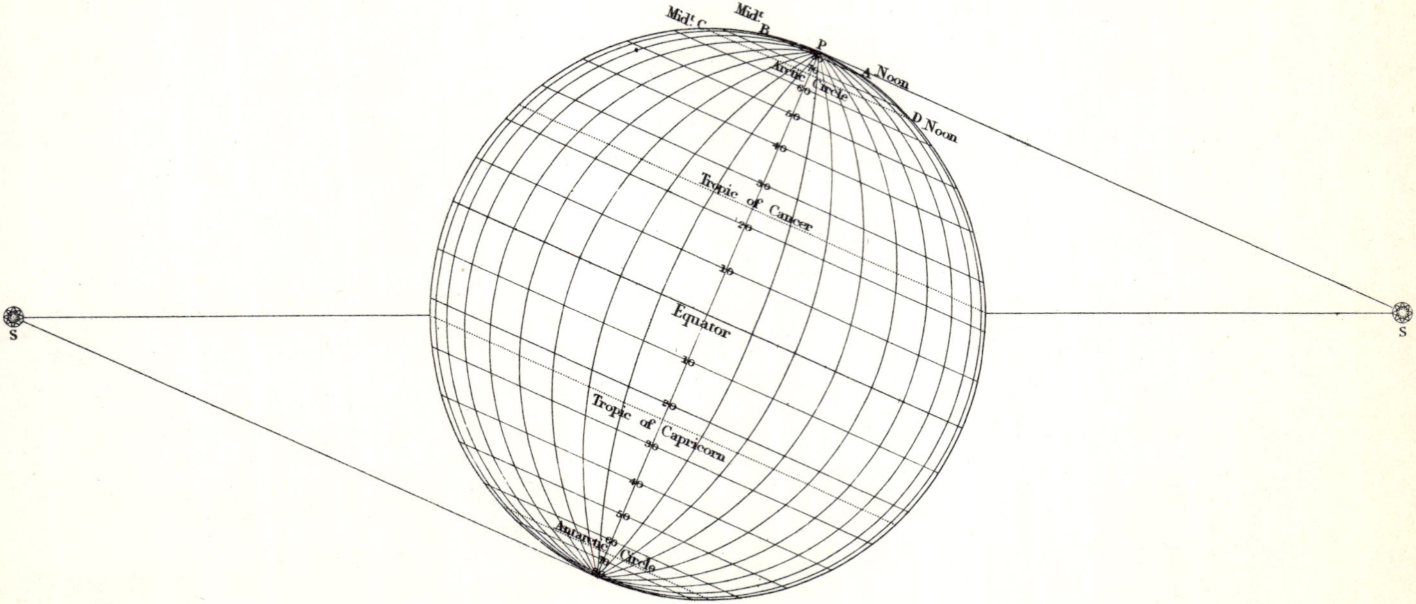

Sidy Hall Sculpt

spherical form of the globe, they exhibit great differences in the length of day and night. The sun, S, being placed at an assumed distance, it may be seen, that the ray A, proceeding from the sun to the Pole, P, from which the sun appears at an angle of 23° 28′ above the horizon, cannot, by the diurnal motion of the earth, be either raised or depressed, as there is nothing in that situation to intercept it. But, in the latitude of 80°, and at the point B, at midnight, when the sun is under the Pole, the segment of the earth that lies between that latitude and the Pole will, by its convexity, reduce the altitude to 13°. At the Arctic Circle, C, at midnight, the segment contained between it and the Pole being equal to the altitude of the sun at that point, he will, of course, appear in the horizon. An observer, at the point D, on the Arctic Circle, will perceive the sun on the meridian, at an angle of 46° 56′, with the horizon. But, when the observer is carried half round that circle, by the diurnal motion of the earth, which brings midnight, as at C, the sun will appear in the horizon; his depression being equal to the segment C P D (46° 56′). Hence it appears evident, that the altitude of the sun at midnight will increase as this segment becomes shortened, or, in other words, as you approach the Pole; and there, at the summer solstice, the segment being reduced to a point, he will pass round the Pole at nearly the same altitude.

The diameters of the circles of latitude at 10 and 20 degrees differ but very little from that of the Equator; and, consequently, the days do not vary much in length: but, above the latitude of 20°, it may be seen, that towards the Pole the diameters diminish very fast, keeping the sun longer in view as they become shortened, till beyond the Arctic Circle, where, at the summer solstice, he never disappears.

Notwithstanding all that has been said for the open state of the Poles, two instances of modern experiment have proved, beyond a doubt, the impracticability of at present penetrating the Northern Polar Circle. Captains Phipps and Ross, in their respective attempts at different points within the Arctic Circle, have reached the utmost navigable limit; but, in both cases, they were entangled with land, from which, probably, arose the impediments of ice they met with.

As the northern termination of Greenland has not yet been discovered, it may not unlikely extend to the northward of Spitzbergen, and thence to the eastward, supporting that glacier of ice along which Captain Phipps coasted in search of an opening.

From the direction of the east coast of Greenland, and the position of the northern shores of the Arctic land in general, it is not improbable that a range of islands extends quite round the Polar Circle, terminating the northern extremities of Europe, Asia, and America, and forming channels which will be constantly encumbered with ice. The disjoined state of lands already known in high latitudes supports this conjecture.

We are credibly informed that the latitude of 81° 50′ was reached by Captain Scoresby, senior; but previous accounts cannot be equally depended on. The Dutch navigators, whose method of observation, from the imperfection of their instruments at that time, was subject to much inaccuracy, pretend to have been driven by gales and currents into the latitude of 88°; and, on one occasion, into 89° 40′; but these accounts are void of credibility. In the Edinburgh Review some more modern voyages are taken notice of, which appear to be well authenticated. (See No. 58. p. 331.) "In 1616, Baffin advanced in Davis's Straits as high as the latitude of 78 degrees. The same skilful navigator had, two years before, penetrated in the Greenland seas, to the latitude of 81°, and seen land as high as that of 82°, lying to the north-east of Spitzbergen; but it is mortifying to remark, how little progress has been made in geographical discovery since those early and intrepid adventurers explored the Arctic Regions with their humble barks, which seldom exceeded the size of fifty tons.

We must pass over a very long interval to obtain authentic information. In 1751, Captain M'Callam, whom Barnington calls a scientific seaman, sailed without obstruction from Hackluyt's Headland, as high as the latitude of 83½°, where he found an open sea; and the weather being fine, nothing hindered him from proceeding further but his responsibility to his owners for the safety of the ship. Captain Wilson, about the end of *June*, 1754, having found the sea quite clear as far as he could descry, advanced to the latitude of 83°, till, not meeting with any whales, and beginning to apprehend some danger, he shaped back his course. At this very time Captain Guy, after four days of foggy weather, was likewise carried to the same point. The Polar Seas at this period must, indeed, have been remarkably open; for one of the most extraordinary and best authenticated voyages was performed in 1754, by Mr. Stephens, a very skilful and accurate observer, whose testimony is put beyond all manner of doubt by the cool judgment of the late astronomer royal, Dr. Maskelyne. This navigator informed Dr. Maskelyne, that about the end of

May he was driven off Spitzbergen by a southerly wind, which blew for several days, till he had reached the latitude of $84\frac{1}{2}°$, and that in the whole of this run he met with little ice, and no drift wood, and did not find the cold to be anywise excessive.

The credibility of these latter statements of the Polar Sea having been penetrated, appear scarcely to admit of being called in question; particularly that of the voyage related by Mr. Stephens; but, it is much to be regretted, that the accounts of these voyages were not published with such details as would corroborate the general statement, which would have been much more satisfactory than traditionary report.

Mercantile pursuits have not afforded equal means for obtaining information of the southern regions; nor have experiments for arriving at the South Pole been persevered in by governments or public boards of science.

The barrier of ice which Captain Cook met with in latitude 71° 10′ was considered to be the glacier of the ice of the Pole, and consequently closed all speculation on the possibility of reaching it.

The continents of the two hemispheres terminate at very different points of latitude. The southern extremity of the continent of Asia lies to the northward of the Equator, and those of

Africa and America in the south, terminate in mere peninsulas. The South Pacific and Atlantic Islands are inconsiderable when compared with the expanse of ocean in which they are scattered, whilst the lands of the northern hemisphere terminate within the Arctic Circle. The western extremity of South Shetland lies within the Antarctic Circle, and that is the most southern land which has yet been discovered.

By a glance at the map of the Polar parts of the two hemispheres, it will be seen how many more points of access there are to the South Pole than to that of the North. The only openings to the northern Polar Regions are by Bhering's Straits, and by the Spitzbergen Sea, forming together not more than one ninth of the Circle of the seventieth degree of latitude.

The Antarctic Regions are differently circumstanced as regards land, for we know of none to the south of 69½; and that is reported to be an island of small extent, and probably is a part of the Archipelago of South Shetland.

The difficulty attendant on the navigation of the Antarctic Sea, so far as I have seen, consists in having to pass through chains of ice islands, floating between the latitudes of sixty and about seventy-one. Within little more than this portion of both hemispheres, probably, the principal ices will be met with.

In standing southwards there is little doubt but that heavy field-ice would be fallen in with, which had been formed in bays or straits, and which had thence drifted into deep water. These obstacles, however, though a little embarrassing, might perhaps without much difficulty be passed.

Two Russian ships on discovery in the year 1821, are reported to have reached the latitude of 70°, and it is said were prevented by ice from going farther.* I reached about 255 miles nearer the Pole, and met with no such obstruction.

The barriers to the attainment of experimental knowledge are, however, often produced by an unlucky concurrence of circumstances. The noblest efforts are frequently blasted by some untoward event, which not only, perhaps, affects the interest of the persons engaged, but leads to false conclusions as to the possibility of ultimately obtaining the object desired.

* Bellinghausen's Voyage. — The Russian voyage of discovery towards the South Pole did not reach so high a latitude as Captain Weddell, whose voyage is noticed at p. 146. For the chief of the expedition, Captain Bellinghausen, says, "We continued our cruise to the south-east, sailing between large masses of ice; but, notwithstanding all our efforts, we never could pass the 70° of south latitude, and this only in one place. In all others, we could only advance 69½°." — Edinburgh Philosophical Journal, No. 23. p. 177.

Probably no part of science is more subject to erroneous conclusions than that of hydrography. Supposititious islands have been seen through a hazy atmosphere which in reality never had existence; and those which have been actually seen have been sometimes incorrectly laid down, by reason of adverse circumstances, such as having been seen at a great distance, or by reason of darkness or fogs.

The most patient and diligent research is always necessary to the attaining a correct knowledge of those parts of science of which I have treated in the foregoing pages: and if I have contributed, by my private adventure, to the advancement of hydrography, I conceive that I have only done that which every man would endeavour to accomplish, who, in the pursuit of wealth, is at the same time zealous enough in the cause of science to lose no opportunity of collecting information for the benefit of mankind.

SECOND VOYAGE

OF

THE BEAUFOY

TO

TIERRA DEL FUEGO.

ADVERTISEMENT.

Some particulars of a second voyage, performed by the Beaufoy in the South Seas, have been communicated to me by Mr. Brisbane; and I shall in the following pages offer such remarks as seem to me to be possessed of interest, in consequence of their conveying additional information on the subject of our former transactions in the Southern hemisphere.

JAMES WEDDELL, R. N.

SECOND VOYAGE.

THERE having been no specific object of hydrographical discovery either projected or attempted in this adventure, I would not have thought necessary to record the circumstances, were it not that Mr. Brisbane, following my instructions, in the prosecution of his voyage, revisited those peculiar people the Fuegians.

The progressive improvement of a friendly tribe of men, originally found in a rude state, cannot be a matter of unconcern to the generally benevolent part of mankind; and under that impression I have ventured to bring forward some further observations on the condition of these uncultivated Australians.

Although little as yet can be said of their advancement in knowledge, they have decidedly evinced a mild and pacific disposition, and also an anxious desire for the assistance of strangers.

Considering the cruelties which have been committed by the greater number of other savage nations, which have been almost always found untractable and ferocious, the humane disposition possessed by the Fuegians merits our attention.

The object of the Beaufoy's voyage was to procure the furs of seals and other animals in the South Seas.

Mr. Brisbane sailed from the Downs on the 23d of August, 1824; and, after coasting eastern Patagonia and touching at the Falkland Islands, on the 16th of October, 1825, he arrived at Tierra del Fuego, and anchored in Maxwell's harbour.

On the 18th, a party of about twenty of the natives came along-side the Beaufoy, in their canoes, and after a little ceremony on their part, by way of salutation, they hurried on board.

Of these Fuegians, several had been visitors on board the Jane and Beaufoy in the year 1823, and though nearly two years had elapsed, they, at once, knew Mr. Brisbane and several of the crew. In order to be identified as former friends, the medals which had been given them on the Beaufoy's preceding voyage were produced; but after this interview they were never to be seen: probably from fear of having them reclaimed.

Full liberty was given them to come and go throughout the day, and, till the 17th of December, a number of the natives were frequently on board. Mr. Brisbane's account of their behaviour, while he was among them, strongly marks the uniformity of their character. They conducted themselves in the same pacific manner as formerly, and by this further communication, their knowledge of the advantages of the arts and intelligence possessed by us appeared conspicuously. Their sick applied regularly for medical aid, and the women even presented their afflicted children for assistance.

The practice of pilfering was continued with their usual dexterity, but never aggravated by ferocious insult on being detected. Their petty thefts were sometimes, however, accompanied by ingratitude; as, particularly, in one instance of a man, who, while in the cabin getting a wound in his leg dressed, took that opportunity of requiting the favor by stealing a tumbler.

No doubt the principal object of this theft was to obtain a glittering substance; for while I was among those people, I endeavoured to impress on their minds the convenience of having a well constructed vessel for holding liquids, by giving them several articles of that description. All these were accepted, but never made use of for the purpose I had intended. The buckets, and other iron-bound utensils were broken down in order to obtain the hoops; and to possess these, every consideration connected with our ideas of comfort was sacrificed.

Their own rudely-formed calabash, made from the bark of a tree, could be better endured than to suffer their precious metal to remain fastened up with any other substance to form a vessel for a similar use.

In each canoe they generally carry a large calabash, containing about six gallons, which is filled with water on leaving the shore; and their mode of drinking out of it is through the thigh-bone of the albitross, which is inverted into the mouth of the vessel.

Several amusing absurdities were played off by the natives: but, as I have described their ludicrous character in the Journal of my visit in 1823, it is unnecessary to repeat the further instances of their tricks.

Mr. Brisbane frequently employed them in the labours of the ship, at which they were by no means inactive. Though they still were exceedingly fond of a repast of seal-fat, and other gross substances, they frequently partook of ship's fare with apparent relish; but spirituous liquors they could not be brought to like.

Their friendship and confidence was manifested by inviting our people into their wigwams; a privilege which was not conceded during my stay among them.

No appearance of a sense of religion was discoverable. Mr. Brisbane frequently observed them gabbling, for a quarter of an hour together, seemingly to the water; but nothing conclusive could be drawn from this circumstance.

In an excursion into the woods two dead bodies were found stretched on the ground, in such a manner as conveyed an idea that they had been placed there by way of sepulture. Mr. Brisbane had them interred, and frequently requested their countrymen to accompany him to the spot, that he might show them the nature of burial; but they always refused to proceed in that direction. Most probably this arose from a feeling peculiar to them, in relation to their departed friends.

Mr. Brisbane's attempt to instruct the natives in this particular could scarcely be expected to succeed; as we must suppose that, before they can acquire proper notions regarding the performance of a duty which calls forth the finest sympathies of our nature, they must be assisted by foreigners in the simple means of obtaining a better subsistence. In consequence of their local disadvantages, nature does not afford them that easy introduction to a cultivation of the arts that almost all other people have enjoyed in their advances to a state of civilization.

On visiting Indian Cove the iron pot of two hundred gallons, which is mentioned in the journal of my voyage, and which we left there, was found remaining in the same situation; though from the bruises which appeared on its sides, numberless stones had in vain been thrown with a desire to break it. Did the natives but know the value of oil, and the method of making it from the blubber, they might turn the pot to good account, from the dead whales which are sometimes thrown upon their shores.

The crew of the Beaufoy carried on a barter with the Fuegians for their manufactures of ornaments, &c., which are already described in my Journal. Otter skins formed the most essential articles they had to offer; and their knowledge of trade in this commodity was latterly so much improved that their exactions were comparatively exorbitant.

A few words of the Fuegian language was, of course, obtained by Mr. Brisbane; but, owing to his sailing almost immediately after his arriving in England, and his not having inserted the words in his Journal, I am unable to state them.

The skin of the otter of Tierra del Fuego is

20

nearly of the same quality as that which we have in Scotland; but, from their scarcity, they are not of sufficient value to realize a profitable trade.

I have little doubt that, about the Straits of Magellan the otter must be much more numerous; and that on the Patagonian side of the Straits a variety of other fur-bearing animals may be found.

On the 17th of December, the Beaufoy being prepared for sea, Mr. Brisbane took leave of his Fuegian friends, in number about forty, and proceeded towards the eastern coast of Patagonia.

Owing to his being much occupied in business, he had not frequent opportunities of adding to the hydrography of the parts which he visited. He sailed through the Straits of St. Francis, which in my chart of Cape Horn is mentioned as being seen through from Saddle Island.

In the chart of these parts, published by Faden, low land is laid down running across this Strait, and forming a bay, which is called the "Bay of St. Francis." This strait is spaciously navigable, and, in peculiar situations of ships on this coast, might be found of the utmost consequence.

The winds and weather at that season appear

to have been much the same as I have described them in the Appendix to my voyage.

In the latitude of 46° on the coast of Patagonia, Mr. Brisbane succeeded in killing an animal of the lion species, though not before he had destroyed a large bull dog. The skin, together with the skull, was brought home and given to the museum of Edinburgh college. Professor Jamieson characterises the animal as having been an individual of the species Felis Concolor, or Puma, sometimes called the American lion.

Mr. Brisbane continued his voyage in the acquisition of his cargo till the 15th of January, when he shaped his course for England, and on the 29th of March he arrived in the Downs, after an absence of about eighteen months.

THE END.

London:
Printed by A. & R. Spottiswoode,
New-Street-Square.